Dharamjit Singh, born in Lahore in 1922, has a degree in History and Political Science, and an M.A. in English Literature. He is widely travelled and speaks several European languages. He has worked with the governments of various countries on visual media projects, and from 1951–4 was head of the photographic section of Unesco in Paris. As a photographer, his work is of top international level and has appeared in such magazines as *Life* and *Harper's Bazaar*. He has also done advertising work for ICI, Shell, and Kodak. As a writer, he has written for many journals, for television in the U.S.A., and for advertising agencies in London. Among his many publications are two books on the stories and system of Indian cookery, *Yoga and Indian Art*, *History and Ideas of the Sikh People*, *Classic Cooking from India*, and *Rice Cookery*. He won the Bharitya Vidya Bhavan Award and medal for *Indian Art and Psychology*.

D1012250

DHARAMJIT SINGH

Indian Cookery

PENGUIN BOOKS

Penguin Books Ltd, Harmondsworth, Middlesex, England
Penguin Books Inc., 7110 Ambassador Road, Baltimore, Maryland 21207, U.S.A.
Penguin Books Australia Ltd, Ringwood, Victoria, Australia

—

First published 1970

—

Copyright © Dharamjit Singh

—

Made and printed in Great Britain by
Cox & Wyman Ltd,
London, Reading and Fakenham
Set in Monotype Imprint

THIS BOOK IS DEDICATED TO
MY FAIRY GODMOTHER
MRS HENRIETTA TEN EYCK:
MANHATTAN AND NEW JERSEY,
18??–1957

I would like to thank Mark Longman who inveigled me into writing this book and who must bear the result, 'bon gré, mal gré'; also Miss Georgina Horley for her meticulous and arduous help in preparing the book.

Contents

Introduction

THIS is a practical cookery book designed to enable you to produce genuine Indian food in your own home. The early chapters describe the important role of aromatics and the techniques and styles of Indian cookery, as well as the basic ingredients and the kind of utensils you will need.

As with the French and the Chinese, Indian cookery has a system, an architecture of its own, though little is known of it outside India, and even in India it remains unrecorded. The knowledge and skill of Indian cookery has been handed down by word of mouth and practical example. Only when this tradition has been endangered has an attempt been made to rationalize and record it. Such a danger exists today: the master cooks employed by princes and in the great houses are now seeking other work, the days of the great chefs are past, and even in Indian homes – until recently, the stronghold of high-class cooking – there is a deterioration in cooking standards. New generations are growing up with no knowledge of the superb traditions of Indian cooking. They have no point of reference and can neither act as patrons nor educate others as has been the case in the past. While this book is meant for the Western reader with an interest and enthusiasm for Indian food, I have attempted to describe the background tradition to a great cuisine as well as to set out the practical steps necessary to produce results like those of the great chefs, and the cooking once done in Indian homes.

These chefs of the past regarded themselves as artists; they had a sense of dignity that showed in the food they produced. Few master-chefs aspired to all-round proficiency. One would be a wizard with pilaus, another would specialize in the barbecue, or cooking on the spit, a third would be a master of the *korma*, or braised meats. Vegetables would be the pride of another class of chef. The sweetmeat-makers, dealing with sugar and almond paste, pistachio, rose water, musk and sandalwood, rose petal jams and preserved fruit of all kinds, traditionally

9

possessed a jovial, even rollicking sense of humour. The chefs of salt and seasonings were sterner, conscious of the dignity of their calling. Both produced, and still do, food of mouth-watering taste and aroma.

THE INDIAN MENU

Until some twenty years ago an Indian meal usually consisted of a meat and fish dish; five or more vegetable dishes, one of which would be of lentils, and another of rice; several pickles and chutneys, including a chutney made from fresh herbs and fruit or vegetable; yoghourt and salad; and a sweet dish. These dishes would all be put on the table at the same time, not served one after the other in courses, as in the West. The diner composed his own meal from those dishes he preferred, and he ate them in whatever order or combination pleased his palate. This he does still, but in most households meals have been reduced in quantity and elaboration just as they have been in Europe. A more usual meal will now consist of one meat or fish dish, two vegetable dishes, lentils or rice, not more than three pickle or chutney accompaniments, yoghourt, perhaps a salad, and a sweet dish.

The right mixture and balance of flavours and textures is the essence of good Indian cooking. Dishes might include a dry and a moister dish, a bland and a fiery dish, one served chilled, another piping-hot, a sweet and a sour – or combination of both in a *chasnidarh* – a preserved chutney and a fresh one, a light and a rich dish. Some Westerners are aghast at serving starch with starch, as when lentils accompany a rice dish, but the contrast may be made by using plenty of butter or sauce in the cooking of one of the starchy foods, or the palate may be refreshed with yoghourt, a green vegetable, or a salad.

Normally no tea or coffee is taken after meals in India, but in winter nuts or dried fruits are handed round.

Many Indians are vegetarians and for them lentils and similar pulses play an important part in the diet, and lavish, variously flavoured and treated dishes of these appear at all meals, so that the total number of dishes may be increased.

Indian breads, *poppadoms* and fried appetizers, such as

onion rings, juliennes of pimento or ginger, or roasted chillies may also accompany the meal.

For the average Western family probably one main dish, a vegetable dish, a simple rice recipe, if rice does not form part of the main dish, and a chutney and some yoghourt would make an excellent introduction to Indian cooking. The unfamiliarity of the work always slows one up when trying new dishes, so it is wise not to be too ambitious at first. It is worth investigating local Indian food shops, for these often sell Indian puddings complete, or sweetmeats such as halva; and a variety of Indian breads.

The chapter on techniques and styles of cooking is designed for reference. When a recipe calls for a specific method, its description will be found in the preliminary chapters. These techniques belong to the Indian home and should be easy to reproduce in your own kitchen, especially with the aid of modern equipment and appliances.

Measurements used are in Imperial, or British Standard, measures (see Appendix, p. 257 for tables). For the most part, I have chosen to indicate quantities of spices and other aromatics in table-, dessert- and teaspoons for these are always to hand; in certain cases, where it is more convenient, the weight is given in ounces. Always level ingredients for all spoon and cup measurements. Keep in mind that doubling or halving a recipe may produce small changes in the consistency of the sauces: because of the rate of evaporation, halving may produce a thicker result unless more liquid is added; doubling may require slightly less liquid.

The nomenclature of Indian dishes is rather complicated. Each section is divided into separate preparations: curry, korma, *tandoori*, *parcha*, etc. Yet there are many variations of the same style which all come under the one name. For the sake of this book, names denoting special techniques are given in all cases where the recipe has no other name. The ancient chefs often named recipes after some epoch or personage. Thus Shah Jehan, the builder of the Taj Mahal, has many dishes named after him, indicating that they possess a certain grandeur. Some of these names and titles are over fanciful and have been modified. For the rest, each recipe is given its name in Hindi followed by an English or French equivalent where possible.

Most of the ingredients and aromatics mentioned in this book should be readily available. London and many other big cities have numerous Indian grocers, even supermarkets and some small grocers now carry a range of aromatics. If you have any difficulty in finding ingredients, the following London stockists have a very wide range of goods and all supply by post:

The Bombay Emporium, 70 Grafton Way, Tottenham Court Road, W.1.

The Far East Exotic Supplies, 34 Greek Street, W.1.

Hustlers, 35 Rupert Street, W.1.

Patak Spices Ltd., Drummond Street, off Tottenham Court Road, W.1.

Kettner's, Old Compton Street, W.1. (for oriental wine and sherry).

I have indicated where a particular ingredient is optional and in some recipes I have suggested substitutes. Do not hesitate to make slight alterations in quantity and ingredient, especially in the matter of aromatics where flavour and taste may often vary, and are in any case so much a matter of personal taste.

Recipes are for an average of 4–6 servings except where otherwise stated.

CHAPTER ONE

Aromatics: The Heart of Indian Cooking

AROMATICS – spices, herbs and seasonings – are the vital core of Indian cooking. The dictionary describes these plants, flowers, roots, barks and fragrant seeds in dry, though informative, detail. Such description cannot explain the subtle aromas, the intriguing undertones, the appetizing nuances which we can achieve through the use of aromatics. Between pungency and fragrance, the two ends of the aromatic scale, Indian cookery can ring an amazing number of culinary changes – aromatics are all individual in taste and enjoyable in their own right, even cayenne or hot chilli pepper has its own piquant taste. The use of aromatics, combined with the techniques and styles of cooking as outlined in Chapter Three, gives Indian cooking its unique character. Some Indian food is light, barely brushed by the breath of a single herb; some rich and grand, but if in the true tradition never heavy.

Aromatics fall into three main groups: spices – usually dried roots, barks, or seeds used whole, crushed or powdered; herbs – usually the fresh leaves, stems, or flowers of herbaceous plants; and the bulbous group, almost invariably used fresh – onions, garlic, shallots. To these must be added sweet and sharp flavourings – sugar, honey, salt, citrus juices, vinegar; and a miscellaneous group including natural ingredients like almonds, and manufactured products such as rosewater and pickles.

All aromatics must be stored in airtight containers in a cool, dry place, as they tend to lose their freshness if exposed too long to air, heat or moisture. In very wet weather, when some aromatics may absorb moisture, they can be spread out on a tray and placed in a very low oven with the door slightly open, then re-sealed in their containers.

SPICES

Spices are stronger than herbs, but they can be used in combinations without loss of flavour; herbs are more difficult to mix. This holds true for both Indian and Western cooking.

Among spices, the main aromatic (over a hundred are used in Indian cooking), is *turmeric* (haldi), the powdered form of a knob-hard root related to the ginger family, which comes into most Indian recipes. Its colour varies from canary to saffron yellow. Its natural aroma is most appetizing, and on its own is sufficient to produce delicious food. Turmeric is the basis of most spice combinations of the type known as 'curry-powder'.

Fenugreek (methe) is a hard lentil-type seed, used in powdered form. Its colour is dark fawn, and its astringent aroma is characteristic of packaged curry powders. This spice is not used extensively as it tends to be overpowering, but in small quantities, especially with vegetables, it imparts a delightful aroma. Fenugreek leaves belong to the spinach family, of which many varieties are used in India. When dried, the leaves are used as a herb.

Coriander (dhanyia) when of the best quality is unmatched for its fresh, delicate, spring-like aroma. It is used in powdered form, or, when roughly bruised, to give certain dishes a crusty texture. Green coriander leaves (classed as a herb) give a very delicate aroma.

Cumin (zeera) is pungent, even sharp, and astringent. There are many varieties of cumin including the dark one from Kashmir. It is a caraway-shaped seed, usually medium brown. Some varieties can be crumbled between finger and thumb, others may require a pestle and mortar.

Ginger (soondth) is the powder of a root which, in its fresh or green form (adrak) is highly prized in Indian cooking. Dry ginger is more pungent, and valuable for the zest it gives to blander spices.

Saffron (kesram, hence zaffaran and saffron – originally from the Sanskrit) is the name given to the fragrant stigmata found in the crocus flower. It is a regal spice, of matchless aroma, and the most costly in the world. Seventy-five thousand flowers are needed to make one ounce of pure saffron; each filament can colour seven hundred thousand times its own weight in water.

Fennel seed (soonf) has a sweetish aniseed taste and is invaluable for use with fish and shellfish, and for many vegetables. Green fennel leaves (classed as a herb) are used for the delicate aromatizing of steamed food.

Lovage (ajwain) is allied to the liquorice family. A powerful spice, it must be used in moderation.

Then there are nutty spices like *poppy seeds* (khus-khus), *sesame seed* (til); 'festive' spices like *cardamoms* (elaichi) – green, large black, and bleached; *cinnamon* and *cassia* sticks (dal-chini), *cloves* (laung), *nutmeg* (javatri) and *mace* (jaiphal). Lastly *nigella indica* (kalonji) – wild black onion seeds. These are the main spices.

Mention must be made of curry powders. These are anathema to Indian cooking, prepared for imaginary palates, having neither the delicacy nor the perfume of flowers and sweet-smelling herbs, nor the savour and taste of genuine aromatics. Curry powders often contain inferior spices which with age become acrid and medicinal in taste. They not only mask the natural taste of food, but lend a weary sameness to everything with which they are used. Curry pastes are available in India and in Indian grocer's here, but these are for special preparations like the vindaloo; they are not to be used indiscriminately, and never as a substitute for aromatics. In the Appendix (p. 249) you will find a recipe for an aromatic powder used throughout India. It is known as *garam masala*, and it has many variants. This powder should be used with discretion. It is meant to be sprinkled on food just before it is served, or added towards the end of the cooking. In all cases, its purpose is to add piquancy, and to form a highly aromatic crust on foods which are *bland and simple*. In present-day India, with the deterioration in cooking standards, this powder seems to be included in every recipe. The result is ruinous. In this book, garam masala is added only strictly in accordance with classic usage. It is never used as a curry powder, nor to bolster up missing flavours.

Black, red and white peppers make up the hot seasonings; some are bland, a few incendiary. Black pepper is the most aromatic. Some varieties from Malabar can be broken with the fingers, and have an intriguing flowery scent. Husked or white pepper is faintly medicinal. Paprika pepper comes from the bright red, ripe pimento (or pimiento) capsicum, which is dried, pounded and sieved. Called sweet peppers sometimes, pimentos are dark green at first and are often sold in this unripe state, but may be ripened wrapped in tissue and stored in a cool, though not cold, place. They have a gentle aroma and add colour. Fresh chillies may also be bought green or red. They are much hotter – the redder, the hotter. Dried, they turn brownish and become most fiery, and used with seeds inside are the hottest of all. The small birds-eye chillies which, when ground, become cayenne pepper, are also used for very hot dishes.

Note: Great care should be taken when preparing fresh hot peppers not to get any of the juice on delicate parts of the skin or in the eyes as it can be extremely painful. Do NOT take a bit to 'see how it tastes' – the effect is quite overpowering.

HERBS

Herbs can be divided into two groups: the gentle and the robust. Dark meats, including game, and some other food preparations require robust herbs.

Basil (tusli) is a sacred herb, and many people do not use it; it is however a very strong aromatic, though limited in usefulness.

Fresh coriander leaves (dhanyia) are one of the most delicate of all herbs, and easy to grow. Use like parsley for sprinkling on prepared food, for flavouring broths, and, when pounded or minced, as a base for sauces.

Mint (pudeena) needs no introduction. In Indian cooking it is used with lamb, chicken and vegetables together with other spices.

Kari phulia or sweet nim leaves are available in London, in fresh or dried form, from Indian grocers' shops. They are similar in appearance to bay, but smaller and thinner, the aroma having just a suspicion of truffle. They can be used minced, or steeped in a dish to release the intriguing aroma. Sometimes they are fried in butter and then removed before the food is cooked in the aromatized fat.

Various kinds of *thyme*, including wild and lemon thyme, are used in Indian cooking, mostly for roasts and food cooked on a spit.

There are countless other herbs in common use, but they vary from district to district and may not be generally available.

As in French cooking, Indian herbs and spices are used to make up a *bouquet garni*. They are tied in a fine muslin bag and removed before the dish is served.

Dried herbs are about twice as strong as fresh or green herbs, so use a little less than half the specified quantity if you substitute dried for fresh. Herb juice is also used and produces very refined cooking. Green herbs like coriander or mint can be used raw, or may be scalded, dried in a cloth and then ground in a mortar; they are sometimes put into a muslin bag and the juice squeezed out – this is especially good with steamed (dumned) food as well as roasts and grills.

The pungent aromatics are shallots, garlic and onions; these figure prominently in Indian cooking, and are used for the flavour and body they give to the various sauces.

In European versions of Indian dishes, thickening is invariably dependent on the use of cornflour or flour. This is seldom correct. Juices from the meat and vegetables, together with onions, pounded green (i.e. fresh) ginger, chopped parsley, coriander or mint, and spices, mostly provide the thickenings in Indian dishes. Many cooking methods use no onions or other thickening of any kind. In fact, as you work your way through the book, you will find numerous dishes that are dry and crisp, without gravy or sauce. It is the crusty gilding by spices on the surface of the food which is the special feature of this style of cooking.

SEASONINGS

Salt is the best known of all seasonings. If possible use the zesty, pungent, rock salt available in India. Black salt also adds variety. There are various kinds of spiced salts (one recipe is given in the Appendix on p. 249) which are used to aromatize grills, hors d'oeuvres and drinks such as tomato juice.

Sweet seasonings include sugar and honey, raisins and other dried fruit. Honey is the most aromatic, but its flavour is too

17

strong for many dishes. Brown or whole sugar has more flavour than white, and is also more nutritious.

Acid seasonings like lemon or orange juice, oil from the zest of citrus fruits, green mango, green papaya, pomegranate, tamarind (see Appendix p. 254), dried mango powder and other verjuices are used in Indian cooking. Dried pomegranate seeds can be treated in the same way as tamarind, or used finely ground to add a piquant flavour. When such seasonings are not available, lemon and lime juice can be substituted.

CHAPTER TWO

Basic Ingredients and Preparations

BASIC INGREDIENTS

IN all cooking, whether simple or gourmet, the food should be light and digestible. To a great extent, this will depend upon the quality of the basic ingredients. Indian cooking uses fats and oils, dairy products and starches, nuts, fruits and vegetables as in the West, but because a few ingredients may be unfamiliar, a brief account and description follows.

Indian food is cooked in *ghee* (or *ghrt* as the ancient Indians called it) or clarified butter (see Appendix p. 252). It is a concentrated form of butter, heated to rid it of all impurities and moisture. Ghee has a burning point higher than the best oils, which makes it the perfect cooking medium for frying, sautéing, and searing meat and aromatics.

Ordinary butters may be used as a substitute if certain rules are followed: use unsalted butter only, as salt will burn, blacken and may cause spluttering; reduce the stated amount of butter by $\frac{1}{4}-\frac{1}{2}$ oz. (according to the total to be used), and in its place first heat in the pan for 1 minute 1 dessertspoon–1 tablespoon good oil before putting in the butter. The oil allows the frying temperature to be reached with less risk of burning the butter. Clarified margarines make an economical substitute if similarly used with oil. White cooking fats, except lard, are satisfactory from the temperature point of view, but should be used in combination with a proportion of butter for flavour and appearance.

Olive oil, sunflower oil, mustard oil, groundnut oil, sesame oil (til oil – also called *gingelly* in India) are some of the oils used for cooking. If the quality of your oil is uncertain, use a very heavy saucepan with an asbestos mat underneath, and gently heat the oil for about ten minutes. This will rid it of excess moisture. Any oil or fat used for deep frying should be carefully

19

strained after use through a double thickness of fine muslin, then stored in a cool place.

Milk, cream and yoghourt are much used in Indian cooking, particularly in pilaus and braised meat dishes. They help flavours to penetrate the meat or vegetable, and serve to thicken sauces. All three absorb flavours from other foods, so always keep them well covered while storing. Make a point of using the freshest cream and the thickest yoghourt (see Appendix p. 250) available. Indian yoghourt is used for both sweet and savoury dishes; its consistency is near to that of a thick jelly.

Eggs are used for binding forcemeats, or the minced meats of the *kofta*, *kabab* and *kofta-kabab* styles. They go into various batters, stuffings and rice preparations. Hard-boiled eggs make an egg curry; chopped, they are used as a garnish. Eggs are used in some sauces; they are scrambled and placed inside the breast of a chicken; they are used in desserts.

There are various flours, including white refined flour, whole-wheat flour and those made from other grains, including rice. There is also the flour called *bessan*, made from chick-peas. Bessan is more aromatic and less starchy than refined flour. It is excellent for batters, and is used extensively in the preparation of fish where it acts like a blotting paper, absorbing superfluous oils and the fishy odour.

Shelled nuts such as almonds and pistachio are used in many dishes from rice pilau to sweets and desserts. Take care that they are not old or rancid, or of poor quality. Ready-bought ground almonds are about as useful as sawdust; the essential oils and characteristic aroma tend to escape once the nut is shelled and, more especially, once it is broken or cut up. Almonds may be blanched in the usual way by pouring boiling water over them. But soak them overnight in cold water, and the skin slips off easily, leaving the almonds moist and at their best as regards flavour.

Dried fruits such as prunes or apricots are used with some chasnidarh, or sweet-sour styles, and are included in some of the mixtures which go inside kababs or certain braised meats.

Of the vegetables, tomatoes do not really belong to the Indian tradition, though they were introduced to the country by traders in the sixteenth century. The dark mahogany red of some curries and kormas is *not* due to the use of tomatoes (or should not be), as they tend to mask the flavour and aroma of aromatics. They make a useful addition to certain dishes, but should be used with caution and subtlety.

BASIC PREPARATIONS

The quality of many dishes depends on the preparation of stocks and broths, batters and marinades, stuffings, forcemeats and pastes, milks, creams and syrups. Here we can briefly consider these preparations and their role in Indian cooking. It is attention to these basic preparations that will make all the difference in developing skill in genuine Indian cooking.

Akni is the Indian court bouillon, made from water and herbs (see Appendix p. 253 for recipe). This aromatized water is used for rice dishes and for steaming vegetables, where only the barest suspicion of aromatization is needed. You can make up your own recipes for akni provided that you keep in mind the basic principle that the aromatics must suit the food.

Yakhni from meat and bone (see p. 253) is prepared as in Western cooking, though it is generally realized that a proper stock is the result of 12–14 hours of slow cooking. In India, the vessel is sealed with dough once it is simmering, and left overnight by the side of a fire. The long cooking will extract the bone's gelatinous content as no other method can do.

Yakhni is also made from a combination of meat, bones and vegetables. There are two kinds: the plain yakhni or broth, and the double broth or *garhi yakhni*. The double broth becomes a heavy jelly, and is used in layers in the nobler pilaus.

Marinades are generally made with lime or lemon juice, vinegar, yoghourt, cream, juices of green mango or green papaya and oil. There are both cooked and uncooked marinades. They are used to tenderize meat or simply to aromatize food. Marinating meat for several hours ensures that the aromatics penetrate it thoroughly. Pickling food in oil is considered a form of marinade; such a pickle takes a long time to mature and will keep well.

A recipe for Indian cream (*malai*) is given in the Appendix p. 252). Milks are prepared from ground almonds, coconut, pistachio or pine nuts steeped in liquid then strained for later use.

Syrups make chasnidarh (sweet-sour foods) and pilaus, and are used for sweetmeats and desserts. In some recipes, chasni or syrup is used to glaze the surface of the food cooked on spit or grill; tamarind or pomegranate is usually mixed with the syrup to balance the sweetness. This is particularly delicious with duck and pork.

Batters (see Appendix p. 255) are made with white flour as well as lentil and chick-pea flour, and used to coat food for deep frying.

Stuffings are made from puréed vegetables, minced meat, rice, buckwheat groats, eggs, etc., mixed with aromatics and fragrant fungi like the black mushrooms from the Himalayas. They are used to stuff poultry and gamebirds, boned pork and lamb, and small whole lamb.

Forcemeats are made from mutton, lamb, pork, game, or fish, sometimes mixed with a little rice, or with raw lentil finely ground in water. Delicate quenelles are made with these force-meats and either poached in salted, aromatized water, or deep fried to a crusty gold outside, while the inside is fluffy, moist and crumbling. Using banana or papaya leaves as a wrapping, the quenelles can also be baked *en paupiette* in the ashes of a charcoal fire. They can also be baked in the oven, wrapped in aluminium foil. Some forcemeats are poached and served chilled, coated with a cream and yoghourt sauce and accompanied by raw grated cucumber or carrots, or beetroot cooked in akni. Others are used to make kababs or steamed meat cakes.

CHAPTER THREE

Indian Cooking Styles and Techniques

THE function of the whole range of aromatics, basic ingredients and preparations used in Indian cookery is to blend the aromas and flavours, the delicate or heady savour of seasonings, in such a way that we are unable to guess which aromatics have gone to make the alchemy of a dish; or alternatively, to capture the flavour of one main spice by a subtle chemistry of other herbs, spices, seasonings and ingredients. This can come only from an understanding of the separate styles of Indian cooking, and a mastery and control of the cooking techniques.

As you try out the recipes in this book, use this chapter for reference. The main culinary styles are first described briefly, then the techniques on which they are dependent explained, step by step; a brief reminder is often included in individual recipes.

A very important difference between Indian and other cooking is that Indian food is basted with clarified butter, or some of the marinade, where this is used. *Unlike Western cooking, meat is never larded, and all fat is trimmed off before cooking.*

CURRYING or STEWING

Curreari or curry is essentially a stew with plenty of light, delicate, or pungent sauce, this being the great attraction of the dish. The sauce, which is more like a delicious, spiced soup, has as much flavour, if not more than the meat. Almost any meat or vegetable can be curried, but the long, slow cooking is best suited to mature meat like mutton. Vegetables can be included in meat or poultry curries; the most usual ones are peas and potatoes. No cream, yoghourt or marinade is ever used.

Curries vary in colour from light gold to dark red depending on how well the onions and meat are browned and how much paprika is used. Often a light flavour and colour is wanted, and

the yellow of turmeric, which is always used in curry, combines
with the other aromatics to produce a dark gold. Colour is no
guide to taste: the so-called Madras curry is no darker than the
standard north Indian curry, yet it uses hotter seasonings and
many more spices.

Method. Remove all fat and skin from the meat, and wipe dry.
Using a heavy pan, heat clarified butter to smoking point, and
brown the minced onion. Remove onion, raise heat, and add the
meat. Frizzle it well and when half seared, add the aromatics and
fry together on medium heat. Stir constantly to prevent burning.
When the meat is well browned, lower the heat and cook until
the butter separates. It will come to the surface in small globules
or a mass of tiny beads. This indicates that the meat and spices
will absorb no more butter – cooking beyond this point will spoil
the flavours.

This is also the point at which to add salt. Added earlier, salt
would liquefy the meat juices so spoiling the dry sauté. Add
pepper or chilli and water. Boil for half a minute, then cover and
simmer. When the moisture is well reduced add more water just
to cover the meat. Boil again briefly, then cover and cook gently
until tender. Cook uncovered for the last 5 minutes on the
lowest heat possible – a smooth skin will form on the top and the
curry is ready to serve. The onions may be added again at this
stage. If you want a thicker sauce, they should be added at the
same time as the liquid. It cannot be overstressed that the secret
of cooking curries or braised meats lies in cooking the aromatics
with great care until they reach saturation point. Only then will
you get the authentic flavour of Indian cooking.

Vegetables may be added to curry during the later stages of
cooking. Potatoes will take from 15–20 minutes, depending on
size, peas 5–15 minutes depending on whether you like them
soft or just cooked.

KORMA or BRAISING

Korma is meat or vegetable braised with water or stock,
yoghourt or cream (sometimes all) to produce a rich, substantial dish. There are many styles of korma each with

different taste and texture. Some are cooked until a thick sauce is formed; in others the liquid is reduced to a glaze, or the sauce reduced to a delicious flaky crust. The korma is made with finest quality, young meat only. Some kormas are finished by steaming in which case a special technique called *bhogar* is used to give food of superb quality (see p. 26).

The *doh peeazah* is a variation of korma where two lots of onions are used: *doh* meaning two or twice, and *peeazah*, onions. There should be roughly two pounds of onions to every pound of meat. Half the onions are first browned, then the meat added. It is cooked with aromatics and then braised. When the meat is nearly done, the second half of the onions, grated or pulverized, is added. Sometimes the onions are cooked with the aromatics, then pounded and blended, to be added at a later stage with more raw onions. The main feature of the doh peeazah is that the two onion preparations should give different textures and tastes.

Method. Korma is one of the most important techniques in Indian cookery. It is not easy, but once mastered you can produce food of superlative flavour.

Braising uses the minimum of cooking liquor which is absorbed back into the meat together with all the savoury juices it has first extracted. True braising is done on a very slow fire, with charcoal on the lid. If this is not possible, food can be braised on top of the stove, or started on top of the stove and later transferred to the oven. Braising is carried out in several stages, and these are detailed below.

The aromatics in braising are used in two or three stages also. The first are mixed into the marinade, the second added halfway through cooking, and the third towards the end.

Use your heaviest vessel, with a well fitting lid; it should be just large enough to hold the meat comfortably. Choose best quality meat, not too young but certainly not old or stewing meat. Marinate the meat according to your recipe. In some recipes the marinade is drained from the meat and cooked separately with the aromatics to a thick paste, the marinade being added gradually to the meat as it dries. In both cases, the meat is cooked and stirred over very high heat to drive the flavours inside. When all the marinade has dried, the meat is given a final brisk crisping in clarified butter.

After searing, the meat is usually moistened a few times by sprinkling it with a liquid – stock, water or an infusion – about a tablespoon at a time, which is allowed to dry, the meat being stirred before the next sprinkling is added. Only experience will teach you how long the moistenings will take to dry. After about 15 minutes of careful attention, moisten finally, then seal the pot with a ribbon of dough, or by covering with a sheet of foil or greaseproof paper before putting on the lid. Place charcoal on the lid, or put in the oven.

There are two methods of finishing braised meats. The dish is either 'glazed', quite dry of gravy or sauce, or served moist. To glaze, remove lid and stir meat continuously over a fierce heat until the juices form a savoury gelatinous coating. If the korma is to be served moist, the meat is given a delicate steaming – called a *dum* – for 10–30 minutes in a low oven. Indian cooks put charcoal on the lid and place the casserole over the lowest possible heat.

When braising a large piece of meat, the procedure is slightly different. Once well seared, the meat is able to withstand brief periods of boiling.

The bhogar. To make sure that the meat is basted while cooking in a covered casserole, lift out the vessel and shake it well. The liquor will jump, and drench the meat, releasing steam at the same time. This shaking is very important: it is a quick agitation, moving the pan sideways and downwards. This technique serves three purposes: it releases aromatic steam, bastes the meat and helps complete the cooking.

In some forms of braising a fair quantity of cooking liquor *is* used, but always of a quantity that can be absorbed into the meat at the end of the cooking. The meat is removed and the sauce or liquor that has formed during cooking given a bhogar as follows: clarified butter is heated with a selected aromatic and the liquor is thrown in and mixed. It is reduced, covered, to the right consistency, then added to the meat. The vessel containing meat and sauce is covered, the heat raised very high and another bhogar is given. The heat is reduced and the cooking completed with a dum to allow the ingredients to marry.

In some braisings or kormas, the meat is braised as usual, but the sauce is cooked by bhogar in a separate vessel. Meat and sauce are joined at a later stage by a third bhogar (clarified butter heated with fresh aromatics and the food mixed in). The difference in these processes will appear clearly when recipes are actually in use. The true bhogar blends flavours superbly, but is only possible if the casserole is placed in the oven, or the lid charcoaled.

Braising white meat needs even more care than braising red or dark meats. Red meats do not spoil when overcooked, but white meats are ruined. First lightly brown (gild) white meat in clarified butter, or boil in cream, yoghourt, or a mixture of both or double broth, reducing to a glaze*, then frying in clarified butter. Add liquor in very small quantities, and see that it is quite dry before you add more. Shake frequently to keep the meat basted and cook until it begins to stick a little to the bottom of the pan. Test the meat occasionally with a thin skewer. White meat is not cooked for long enough to produce its own gelatine, so the use of double broth or some marinade with a high fat content is recommended.

DUMMING or STEAMING

Dumned food is steamed food in all its many variations. The word *dumned* means 'breathed-in', and the steam which collects in a large, well-sealed cooking vessel is sufficient to cook many kinds of vegetables, fish and meat. Some foods are steamed after an initial browning; others are lightly rolled in butter after steaming. Rice pilau uses a special steaming technique.

Method. Proper steaming requires a special steamer or a large saucepan with a trivet or rack. Use akni, the Indian court bouillon (see Appendix p. 253) and place food on the trivet standing clear of the liquid. (Add more liquid during cooking as needed.) Bring to a fierce boil, seal the lid by covering the pot with sheet of foil or greaseproof before putting on lid, or with a

---

*The term 'glaze' is used somewhat loosely in these pages. Western cooks will know that for the classic European glaze all fat is skimmed from the liquor.

ribbon of dough, and gradually reduce the heat. The steam will both cook and aromatize the food very delicately.

Food can also be steamed on top of a rice pilau or between two layers of rice – completely or partly cooked as a rule. For large pieces of food, some precooking may be necessary as the recipe directs.

To steam vegetables, first cut them into small pieces or slivers, then brown briefly in a very little clarified butter with some herbs. Salt is then added, and a very little (a tablespoon or less) water or akni. Close the lid tightly, raise heat for half a minute and then reduce it. Steam until done, shaking the vessel often to release the steam and prevent sticking. Uncover and serve. The texture should be crisp but tender. Green beans take 5 to 6 minutes; cauliflower flowerets about 5–10 minutes. There are certain special ways of steaming as in the recipe for Dumned Potatoes on p. 175.

BHOONA or FRYING

There are three styles under this heading.

Sukha Bhoona is a simple sauté, using thinnish fillets of best quality meat. It is lightly seasoned with pepper and salt or may have green herbs crushed to a paste and rubbed into the meat.

Dumned Bhoona is a pot roast. The meat may be marinated or rubbed with aromatics; it is then seared, moistened and cooked in a tightly closed vessel in the oven, or over charcoal with more charcoal placed on the lid.

Ard Bhoona is a dry pot roast employing butter only, and no liquid or marinade. The meat is first seared, then placed in a heavy casserole and drenched with butter. The lid is closed tightly and cooking completed in the oven. More butter is added during cooking. The ard bhoona is best with white meats.

Method. The simple sauté (sukha bhoona) uses small pieces of meat or vegetable cooked in a minimum of very hot fat – it should be capable of instantly frizzling the surface. The food must be cooked quickly, and kept moving all the time. Some of the flavour of the sukha bhoona comes from allowing the meat to stick just a little to the bottom of the pan (it must not actually burn, of course) and scraping up the residue with a spatula. White meats should be covered after the initial searing on both sides, and will be cooked in a few minutes. Some people like to serve sautéed meat with a little additional clarified butter added a few moments before the meat is done. This goes well with rice and the various breads eaten in northern and central India.

After a crisp sauté, some food is finished with a gentle dum. This is particularly effective with vegetables, where the late addition of salt helps to extract sufficient moisture to steam the food.

It cannot be over emphasized that really heavy cooking vessels are essential for best results.

In the dumned bhoona (steamed-fried), water or akni is added to the casserole with the seared meat, and in sufficient quantities to leave a generous amount of gravy. The meat is usually in one large piece (two to five pounds) and must be boned, with all fat removed. Cook in a medium oven, and shake the casserole from time to time so that the top of the meat is basted. When tender, leave uncovered in a low oven for a few minutes before serving.

Use your heaviest casserole for the ard bhoona; it must have a tight fitting lid that can be well sealed. Lay a bed of aromatics and any vegetables specified in the recipe. Add the seared meat, drench with clarified butter and seal the casserole. Place in a very hot oven and reduce the heat to low after ten minutes. Add more butter when the first has dried, shake the casserole and return to the oven. Repeat, if necessary, until tender. Meat may be cooked whole, or cut into smaller pieces. Take care that the vegetables are not cut up so small that they become overcooked.

TALAWA or DEEP-FRYING

Talawa means food that is deep-fried. Properly cooked, this food should be crisp, light and truly clean in taste and appearance. Whole or puréed vegetables, small pieces of meat, kababs, shellfish and filleted fish are some of the foods which can be deep-fried, quite apart from fritter-like sweetmeats. Most food requires a batter or coating of crumbs before deep-frying.

Method. Talawa requires a large, heavy saucepan, a wire basket or skimmer and plenty of oil or fat (for safety, it should come no higher than six inches from the top of your deep saucepan). A few simple rules will help you to produce crisp, digestible food.

Use good quality oil (ghee would be the ideal choice, but the amount needed makes it too expensive) and always strain it after use so that small crumbs and burnt pieces of food are removed. Next, see that the temperature of your oil is correct: there should be a thin shimmer of vapour rising from the hot surface. Test by dropping in a little batter, or a cube of bread; this should hiss and sizzle, rising quickly to the surface and turning golden-brown in one minute. The temperature needed will vary very slightly according to the type of food you are frying and the fat used. The idea is to cook the coating at once, thus forming a barrier between the food to be cooked and the oil. This protective layer seals in juices while preventing food from absorbing fat. Do not overcrowd the pan or you will lower the temperature and spoil the food. See that the food is cooked evenly and hold it below the surface occasionally, with a large skimmer. After it has been used for some time the oil will change colour, becoming amber or darkened. It should be rejected at this point as it will only cause food to burn if used again, and may even turn rancid. Oil should always be kept in a cool place after straining. Indian cooks salt food after frying. Carefully dry food before frying (or dipping in batter) as moisture prevents proper frying and may make fat splutter dangerously. For best results, heat your oil very slowly to allow any moisture in it to evaporate.

TANDOORI AND KABABS
or COOKING ON THE SPIT OR GRILL

Now we come to the spitted foods: small or large pieces of food threaded on to a spit and roasted, baked or grilled.

Tandoori is food cooked on the spit in a clay oven. This type of cooking can be done under the grill (the food being frequently turned), on an open fire or barbecue, or on a modern revolving spit. But many people prefer to use the oven, although some of the crisp, dry finish is lost. Indian spitted foods require frequent basting, for the meat is never larded.

Seek Kababs are minced meat croquettes shaped with the hand over an iron skewer, or *seek*, the thickness of a pencil. The layer of meat is thin, and a fierce heat – usually a charcoal or wood fire, but a modern grill will do – cooks these kababs in one minute or so.

Boti Kababs are also made on the skewer. Small pieces of very tender meat are marinated for several hours and then cooked under intense heat, basted with butter. The marinade forms a glaze on the surface.

Kofta is minced meat shaped into small balls then braised in korma style, curried, or even spitted on small skewers. Some koftas are formed over sweet-sour plums, or a paste of minced dried apricots and herbs; some are moulded on eggs and these are called *nargisi* (narcissus). The meat itself is ground very fine, then blended or pounded to a forcemeat. Herbs, seasonings and spices are added, and sometimes cream or yoghourt; an egg is used to bind.

Method and substitutes for tandoori cooking. Cooking on the open fire is one of the oldest methods, and one of the best. The food is crisp because exposure to the air rapidly dries any excess moisture; it also has superb flavour. In India, the *tandoor* is used – a clay oven as high as a man. If you have a closed rotisserie then you can almost duplicate the roasts of India, and, as has already been said, a fair imitation is the now popular barbecue, but that is feasible only in the open air and therefore depends on the weather. The revolving spit fitted inside an oven is useful only in that it allows the meat to revolve and so baste itself.

Spitted foods are first marinated to aromatize and make them tender. The marinade should be used sparingly – only enough to coat the meat and dry on before cooking. Meat must be basted the moment it is dry, but not before. Too little basting produces dry food, but too much produces excess moisture which spoils the flavour.

The spit itself must first be oiled or greased, and the heat should be regulated according to the size and type of meat. Small cubes of tender meat need fierce heat to cook outside and inside simultaneously. Larger pieces which need cooking for a longer period, will start at a very high temperature to seal the surface, and then cook at a more gentle heat. Red meats especially need to be seared so that the juices are sealed within the meat. Do not puncture the brown crust formed by this sealing, or the juices will run out, leaving a dry and flavourless roast. Do not on the other hand, produce so thick a protective crust that the heat cannot penetrate to the interior. White meats need less cooking than red and, having no great concentration of juice, do not require searing. They should be cooked at a temperature that browns as it tenderizes. In both cases, baste well, and allow white meats to become dry and crisp only at the end of the roasting.

GRILLING, ROASTING AND BAKING

Ideally, use a charcoal grill. Next best are electric, gas, or infrared grills. Excellent 'contact' grillers are now available from specialist kitchen shops, consisting of two metal portions with a waffle-type steel grid.

Apply more or less the same rules for grilling red and white meats as for tandoori, except that heat is regulated by altering the grid distance from the meat rather than lowering the heat. Baste to prevent drying, and handle red meat with tongs, not a fork, to prevent piercing the sealed surface. When cooked, white meats will look almondy and opaque; red meats will swell, and be springy to the touch because of the hot juices inside.

For oven roasting, I use one or two small dishes of flour to absorb vapour. In some recipes pastry dough or batter is used as a protective cover for baking food in the oven. This is broken, and only the meat or vegetable served. Meat is sometimes cooked a little first, to drain off surplus fat or oil, and then encased in the dough.

Methods of preparing minced foods for tandoori. Now we come to the techniques for the preparation of forcemeats and meat paste for the various kababs and koftas used in tandoori, grills and roasts.

For minced meats, choose meat that is free of fat, sinew or gristle. Grind finely, using pestle and mortar, mincer, or an electric blender, and then work to a paste. Bind with whole egg or yolk but, with the exception of an occasional recipe calling for lentil, do not thicken. Force through a sieve or squeeze in a muslin bag to expel moisture. Cool before shaping.

Meat pastes may include onions, garlic and other aromatics, as well as chives, coriander leaves or parsley. A little lemon juice, yoghourt or cream may be used during the pounding.

Only the most delicate minced meats are poached; they may also be placed inside banana leaves, foil or cooking parchment, and steamed until set. Some forcemeats are cooked on the griddle or in a heavy frying pan; others are deep-fried until golden.

Rougher meat is used for the kofta. It is minced finely, but not pounded or reduced to a paste, and never sieved. It can be grilled, fried, curried or braised; it may be used to stuff chicken or other meat. Seek kabab can be made from fine or coarser minced meat.

MISCELLANEOUS DISHES

Parcha, or parchment, is a term I have used to describe boned meats rolled up with stuffing and then roasted, baked or braised: loosely, all are kababs of some kind or another. Double pork chops with a wad of mushrooms between come into this section. Food cooked *en paupiette* – in India, wrapped in a banana leaf and cooked in hot ashes, over charcoal, in the oven or over steam – is also a variation of the parcha style. A parcha of whole shoulder of lamb is cooked in a pastry casing. This pastry enables the meat to be cooked without loss of juices and without the application of direct heat to the surface, but it is not eaten itself.

Chasnidarh food is cooked or finished in a sweet-sour sauce. It is usually eaten hot, but if made without fat can be served chilled. Pork, duck, very young lamb, veal and fish of many kinds (but not shell-fish) are best suited to this style of cooking. Sugar and vinegar or lemon or lime juice are used for the sauce, and fruits such as banana and cherries, or vegetables such as beetroot, pumpkin, turnip, carrots and some types of bean add to the appearance and flavour of chasnidarh dishes.

Finally, the *tarka* or *chamak* style: this is of great importance in Indian cooking and indicates a fierce searing with clarified butter and seasonings to flavour or coat and gild the surface of the food. It is essentially a finishing-off process. The food is first cooked quite plain or with just a suspicion of seasonings, and then given a searing at a very high temperature.

There are other minor styles, but these are explained as they occur throughout the book.

Stuffings and Forcemeats. Fine meat paste is used to stuff poultry and boned meat, as well as vegetables like aubergine, fresh pimentos and cucumbers. Though recipes for stuffings are given in the various sections of this book, here is a short list of the type of ingredients which go to make Indian stuffings – true gourmet fare: rice, mashed potatoes, chestnuts, buck-wheat, meat, fish, scrambled or hard-boiled eggs, shredded omelette, mushrooms, celery, green ginger, coriander, parsley mixed with butter, milk, cream or yoghourt, consommé, lemon juice, onions, garlic, bay leaves and the whole range of aromatics, chillies, fresh or tinned pimentos, cheese, almonds, dried fruits, cooked fruits, capers and pickled gherkins, pickles and chutneys of all kinds and the oil, brine or sauce from various pickles, chopped liver and kidney, brains and sweetbreads, bamboo shoots and lentil sprouts (see p. 194). This does not exhaust the possibilities, but gives some indication of the variety of ingredients.

The techniques of cooking which follow are similar to those used in Western cooking.

BOILING

Except for brief periods, meat should not be fast-boiled. Correct application of heat is the secret of cooking, and boiling hardens the outer surface of meat, while the inner part remains uncooked. White meat becomes stringy and hard right through because the albumen has hardened. One or two recipes in this book call for a brief boiling in cream or yoghourt which, because of their fat content, help to penetrate the tissue and moisten it.

POACHING

The liquid for poaching is kept just below boiling point: the surface of the water should be steaming hot, but never bubbling. There must be enough liquid to cover the food completely.

SIMMERING

A prolonged poaching. The water must never boil, save for a
few stray bubbles which indicate that the liquid is sufficiently
hot to extract the juices and flavour of the meat and to soften the
fibres. Small pieces of meat are added to the boiling water, and
heat quickly reduced. Large pieces are placed in cold liquid and
brought rapidly to the boil. Use a large quantity of cooking
liquor for small poachings, but for one large piece like a whole
fish or chicken, choose the smallest pan that will hold enough
liquor to poach safely.

CHAPTER FOUR

Batterie de Cuisine

COOKING UTENSILS

I DO not want in this chapter to produce an exhaustive list of the utensils and implements used in preparing Indian food, but rather to discuss the most important ones and to describe the present-day transition from the traditional to the modern.

Gas and electric cookers are finding their way into kitchens in the towns and cities of India. There remains no substitute for charcoal cooking and for the special flavour it imparts to food, but we must accept this change and learn to adapt the techniques for charcoal and wood fire to the use of heat 'on tap'. Gas cooking affords a greater degree of control than electric, and has the advantage of a naked flame for glazing and searing. However, new electric cookers are being introduced with quick-control elements, and the new infra-red grills allow an extension of cooking techniques. The oven, whether gas or electric, is well suited to the dum technique, so similar to the French *daube*. In former times *daubières* had deep lids so that they could be covered with live charcoal, and this is still the practice in India today. Charcoal burning barbecues are an excellent substitute for the Indian *anghiti* (brazier) used for grilling meat kababs and minced meat preparations and even placing food direct on charcoal.

If you can afford two really heavy vessels with heavy lids, you should be able to produce all the recipes in this book. They should be of 3 to 5 pint capacity. Heavy metal transmits heat evenly and prevents food burning or scorching; it also retains heat, so that the vessel can be removed from the fire for a short time and the food remain hot. Modern Scandinavian casseroles made of heavy metal are ideal. With glazed enamel, however, I find that food tends to stick to the bottom. Cast aluminium

36

comes in heavy weights and, though difficult to find, makes very good cooking utensils. In addition to two heavy saucepans, a heavy frying pan or skillet is desirable, an iron griddle or 'Mijoska' (called *tawa* in India) which can be used under the pan to reduce heat and for making Indian breads, and asbestos mats for further control of heat at low temperatures. One heavy (fish) kettle, about 12 to 14 inches long is useful: it allows the quick evaporation so necessary for certain types of cooking. It also enables one to make a flat bed of the food instead of piling it up. A covered roaster is a good substitute.

Earthenware, both glazed and unglazed, is used in India as in Europe. It transmits heat gently and is ideal for long, slow cooking. An earthenware casserole will gradually acquire a characteristic and unmistakable flavour of its own; oven glassware may be used as well, but it adds nothing of itself to a dish. Food keeps extremely well in earthenware, so it is good for a dish like Vindaloo (p. 51) which must be cooled for a day before reheating. And for rice pilaus and such preparations, an earthenware casserole will give the finest result.

A pestle and mortar or an electric blender is essential. Old Victorian brass or iron pestles and mortars can still be found occasionally in London markets or country auctions. The porcelain type can be bought in several sizes from a chemist or most kitchen equipment stores and will cope well with every kind of pounding except liquid. Acid ingredients should never be used in a metal mortar. It is best not to use the smaller sort of electric blender with a plastic beaker as these can shatter; some aromatics may also flavour them permanently. In addition to powdering aromatics, a blender will liquefy or purée foods, especially fruits and vegetables. Again the small blenders may not mince dry meat or fish, and the makers' instructions should be followed. It can be used in the preparation of pâtés, forcemeats, pastes and marinades. Chick-peas, rice or nuts can be pulverized to a fine flour.

It is essential to have a standard asbestos (not merely wadded) oven-glove to handle pans and lids straight from the oven. You will also need skewers, of two sizes: 20 inches long by $\frac{1}{2}$ inch thick, and 9 inches long and needle thin. Wooden and bamboo skewers are also used in India. They should be oiled and placed in a warm oven and this treatment repeated several times, in order to season them. Wooden ladles are useful for they do not rob a casserole or saucepan of its valuable heat; nor can they be damaged by acid foods which attack some unlined metals. A strainer is used frequently in Indian cooking, and a sieve is essential. Use a large square of muslin (not cheese cloth) for straining broths, and another square of cotton or fine poplin for squeezing surplus water from yoghourt and cream (see p. 250). Graters, rolling-pins, chopping boards should be found in every kitchen and you should have a collection of really sharp, good-quality chefs' knives. Keep several yards of cheese cloth handy; it is extremely useful when steaming rice and helps to keep it perfectly dry and fluffy.

I am enthusiastic about modern appliances. The blender has already been mentioned. Mincers, whether manually operated or electric, are useful not only for taking the hard work out of mincing meat or fish, but also for grinding spices and other ingredients. If you own a mixer, it will be pressed into daily use and act as a substitute for the *massalchi* or cook's assistant – rare now, even in India. Many gadgets are surprisingly good: syringes for separating fat from gravy, parsley choppers, onion slicers and the garlic press. However, if too much work is done for you, the satisfaction which comes from manual dexterity and skilled judgement, and provides half the fun of cooking, will be absent.

Finally, a taboo. Use of the pernicious pressure cooker grows daily. There are certain vegetables which can stand up to rapid boiling, as well as some soups and stocks, for which the pressure cooker may be admirable. But the difference between lentils or beans cooked by traditional methods, and those cooked in a pressure cooker is considerable. It is death to meat: the food will emerge tenderized but flavourless. Only in an emergency does it prove its worth, for then foods of many kinds may be cooked in a short time and so save the day. Compare pressure cooking with the Indian style called *dum* or the French *daube*. Here, a ribbon of solid dough is used to seal the casserole. Pressure is slight, the heat very slow. Unlike the pressure cooker which drives in moisture by force, dum cooking first seals the surface, then cooks the interior and finally, extracts the juices. The difference is fundamental.

SERVING DISHES AND PRESENTATION

In India there is no table setting as in the West. Food is served on brass, copper or silver platters with raised edges. This is the *thal*, and the smaller one is the feminine, *thali*. Food is then placed in individual bowls made of metal and earthenware. These *katora* or *katori* keep the food hot, and prevent it from mixing, which is the natural consequence of eating from a plate.

It is the traditional serving vessels, of vivid enamelled metals, of porcelain, of metals engraved and chased, of brass on steel, and gold in silver, rather than the food itself, that form the focus of display. Garnishing and decoration of food is kept simple: a sprinkling of freshly chopped green herbs, the various colours of rice, patterns in gold-leaf on some sweetmeats.

In India it is traditional for the kitchen and dining-room to be one. A separate room is reserved for formal dining, and large gatherings may be accommodated under awnings (usually of hand-blocked cloth) and marquees. Food is also served in different parts of the house as mood and the season may incline one. The joint-family system of an Indian household, now breaking up, especially in the cities, meant that the kitchen was in use for several hours. In the sunny months of winter, food may be eaten out of doors. Indians normally sit on woven mats, small carpets, or small wooden seats, raised no more than one inch from the floor; his thali is placed on another (higher) wooden, marble, stone or forged-brass table. In well-off families, cotton sheets – hand-blocked in the old days and of many colours, now too often white – are spread out to protect the carpets. Paintings show that at one time embroidered sheets were used to cover the laps of diners and so act as napkins. Food is placed in the middle of the sheet, or on the side, and is handed in by a server. Gaily coloured cloths of cotton or silk are used to wrap around the serving dishes. The cloths are untied and the food served, then the cloths are folded back loosely around the container.

For the modern table, I use carefully selected pieces of Indian cloth, chosen for colour and texture. Cloth squares of arsenic red, lapis lazuli, magenta and sombre grey look attractive against a plain white table cloth. For a table setting, I provide small deep bowls and one large plate.

CHAPTER FIVE

Expertise

I AM often asked whether it is possible for anyone other than an Indian to produce authentic Indian food. How can someone who has never lived in the country understand the subtleties of the Indian cuisine? This question is important. Without a definite answer the recipes in this book become pointless, 'like flowers growing in the sky', as they say in India.

This book has been written for Europeans and for Indians too. It attempts to define for the first time the system and structure of Indian cookery. The methods are clearly explained; there are general chapters on style and technique. Yet there is more to cooking than an understanding of principles and a knowledge of techniques. The heart of any country's cuisine lies in the tradition and sensibility of its people, and something must be known of this in order to develop real sympathy with the methods and logic of Indian cooking.

There is a widely held belief that Indian cooking owes much of its ingenuity to the chronic poverty of its people. Nothing could be more wrong. From early times until quite recently India has been *the* country of riches. This wealth was founded on the prosperity of the merchant classes, of the small traders and the workmen. The farming communities have always been affluent. I have chosen the following extracts, from the chronicles of Portuguese and Arab travellers of the sixteenth century, to illustrate this point.

Visiting Vijyanagar in the Deccan, Domingo Paes of Lisbon wrote in 1537:

These dominions are very well cultivated and very fertile, and are provided with quantities of cattle, such as cows, buffaloes and sheep; also of birds both those belonging to the hills and those reared at home, and these in greater abundance than in our tracts. The land has plenty of rice and Indian-corn, grains, beans, and other kinds of crops which are not sown in our

parts; also an infinity of cotton. Of the grain there is great
quantity . . .

And of the capital itself, Paes writes:

This is the best provided city in the world, it is stocked with
provisions such as rice, wheat, grains, Indian-corn, and a certain
amount of barley and beans and moong (lentils), pulse, horse-
gram (channah), and many other seeds which grow in this
country and are the food of the people, and there is a large store of
this and very cheap. . . . There is much poultry; they give three
fowls in the city for a coin worth a vintem, outside the city they
give five fowls for a vintem.

In the country there are many partridges . . . as also quails
and hares, and all kinds of wild fowl, and other birds which live
in the lakes and which look like geese. All these birds and game
animals they sell alive and they are very cheap for they give six
or eight partridges for a vintem, and of hares they give two and
sometimes one. Of other birds they give more than you count,
for even of the large ones they give so many that you would
hardly pay attention to the little ones they give you, such as doves
and pigeons and common birds of the country. . . . The sheep
they kill every day are countless, one could not count them, for
in every street there are men who will sell you mutton so clean
and so fat that it looks like pork; and you also have pigs in some
streets of butchers' houses so white and clean that you could never
see better in any country; a pig is worth four or five fanams. Then
you see the many loads of limes which come in each day, such as
those of Povos [near Lisbon] are of no account, and also loads of
sweet and sour oranges, and wild brinjals (aubergine) and other
garden stuff in such abundance as to stupefy one.

Domingo Paes goes on to speak of the oil and milk sold, and
the rearing of cows and buffaloes for dairying, of pomegranates,
grapes and other food-stuffs. With this abundance and general
prosperity, it was possible for a cuisine to evolve where even the
humblest could boast of some delectable fare.

The second extract is from a collection of classical tales which
mirror the domestic and thereby the culinary scene. This folk-
tale portrays the care lavished on cooking, and the pride in
perfection:

Once upon a time, the eighteen-year-old son of a millionaire began to worry about finding a wife with all the necessary qualities. He had to find her for himself. Travelling in the guise of an astrologer he took with him two pounds of unthreshed rice. To all the daughters of rich and poor families that he met he asked, 'Are you able, my dear, to prepare a complete meal for us with these pounds of rice?' He was mocked and thrown out. During his wanderings as an astrologer, which brought him into contact with many households, the millionaire saw a girl of surpassing beauty whose family had run through a fortune and were reduced to comparative poverty. His heart went out to her, '. . . however, I shall not marry her before I have tried her; for those who act without circumspection inevitably reap repentance in abundance.'

So he asked with a kindly look, 'Would you be able, my dear, to make a complete meal with this rice?' He showed her the two pounds of unthreshed rice.

The girl gave her old maidservant a meaningful glance, whereupon the woman took the two pounds of rice from him, sprinkled and rubbed it thoroughly and placed it on the terrace. Then she washed the girl's feet. The girl then dried the sweet-smelling rice, measure by measure, repeatedly turning it over in the sun, and when it was thoroughly dry, she spread it on a hard smooth part of the floor, threshed it very very gently with the edge of a reedstalk, and finally took all the rice grains out of the husks, without breaking them.

Then she said to the old servant, 'Mother, jewellers want these husks, they use them to polish jewellery. Sell them, and with the pennies they give you, buy good hard firesticks, neither too dry, nor too damp, a small pan, and two shallow bowls.'

When the servant had done that, the girl placed the rice grains in the shallow mortar of kakuba wood with a flat, wide bottom, and began pounding them with a long, heavy, iron-tipped, smooth bodied pestle of khadira wood that was slightly hollowed in the middle to form a grip. She tired her arms in a charming play of raising and dropping, picking up and picking out single grains, which she then cleaned of chaff and awn in a winnowing basket, washed repeatedly in water, and after a small offering to the fireplace, dropped in boiling water, five parts water to one part rice.

As the grains softened and began to jump, and swelled to the size of a bud, she lowered the fire, and holding the lid on the pot, poured out the scum. Then she plunged her ladle into the rice, turned the grains with the ladle, and having satisfied herself that they were evenly boiled, turned the pot upside down on its lid, to let the rice steam [dum]. She poured water over the fire-sticks which had not burned up entirely, and when the flame had died down and the heat was gone, she sent this charcoal to the dealers. 'Buy with the coin you receive as much of vegetables, ghee, curds, oil, myrobalan and tamarind as you can get.'

When this had been done she added two or three kinds of spices, and once the rice broth had been transferred to another bowl, placed on wet sand, she cooled it with gentle strokes of a palm-leaf fan, added salt and scented it with fragrant smoke. Then she ground the myrobalan to a fine lotus-sweet powder, and finally relayed through her servant the invitation to a bath. The old nurse, clean from a bath herself, gave the disguised millionaire youth myrobalan and oil, whereupon he bathed.

After his bath he sat down on a board placed on sprinkled and swept paving stones. . . . He touched the two bowls that were placed on a light, green banana-tree leaf from her own garden – a quarter of one leaf was used – and she set the rice broth before him. He drank it and feeling happy and content after his journey let a sweet lassitude pervade his body. Then she served him two spoonsful of rice kedgeree and added a serving of butter, soup and condiment. Finally she served him the remaining boiled rice with yoghourt mixed with mace, cardamoms and cinnamon, and fragrant cool buttermilk and fermented rice gruel. He finished all the rice and side dishes. Then he asked for water. From a new pitcher with water that was scented with the incense of aloe wood, permeated with the fragrance of fresh bignonia blossom and perfumed with lotus buds, she poured out a thin, even stream. He held his mouth close to the vessel; and while the snowcold sparkling drops stung and reddened his eyelids, his cheeks tickled and thrilled at the pleasurable touch, his nostrils opened to the fragrance of the lotus buds, and his sense of taste delighted in the delicious flavour, he drank water to his heart's content. With a nod of his head he indicated that she stop pouring, and she gave him, from another vessel, fresh water to rinse his mouth . . .

CHAPTER SIX

Meat

THE meats most frequently used in Indian cooking are mutton, lamb or pork. Most Indians do not eat beef. However, beef can be substituted for some of the darker portions of mutton; veal can sometimes be used for the white portions of lamb, such as saddle (*rarrah*). The meat used for currying or stewing should be mature mutton not more than two years old, and for braising, about one year old (beef is best for braising when about four to five years old). Older meat is fit only for the stock-pot. Lamb is used for grilling and roasting.

There is much confusion about mutton so a few facts may be helpful. Mutton is matured lamb. It is best from the age of eleven months up to a maximum of two years. The winter or grass lamb is an animal which has had a full winter's grazing. It should not be over eight months old. Baby (spring) lamb is an animal as yet unweaned. It has never been grazed, and should be two to three months old. Baby lamb is treated as white meat, and mutton as dark or red meat. Baby lamb is used for the skewered meats, especially the *barra* or *barg* kabab. It is used for ard bhoona meats, where the meat is cooked in a sealed vessel with no moisture save butter. Meat for these dishes must be as tender as possible. Superb as baby lamb is, it will not do for korma or braised meats. It is too fatty, and the flesh has had no time to develop the juices of an animal between eleven and twenty-three months old. Baby lambs are sometimes cooked whole for feast days. If the animal is roasted on the spit, it is then coated with edible gossamer-thin leaf made from pure silver and gold :* the legs gold and the body silver. The use of this incredibly fragile gold and silver tissue is traditional, and is found in many dishes; all rice pilaus may be gilded as well as sweetmeats and confectionery. Eating gold and silver in this

---

*In London edible gold and silver leaf is sold in book form from F. Winter & Co. Ltd, 56 Whitfield Street, W.1.

form is an exotic way of getting your daily ration of roughage and minerals. Whole spitted baby lamb is sometimes stuffed with chicken, which in turn is stuffed with eggs and kofta. Whole baby lamb is also used in pilau rice preparations. This, however, is very advanced cookery and does not concern our book.

It will be noticed that most of the recipes use onion, and yoghourt is used as the French would use wine. The onions do not leave any distinct taste; they help to flavour and thicken the sauce. Yoghourt, likewise, leaves no flavour or taste of its own. It helps to tenderize meat, and to carry the aromatics inside the fibres; it also helps to thicken the sauce.

The preparations throughout this book use varying amounts and kinds of aromatics. Some are crusty, others piquant, others again bland, some pungent. Whatever the style of cooking, the food should have a clean appearance and taste. Overspicing food has become fairly common in modern Indian, but there are many preparations which need the merest suspicion of aromatics. Lamb chops can be cooked with a modicum of black pepper, one or two cardamom seeds and a touch of garlic; some skewered meats use only green sieved mango pulp, and black pepper. There are others whose glory is the rich mantle of a score of aromatics. True Indian cooking has flavour and taste, but above all aroma and scent.

TURRCARRI (CURRIES)

Curries are stews aromatized and cooked with water according to the Indian fashion. This cooking liquor is distinct from the sauce or juices of the braised meats (kormas). The liquor of the curry usually comes 2 inches above the surface of the meat; it often has more flavour than the meat itself. Left-overs are not used in Indian curries or other preparations. A long, slow simmering process is required to extract the juices from mature meat, and to soften the fibre to the stage where the meat becomes very tender. Use of heavy saucepans and slow cooking over gentle heat ensures that the result is not stringy or fibrous. Slow simmering also helps to blend the various ingredients. This style, the turrcarri, is the only preparation with a generous, soup-like cooking liquor. The meat should be lean, and free of fat, skin, rind, hair, gristle and any membrane. Ghee can be used, or clarified margarine, vegetable or animal fat, but not oil.

Mhaans Turrcarri Sadah (*Simple Mutton Curry*)

1½ lb. boned shoulder mutton	¼ teaspoon cayenne
1 oz. clarified butter	¼ teaspoon salt
1 small onion grated	1 tablespoon chopped parsley
1 teaspoon turmeric	or coriander leaves
1½ tablespoons ground coriander seeds	

Prepare the aromatics as listed above. Heat half the butter and brown the onion. Remove and reserve. Wipe the mutton with a damp cloth, dry well, and cut into small cubes. Heat the remaining butter and sear the meat over a high heat, then stir and brown on medium heat for 10 minutes. Add turmeric and half the ground coriander seeds. Stir and cook for 1 minute over low heat or until butter separates from the meat. Add browned onion and cayenne, stir, and cook another minute over low heat. Season with salt, and moisten with ½ cup water. Boil briskly and dry off moisture. Add enough water to come 2 inches above the meat, and keep this level constant. Bring to boil and cover; lower heat and simmer gently until meat is tender – about 1 hour. Then add remaining ground coriander, and chopped parsley or coriander leaves. Stir and cover, keeping just below a simmer for about 15 minutes. Serve.

Quartered potatoes can be added to the curry during the last stage of cooking. They absorb the flavour of the meat and aromatics, and are delicious. To make the curry hotter, whole red chillies may be crisped over low heat in a dry frying pan, then crumbled into the curry half-way through the cooking.

Mhaans Turrcarri Khasta (*Piquant Mutton Curry*)

For broth:

1 lb. mutton bones, cracked	Salt
1 small grated onion	1 crushed clove garlic
2 pints water	

For curry:

1½ lb. mutton or stewing beef

4 medium onions minced

4 medium onions cut in rings

3 oz. clarified butter

A little oil

1 tablespoon freshly ground black pepper

2 tablespoons dried mustard seed

1 teaspoon paprika

½-inch stick cinnamon, ground

2 teaspoons ground fenugreek seed

1 inch minced green, or ¼ teaspoon ground ginger

4 crushed cloves garlic

2 tablespoons minced mint leaves

¼ teaspoon salt

Good pinch asafoetida

Pound, chop, grate, etc., all aromatic ingredients before beginning the cooking.

Make a thick broth with the cracked bones, grated onion and the garlic clove. Cool, clear and skim off fat. Make a paste of minced onions, freshly ground black pepper, paprika, mustard seeds, parched or roasted lightly in a frying pan, and ground cinnamon. Cut meat in medium-sized cubes and gash all over with the point of a very sharp knife. Add a few drops of oil to the spices and rub them into the meat. Marinate for 2 hours. Heat the butter, add a layer of cubed meat, top with a layer of onion rings, dust lightly with half the fenugreek, and sprinkle with ginger and garlic. Put in another layer of meat, and top with onion rings; add any remaining aromatic mixture, fenugreek and the mint. Add salt, and cover with the broth. Bring to boil, cover and simmer on very low heat until meat is tender, about 1 hour. Replenish with broth to keep liquor constant at 2½ inches above the meat. Before serving aromatize with the asafoetida, and mix lightly over medium heat. Leave covered for 10 minutes, and serve.

Gurdakupura Turrcarri (*Kidney Curry*)

1¼ lb. lamb or veal kidneys (weighed without suet)

2 onions minced

3 oz. clarified butter

1 teaspoon turmeric

1 tablespoon sesame seed dried in oven

¾ tablespoon black cumin

Good pinch cayenne
2 skinned and seeded, ripe
 tomatoes

2 dried, powdered bay leaves
¼ teaspoon salt
Good pinch mace

Grind, pound, etc., the aromatic ingredients as far as possible
beforehand, similarly prepare vegetables. Steep the kidneys in
very lightly vinegared water for 24 hours, preferably in the
refrigerator. Wash kidneys in running water and dry well.
Halve and remove any membrane. Fry minced onions in butter
until golden brown then add sesame seeds with turmeric, cumin
and cayenne. Add the kidneys and fry five minutes over medium
heat, stirring all the while, until the butter separates. Add
tomatoes, dust with powdered bay-leaf and season with salt.
Moisten with ½ cup water, and sprinkle with mace. Cook until
dry. Add another ¼ cup water, and cook until dry. Now fry until
dark red. Stir all the while and do not let meat or aromatics
scorch or burn. Moisten with enough water to come 2 inches or
more above the meat. Bring to the boil, cover, and simmer over
gentlest heat until kidneys are quite tender. Open the lid a little,
wait until butter separates, then serve hot.

Saluna Shikar Mhaans (*Pork Curry with Eggs*)

2 lb. pork chops
6 hard-boiled eggs
2½ oz. clarified butter
2 red or dried chillies
1 teaspoon turmeric
1 inch orange peel finely
 chopped
¼ teaspoon salt
8 small turnips
3 cardamoms
¼ teaspoon grated nutmeg

½ inch pounded cinnamon
 stick
1½ tablespoons ground
 coriander seeds
1 each red and green pimento,
 cut into julienne strips
1½ inches fresh grated ginger,
 or ½ teaspoon powdered
 ginger
½ tablespoon minced parsley
 or coriander leaves

Grind, pound, etc., the aromatic ingredients, as far as possible
beforehand; also prepare the vegetables. Heat butter and sear
pork chops, then lower to medium heat, turning occasionally,
until meat is well browned on both sides. Remove the chops and
keep them warm. Add the broken red or dried chillies and fry
gently without scorching until the butter is red. Aromatize with

turmeric, stir and fry gently for a minute or so, and add browned chops, turning them in the butter. Add chopped orange peel. Moisten with enough water to come 3 inches above the meat. Bring to boil and simmer until two-thirds cooked, about 50 minutes. Strain liquor, reserving meat, and bring it to boil with salt. Add turnips with cardamom seeds, nutmeg and cinnamon. Dust with coriander seed and cook until turnips are falling apart. Remove turnips, sieve them, and return to the liquor. Put back the pork chops, add red and green pimento and the ginger. Pierce the eggs with a sharp fork or skewer, and add to curry, with parsley or coriander leaves. Cover and cook until meat is tender – about 30 minutes. Then leave on lowest possible heat – using asbestos mat if necessary – for 12 minutes before serving.

Turrcarri Molee (*Mutton Curry with Coconut*)

1½ lb. mutton (or veal)
½ lb. fresh coconut (or ¼ lb. desiccated)
¼ pint milk (or ¾ pint for desiccated)
2½ fl. oz. liquor from fresh coconut, if used
1 inch fresh ginger minced
1 tablespoon ground coriander seed
8 crushed garlic cloves

1 onion sliced in rings
8 small red or dried chillies roasted and bruised
2 oz. clarified butter
2 tablespoons ground fenugreek seed
1 tablespoon poppy seed
3–4 lemon tree leaves
2 tablespoons lime or lemon juice
¼ teaspoon salt

Grate or liquidize fresh coconut with the ¼ pint milk, afterwards straining off liquid for use and reserving grated coconut in muslin. Put desiccated coconut in muslin and steep for 2 hours in the ¾-pint boiling milk, 'pounding' a little at first, then strain liquid, reserving coconut tied in muslin. Parch or roast, pound, chop, etc., all aromatics.

Heat half the infused milk, add meat, cut in thin strips, with ginger, coriander, garlic, onion and chillies. Add salt, bring to boil, simmer until two-thirds cooked (about 45 minutes). Strain natural coconut liquor into rest of infused milk. Heat butter and 'dry' meat mixture, stirring well. Aromatize with fenugreek, add poppy seed, and cook until these are pale golden. Add mixed liquids, bag of coconut and lemon leaves, and simmer until meat is tender, about 15 minutes. Leave on lowest heat 10 minutes. Add juice, stir well, remove bag of coconut, and serve.

Turrcarri Molee Badam (*Almond-Coconut Mutton Curry*)

4 tablespoons ground chirongi or cashew nuts
¼ lb. fresh coconut, or 2 oz. desiccated
24 blanched almonds
¼ teaspoon ground dry ginger
1¼ teaspoons turmeric
1 tablespoon poppy seeds
2 tablespoons ground fenugreek seed
1½ tablespoons sesame seed
1 teaspoon freshly ground black pepper

1½ lb. boned mutton
2½ oz. clarified butter
3 medium onions
8 cloves
¼ pint milk
2 oz. tart gooseberries or rhubarb
½ teaspoon salt
2 green chilli peppers
4 crushed cloves garlic
Juice of 1 lime
1 tablespoon chopped chives

Prepare the aromatics as listed above. Make almond-coconut paste: grate coconut, or pound desiccated coconut, and place in blender with blanched almonds and chirongi nuts, using a little water to make a paste. Reserve.

Make aromatic paste: grind or blend poppy, sesame and fenugreek seeds and black pepper, and mix with turmeric and ground dry ginger. Reserve.

Cut mutton into medium sized cubes. Heat the butter and add meat with cloves and minced onions. Brown well, stirring over medium heat about 12 minutes. Add aromatic paste, and fry over low heat, stirring well until butter separates. Moisten with milk and bring to the boil; add sieved gooseberries or rhubarb to acidulate the curry. Enrich with almond-coconut paste. Season with salt, and aromatize with crushed garlic and whole green chilli peppers. Simmer until liquor is reduced. Moisten with enough water to cover the meat. Cook until tender, about 45 minutes, and then leave, covered, over very low heat for 20 minutes. Acidulate with lime juice and sprinkle with chives before serving.

Khargosh Ka Saluna (Hare Curry)

1 medium-sized hare
1 teaspoon freshly ground
    black pepper
5 cardamoms
4 bay leaves
1 teaspoon juniper berries
1 tablespoon mustard seed
6 cloves garlic

2 tablespoons minced parsley
    or kari phulia leaves
Good pinch cayenne
½ teaspoon ground ginger
½ teaspoon paprika
3 oz. clarified butter
¼ lb. shallots
½ teaspoon salt

Parch or roast, pound, chop, etc. all aromatics. Joint the hare and half-cook (about 1–1½ hours depending on age of hare) in water aromatized with crushed garlic. Meanwhile take cardamom seeds (including husks), mustard seeds, juniper berries, bay leaves and black pepper, parch in a frying pan, and grind down. Strain liquor from hare and reserve, keeping hare warm. Heat butter and fry the chopped shallots until golden. Put in pieces of hare and stir over medium heat for about 5 minutes. Add the ground spices, stir and cook for another ½ minute. Aromatize with mixed ginger, cayenne, and paprika. Moisten with a few drops of water, stir and cook until dry. Moisten with garlic cooking liquor. Season with salt, top with enough water to cover hare by 2 inches, add the kari phulia leaves, and bring to the boil, then simmer on lowest heat until tender (about 1–1½ hours). Leave to cool and keep for a few hours, preferably overnight. Re-heat without boiling and serve.

Vindaloo (Vinegared Pork Curry)

Here are recipes for that lusty Western Indian pork preparation marinated and then cooked in vinegar. The dish is traditionally made with pork, but is equally good with fatty duck or goose. As the molee style uses coconut, so the vindaloo style depends on vinegar. The recipe for pickled vindaloo can be used for venison, boar and game meats. It is extremely appetizing, and a useful standby. The pickled meat is drained and grilled, or it is cut very thin to make an exotic sandwich. The meat can be packed in vacuum jars, or in sterilized tins, and taken along on picnics, and certainly on longer treks or when camping. The vindaloo is a full-bodied dish. The quantity of red pepper is entirely a matter of discretion.

2 lb. boned pork	2 teaspoons ground mustard seed
2 oz. clarified butter	
14 cloves garlic	1 tablespoon turmeric
½ teaspoon each cardamom seeds, cinnamon, cloves, black pepper seed	1 tablespoon cumin seed
	1 teaspoon onion salt
2 tablespoons coriander seed	2 inches fresh, or 1 teaspoon ground ginger
½ teaspoon cayenne	6 bay leaves
1 teaspoon salt	1 cup wine vinegar

Parch or roast the coriander seeds in a frying pan and remove the husks. Lightly roast the cumin seeds. Grind these down with all the aromatics except the mustard seeds and bay leaves, and make into a thick paste with a little vinegar.

Heat ½ oz. of the butter and fry the garlic to a light gold. Remove, crush and reserve. Wipe the pork with a cloth soaked in vinegar and cut into large cubes. Gash or prick the pork cubes and rub in the aromatic paste. Lay the bay leaves on top of the meat and cover with vinegar. Marinate for 24 hours in a cool place or in the refrigerator. Turn and mix well every 4 hours. Fry the mustard seeds in butter and when they are lightly browned put in the pork with its marinade, and the bay leaves. Bring to the boil and close the lid tightly. Simmer over very low heat until meat is tender. If more moistening is required, hot water may be added. The juices of the vindaloo are midway between the sauces of braised meats, and the liquor of a curry. It can also be made using only ½ cup vinegar and making up the rest with water.

Sometimes the vindaloo is made without butter and served chilled. For this, the pork is drained and placed in a hot saucepan, when it begins to stick the marinade is added, a tablespoon at a time until it is perfectly dry. Repeat 4 times, then cover with remaining marinade and cook as above. Serve chilled.

Pickled Vindaloo is prepared as follows. Use very fat pork and wash it thoroughly in vinegar. See that your hands are free of moisture, and use wooden ladles. Rub pork with the aromatic paste, after gashing with a stainless steel knife, place in a covered saucepan and cook gently till all moisture has dried off. Heat a generous quantity of best mustard or olive oil in an earthenware pot or casserole. Grind down more aromatics with vinegar and steep in a little lukewarm oil for 5 minutes. Place pork in oil and add the second aromatic paste. Mix well, and simmer very gently until meat is tender. Cool and place the pork in an earthenware or stoneware jar. Sprinkle with whole peppercorns and bay leaves, top with the heated oil, covering the pork to a depth of 2–3 inches. Seal. When required, drain thoroughly and slice very thinly. It is eaten between bread rolls, or rolled up in a chappati or nan bread. The pickle can be grilled (or lightly fried) quickly on both sides, and served either with a garnish, or with vegetables and rice, or bread. The flavoured oil can be used to aromatize sauces and curries. A successful pickle takes many weeks to mature. Recipes are given in Chapter Fourteen both for fish and dark meat.

KORMAS (BRAISED MEATS)

The kormas require much greater attention than do curries. The method of braising has been described in an earlier chapter (pp. 24–7). Variations of this technique will be used with the preparations that follow – some of the best of any cuisine. Yoghourt and cream are used with verjuices to marinate and thicken the preparations.

Korma Sadah (*Simple Braised Mutton*)

1½ lb. boned mutton or lamb	¼ teaspoon salt
2½ inches fresh or ¾ teaspoon ground ginger	4 oz. clarified butter
5 shallots	½ teaspoon dried basil
6 cloves	½ cup yoghourt
5 cloves garlic	Good pinch mace
2 oz. coriander or parsley leaves	1 tablespoon chopped chives
	½ teaspoon paprika

Wipe meat with a damp cloth and pat dry. Cut into almond-sized pieces. Grind the ginger with shallots, cloves, garlic, and mix with minced coriander leaves to make a paste, adding the salt and scant 1 oz. butter. Rub this over the meat. Heat half remaining butter in a heavy pan and put in the meat. Cook and stir until dry. Aromatize with basil and whipped yoghourt. Boil until dry (boiling such small pieces of meat is permissible, for the inside and outside is cooked simultaneously). When dry and sticking a little to the saucepan, enrich with remaining butter, mace and chives. Cook gently until brown, then raise heat, stirring all the time until meat is well reddened. If the meat is not yet tender, add a sprinkling of water, and dry off; repeat if necessary. Add paprika, mix well. Place, covered, in a slow oven for 25 minutes. Serve.

Shikar Korma (*Pork Braised with Honey*)

2 lb. loin of pork
1¼ tablespoons honey
2 oz. clarified butter
½ teaspoon salt
4 grated medium shallots
½ teaspoon turmeric
½ teaspoon ground black pepper

5 fl. oz. whipped yoghourt
1 inch each orange and lemon peel
1 crushed clove garlic
4 ground cardamoms
½ inch splintered stick cinnamon
¼ teaspoon ground mace

Pound, chop, grate, etc., all aromatic ingredients before beginning the cooking. Wipe meat with damp cloth and dry. Cut along the bone and separate the meat into small pieces. Heat a heavy saucepan, and put in the honey. Stir until it sticks to the bottom, but is not caramelized. Moisten with butter, and when hot add the pork. Stir and brown on medium heat for about 10 minutes. Add one cup water, season with salt, boil, then simmer gently until cooked. Dry off all moisture. Aromatize with shallots, turmeric, black pepper, orange and lemon peel. Cook and stir over medium heat until butter separates. Now add beaten yoghourt a little at a time until it is all absorbed, and the butter again separates. Aromatize with garlic, cardamom, cinnamon. Cook on medium heat for another minute. Dust with mace, and close the lid tightly. Keep it on dum, in the oven, or with charcoal on the lid, for 15 minutes before serving.

Khara Korma (Lamb with Whole Spices)

The *khara* style refers to meat prepared with khara (whole) aromatics. The aromatics are kept whole, or are bruised or slightly crushed.

1½ lb. lamb or veal
4 cloves garlic
7½ fl. oz. yoghourt
¼ teaspoon salt
2½ inch splintered stick cinnamon
2½ oz. clarified butter
1 green chilli pepper
1½ teaspoons bruised aniseed, or fennel, or dill seed
8 cardamoms
2½ teaspoons cumin
2 red chilli peppers

10 cloves
2 bay leaves
1 tablespoon peppercorns soaked overnight in lime juice and a little salt
1 tablespoon pomegranate seed soaked overnight in water (optional)
1 tablespoon kalonji (nigella indica)
Good pinch asafoetida
½ teaspoon ground dry ginger

Prepare the aromatics as listed above. Make garlic liquor by steeping crushed garlic in ½ gill warm water for 30 minutes, then straining through muslin. Reserve. Cut meat into cubes 2 inches square, moisten with yoghourt, season with salt and cinnamon, and simmer until yoghourt is dry. Drench with garlic liquor, and simmer until dry. Add more sprinklings of water until meat is tender and very dry. Fry the meat in butter gently until nicely brown and crusty on all sides. While meat is cooking slit the green chilli pepper, remove seed, stuff with aniseed, and add to meat. Stir for a moment or two, and add cardamom seeds with husks just broken open, coarsely broken cumin seeds, broken or whole red peppers, whole cloves, bay leaves, the marinated peppercorns, pomegranate seeds and kalonji cooked until softened. All liquid from these seeds to be reserved. Stir and cook on low heat. Take the moisture remaining from the brined or marinated aromatics, and mix with asafoetida, and ginger. Combine everything and stir. Cook until dry and the butter separates. Close lid and give it a 10 minute dum in the oven. (The advantage of this method is that, when served, the diners can pick out such aromatics as they prefer to eat, rejecting those they don't care for.)

Shahi Korma (Braised Lamb Royale)

Akni:

½ pint water
3 small bay leaves dried and
  powdered

2 inches stick cinnamon
2–3 inches lemon peel

Korma:

2 lb. boned lamb or young
  mutton
4 oz. clarified butter
4 minced medium onions
2 oz. grated fresh ginger
12 ground cardamoms
10 crushed garlic cloves
4 tablespoons chopped mint
4 tablespoons ground
  coriander seed
½ lb. blanched pounded
  almonds
½ teaspoon freshly ground
  black pepper

4 ground cloves
½ pint whipped yoghourt
1 teaspoon paprika
2 oz. blanched split almonds
6 tablespoons raisins soaked
  2 hours in warm water
½ teaspoon salt
1 tablespoon kewara essence
  (rose water)
Pinch strand saffron, or
  envelope powdered

Pound, chop, grate, etc., all aromatic ingredients before beginning the cooking. Make an akni of ½ pint water, bay leaves, cinnamon and lemon peel brought to the boil, simmered 30 minutes and strained. Put in the meat, and simmer until half cooked; about 45 minutes. Drain, dry and reserve. Reduce liquor by half. Meanwhile prepare a paste from the aromatics: heat half the butter and fry the onions until a rich gold; add ginger, cardamom, garlic, mint, coriander, pounded almonds, black pepper, salt and cloves; mix and dry with onions over low heat for a minute; moisten with whipped yoghourt, 1 tablespoon at a time, until the consistency of the paste is that of a purée.

Add meat to paste, and cook on medium heat, stirring continuously. Add broth from meat and cook meat until tender. Dry off all moisture and give it a bhogar in paprika and the remaining butter, as follows: push meat to one side of the pan, away from heat, add butter, then paprika, allowing the mixture to get very hot. Ladle the meat on to it and start to fry, cover, shake, uncover and stir vigorously until meat is lightly browned and butter separates. Add split almonds and raisins and season with salt. Finally, add kewara essence. Seal lid at once and place in gentle oven. Take out after 50 minutes, unseal, and add saffron previously dissolved in a very little boiling water. Mix and serve.

Korma Badam Malai Khatai (Piquant Almond Cream Lamb)

2 lb. boned lamb
4 chopped onions
3 oz. clarified butter
¼ pint each double cream and moisture-free yoghourt (see Appendix p. 250)
4 crushed cloves garlic
2 tablespoons chopped chives
1 teaspoon freshly ground black pepper

1 teaspoon salt
Pinch saffron strands steeped overnight in 4 tablespoons boiling water
1 tablespoon roasted ground poppy seed
2 inches fresh ginger
4 crushed cardamoms
4 oz. blanched pounded almonds
Juice of 5 limes or 3 lemons

Parch or roast, pound, chop, etc., all aromatics. Squeeze yoghourt and cream separately to expel all moisture. Reserve. Wipe the meat with a damp cloth, dry, and cut into almond-sized pieces. Heat half the butter and brown the chopped onions. Remove, drain, and reserve. Fry meat in remaining butter until dark gold. Mix garlic with ¼ cup water, strain into meat, and dry on brisk heat. Grate the fresh ginger, mix in ¼ cup water, strain over meat, and dry off on high heat. Stir well. Aromatize with black pepper and roasted poppy seed, ground finely. Moisten with the yoghourt and the salt and stir, cooking over medium heat until dry. Mix the chives with the almonds, and add to the meat. Stir and cook for a scant minute. Enrich with cream, saffron and crushed cardamom seeds. Stir and cook until reduced by half. Add the lime juice, stir, and cover well. Place in gentle oven for 20 minutes, shaking the casserole a few times during this period, then serve.

Korma Rogan Josh (*Cinnabar Braised Lamb*)

The colour of this dish is a very dark russet, or cardinal red. Beetroot juice and the cooking technique produce the cinnabar colour.

2 raw beetroots
2 lb. boned lamb
6 minced large onions
4 oz. clarified butter
1½ tablespoons coriander seed
2 teaspoons ground fenugreek seed
2 whole red or dried chillies
1 teaspoon kalonji
4 fl. oz. yoghourt
3 teaspoons black cumin seed
2 teaspoons black peppercorns

1 grain of asafoetida
2 teaspoons turmeric
1 teaspoon garam masala
1 teaspoon salt
8 cloves garlic
1 teaspoon ground ginger
1 tablespoon paprika soaked in 4 tablespoons water
3 black cardamoms
2 bay leaves
1 tablespoon lime juice
3-4 kari phulia leaves

Clean the beetroots very thoroughly and boil, reserving ¼ cup of the cooking liquor (use the beetroots for another dish). Lightly roast and pound all the following, keeping them quite separate: coriander seed (remove husks), fenugreek, chillies, kalonji, cumin, and peppercorns with the asafoetida.

Heat some clarified butter, add onion and bay leaves and fry over medium, then low heat, stirring from time to time until dark brown. Sprinkle with a tablespoon of water, and cook further; repeat five times. The onions should be a dark mahogany red. Remove and reserve. Thinly slice 7 of the garlic cloves and fry in ½ oz. of the butter until russet brown, then remove and crumble in a little water; add remaining raw clove garlic first creamed under a kitchen knife. Reserve.

Wipe meat with a damp cloth and cut into medium-sized cubes. Use remaining butter and sear the meat on high heat. Remove and keep warm. Aromatize the butter with turmeric, coriander and cumin; fry for ½ minute and moisten with whipped yoghourt. Add the chillies, mix and cook gently for 5 minutes. Add the meat and cook until the moisture is dried out. Stir and darken meat further, but do not let the aromatics scorch. Season with soaked paprika. Stir and cook until dry and colour deepens. Moisten a tablespoon at a time with the beetroot liquor. Stir when dry, and add ginger, peppercorns with asafoetida, fenugreek, kalonji and cracked cardamoms. Moisten with ¼ cup water, season with salt, aromatize with browned onions and crumbled garlic, and add 3 or 4 fresh or dried kari phulia leaves. Mix well and cover. Bring nearly to the boil and then simmer on very low heat until tender, about 45 minutes, adding more water if necessary.

Uncover the pan, and stirring continuously cook the sauce over a high heat to a glaze. When only the aromatized butter and aromatic paste remains, sprinkle the meat with the garam masala mixed with lime juice. Mix and fry for 2–3 minutes, then cover well. Place in a gentle oven (or charcoal the lid) for a dum of 30 minutes, before serving.

Korma Sheer (Almond-Milk Pork Chops)

2 lb. pork chops
2 oz. clarified butter
¼ teaspoon saffron strands ground with ½ teaspoon aniseed or fennel in hot milk (see recipe)
½ teaspoon freshly ground black pepper
1 inch fresh pounded, or ¼ teaspoon dry ground ginger
2 tablespoons ground coriander seed

2 pints milk
2 onions
Good pinch ground mace
1 inch crushed stick cinnamon
¼ teaspoon salt
¼ cup rice water or 2 teaspoons cornflour
8 oz. blanched almonds
½ pint double cream

Wipe chops with a damp cloth. Melt butter and add a very few saffron strands with a small splinter of cinnamon. Add the meat over very high heat. Cover, remove from heat and shake the pan several times; replace on medium heat and fry, stirring all the time. Add half the onions sliced thinly, the salt, ginger and coriander. Mix and add milk. Boil (the chops are thin enough not to be spoilt by boiling) until very nearly dry. Keep warm while you grind the almonds, mix with double cream or malai, and strain over the meat. Aromatize with rest of cinnamon, mace and black pepper; add ¼ cup rice water, or 2 teaspoons cornflour and combine well. Aromatize with saffron ground down with aniseed in a little hot milk. Cover and seal with a ribbon of paste. Give it a dum in the oven, or with live charcoal on the lid. Keep in dum for 25 minutes and serve with a sprinkling of chopped chives and the rest of the onions cut thin and fried crisp.

This dish, simmered in milk and finished off with cream, is called *sheer* or *kheer*. Should you use yoghourt and cream it is called *jogurath*, and with milk and yoghourt it is called *lowabdarh*.

Korma Bahadhar Shahi
(Braised Lamb: King Bahadhar Shah-Style)

2 lb. boned loin of lamb
5 egg yolks
6 oz. blanched almonds
½ teaspoon aniseed or fennel or dill seed
½ lb. shallots
¼ teaspoon saffron
4 cloves garlic
5 fl. oz. moisture-free yoghourt (see p. 250)

6 oz. clarified butter
2 inches fresh ginger
2 tablespoons minced coriander or parsley leaves
¼ teaspoon salt
4 fl. oz. double cream or moisture-free malai

Make a paste from the saffron and half each of the shallots, ginger, garlic and aniseed ground down with a little yoghourt. Cut the meat into small dice, rub with the paste and marinate for 1 hour. Heat the butter, add remaining shallots sliced very thinly, and remaining ginger chopped. Brown well, drain and reserve. Fry meat in the butter. When this dries and sticks to the pan a little, moisten with remaining yoghourt and crushed garlic. When dry add little sprinklings of the salt and water until tender. Keep warm. Mince the coriander leaves and mix with a little water. Rub through a sieve, and then strain through muslin. Put aside.

Pound the almonds, mix with cream and pour over the meat. Add the browned aromatic paste and leave on very low heat, over an asbestos mat. Stir in the lightly beaten egg yolks, adding the coriander liquor. Aromatize with remaining saffron and aniseed ground in a little hot water. Cover, and give it a dum of the gentlest kind, not allowing the cream and yolks to curdle: about 18 minutes in a very low oven.

Korma Hazur Pasand (*Special Braised Lamb*)

1½ lb. boned shoulder of lamb
2 oz. clarified butter
4 shallots
2 inches fresh ginger
1 tablespoon ground coriander seed
1 teaspoon kalonji
6 cracked cardamoms
1 inch splintered stick cinnamon
Pinch ground mace
¼ teaspoon salt
5 egg whites
1 teaspoon essence of kewara
2½ oz. each chopped pistachio, blanched almonds and seedless raisins steeped 2–3 hours with pinch ground saffron in ¼ pint hot water

Prepare the aromatics as listed above. Cut a quarter of the meat in thin slices, cut the rest in almond-sized dice and fry in 1½ oz. butter with shallots separated layer from layer, ginger and coriander. Cook until dark gold, and until butter separates from the meat. Remove the thin slices and reserve, keeping warm. Moisten the rest with enough water to cover by 1½ inches and simmer with kalonji until remaining meat is tender, about 25 minutes. Remove this meat also and keep warm. Reduce liquor by half, strain and reserve. Dry pan over high heat, add remaining butter and when hot add cracked cardamom seeds and splintered cinnamon. Give the diced meat a bhogar by throwing it in the pan, clapping on the lid, removing from heat and shaking it. Replace on very low heat, leave for 2 minutes, add mace and shake pan two or three times. Add salt and moisten with the reduced liquor. Simmer and reduce sauce until almost dry. Mix the lightly beaten egg whites with a little water flavoured with essence of kewara and salt. Place in a pan with the meat slices over medium heat. When the egg white is set add contents of first pan, sprinkle with nut and saffron mixture, cover, and place on medium heat for 1 minute, and serve.

Shah Degh (*Lamb Royale Carbonnade*)

For this recipe, the meat is arranged in its pan in layers, and then simmered down to its delicious bedrock. Two cuts of meat are used. Use a shallow pan, no more than $3\frac{1}{2}$ inches deep, and 10 inches or more in diameter. This ensures rapid absorption of steam, and evaporation of moisture. If you have a very large, very heavy frying pan or skillet, it will be excellent for this preparation. For a smaller vessel, reduce the quantities in this recipe.

$1\frac{1}{2}$ lb. boned shoulder or leg of lamb
Lean noisettes from 6 loin chops, each $2 \times 2 \times \frac{1}{2}$ inches
4 fl. oz. yoghourt
4 cloves garlic
8 hard-boiled eggs
$\frac{1}{2}$ teaspoon dried basil
6 cardamoms
2 roasted red chillies
2 fresh green chillies

2 large green sweet peppers
3 oz. clarified butter
3–4 sticks celery
$2\frac{1}{2}$ inches ginger
6 oz. button mushrooms
$1\frac{1}{2}$ lb. white onions
2 oz. parsley or coriander leaves
$\frac{1}{4}$ teaspoon ground saffron strands or 2 teaspoons turmeric
$\frac{1}{2}$ teaspoon salt

Shred the boned shoulder by holding the meat, and with a very sharp, heavy knife, cutting slantwise into slivers. Mix with whipped yoghourt and crushed garlic. Marinate for 30 minutes.

Boil the eggs, chop fine and reserve. Make a paste of roasted red chillies and raw green chilli peppers. Cut the green sweet peppers into julienne strips. Slice the mushrooms medium thin. Slice onions very thin; shred the coriander leaves or parsley. Grind the cardamoms, rub into the noisettes, and sauté them in 1 oz. of the butter until golden on both sides. Aromatize with a little basil and keep warm. Melt rest of butter in a large pan, lightly brown the onions and remove. Put in the shredded meat with its marinade. Stir and fry on medium heat, until butter separates. Strain butter and reserve. Arrange a layer of shredded meat in large pan, season with salt and basil; next a layer of chopped celery and pepper, eggs, mushrooms and onions, sprinkled with more basil. Lay the remaining meat on top and sprinkle with chopped coriander leaves, season with chilli paste and salt. Bury the aromatized noisettes in these layers. Mix the strained butter with ground saffron and enough hot water to cover the top layer by $\frac{1}{2}$ inch. Bring to the boil, then lower heat. Cover and simmer gently until all the moisture has evaporated, about 1 hour. The meat should be tender. If further cooking is necessary, sprinkle in a little water and return to heat. Finally raise the heat high, so that the bottom layer of meat sticks a little, and dry off all moisture. Close the lid, give the pan a dum for 20 minutes either in a moderate oven or with live charcoal. Serve a portion of the slivered meat with each noisette.

Korma Khasa
(Casseroled Meatballs and Spring Vegetables)

1½ lb. boned leg of lamb
4 oz. clarified butter
4 oz. each spinach, beetroot, carrots and white cabbage (or soya greens)
¾ inch stick cinnamon finely splintered
1 red chilli
1 teaspoon paprika
Grain of asafoetida
1½ teaspoons fenugreek seed
Pinch strand saffron steeped in 4 tablespoons boiling water
1 teaspoon cornflour
½ lb. minced meat

2 onions
½ teaspoon ground black pepper
1 egg white
2 tablespoons ground coriander seed
1 tablespoon parched ground mustard seed
¼ teaspoon mace
4 oz. lime juice or vinegar
4 oz. sugar
10 almonds, blanched, slivered, and fried in butter
2 teaspoons black cumin
½ teaspoon salt

Parch or roast, pound, chop, etc., all aromatics. Cut the lamb into almond-sized pieces and fry in heavy pan using about half butter, stirring well, until dark brown. Moisten with a little water and cook until tender. Strain liquor and reserve. Heat ½ oz. of remaining butter, add the sliced red chilli (seeded for milder result) and the paprika, and stir over low heat until butter is a rich red colour. Add half the cinnamon, raise heat high, and put in the meat. Cover the pan, remove from heat, and give it a good shake or two. Then put in a gentle oven or place live charcoal on top and cook for about 20 minutes.

Meanwhile make meatballs or kofta by combining the minced meat, grated onions, black pepper and salt, white of egg, and mustard and shape into marble-sized kofta. Fry them in remaining butter, and reserve. Beat up the sugar and lime juice

with a little cornflour and aromatize with fenugreek ground
with asafoetida. When smooth, put in half the kofta and simmer
to reduce the chasni or syrup to a thick glaze. Simmer the remaining kofta 15–20 minutes in the reserved meat liquor,
aromatizing with cumin. Meanwhile, chop spinach and soya
greens, sliver beetroot, thinly slice carrot, season lightly and
simmer in 2 tablespoons of water until tender.

Take the almond-sized cooked lamb and combine with
slivered almonds, ground coriander, mace and the remaining
cinnamon. Arrange in heavy pan. Add the cooked vegetables
and, on top, arrange the chasni kofta on one side and the meat-
sauce kofta on the other. Sprinkle with saffron water. Cover and
give it a dum in a gentle oven for 15 minutes, and then serve with
a light sprinkling of finely chopped coriander leaves or parsley.

*

The korma khasa brings us to the field of meat and vegetable
cookery. These kormas are made either with a thick sauce, or
with simply the natural moisture and juices of the vegetables and
the butter used for cooking. In these preparations the meat and
vegetables blend, each lending to the other its distinctive
flavour. The dum technique (see p. 27) is of particular importance in blending the flavours, as it is in all kormas and in rice
preparations. It is customary to 'overcook' the vegetables, so
that they really amalgamate with the meat and its juices.

Sagh Mhaans (Lamb with Spinach)

2 lb. spinach
1½ lb. boned lamb
2 oz. clarified butter
6 grated shallots
2 inches fresh ginger
3 crushed cardamoms
1¼ tablespoons ground
    coriander seed
2 teaspoons turmeric
1 green chilli

¼ teaspoon paprika
1 tablespoon mustard seed
Garlic infusion made with
    4 cloves garlic crushed and
    steeped for 30 minutes in
    4 tablespoons warm water
1 tablespoon roasted ground
    poppy seed (optional)
¼ teaspoon salt
2½ fl. oz. yoghourt

Parch or roast, pound, chop, etc., all aromatics. Wash the
spinach well and steep in cold water for several hours. Drain,
chop very fine, cover and put aside. Cube the lamb and fry in

half the butter with the cardamom and three-quarters of the coriander until browned all over. Add grated shallots and continue frying and stirring, until shallots are a dark gold. Mix in the fresh ginger cut in julienne strips and fry together for about 1 minute. Aromatize with turmeric, the rest of the coriander and the slivered green chilli. Stir and fry together for another minute without scorching. Now add the paprika, and stir and fry for a few seconds, scraping the bottom of the pan. Fry the mustard seed, using just enough butter to grease the pan, and when the seeds crackle and snap, add to the meat. Stir and aromatize with garlic infusion. Raise heat and stir vigorously for about 1 minute.

Add poppy seed, top with chopped spinach, season with salt, moisten with whipped yoghourt and cover well. Cook for 1 minute, raising heat and shaking the casserole five or six times. Lower heat, uncover and mix well. Cover again and cook over lowest heat until spinach is velvety and meat is very tender. Moisten with $\frac{3}{4}$ cup water, then stir and cook over medium heat, and dry off all moisture. Now cover and give the casserole a dum for 20 minutes in a gentle oven, or place live charcoal on top and asbestos mat over heat or flame, and serve.

Gobi Mhaans (*Braised Lamb with Cauliflower*)

In the previous recipe, the meat with spinach became velvety and smooth through the moisture from the spinach blending in with the juices and aromatics. For meat and cauliflower, more clarified butter is used, and the cooking prolonged in order to reduce good-sized flowerets to a purée.

1½ lb. boned leg of lamb	½ teaspoon salt
3 oz. clarified butter	Good pinch cayenne
1 large onion	2½ teaspoons turmeric
2½ inches fresh ginger cut in 1¼ inch julienne strips	2 tablespoons mashed and husked coriander seed
2½ fl. oz. yoghourt	1¾ lb. cauliflower
2 small tomatoes skinned and sieved, or 2 tablespoons tomato purée	½ green pimento cut in julienne strips
½ teaspoon paprika	2 tablespoons chopped chives

Grind, pound, etc., the aromatic ingredients as far as possible beforehand, similarly prepare vegetables. Fry thinly sliced onion in butter until dark gold, drain, and reserve. Fry the ginger julienne strips in butter for a few seconds. Add meat and cook over medium heat until well browned all over. Moisten with whipped yoghourt, tomatoes, paprika, salt and cayenne, and, stirring well, cook until reduced to a thick paste. Now aromatize with turmeric and coriander seed. Stir well, and cook another minute. Add cauliflower cut into long-stalked flowerets; sprinkle with pimento strips. Stir and moisten with $\frac{1}{4}$ cup water, then dry off over medium heat. Repeat moistening and drying three more times. Add 1 cup of water. Bring to the boil, cover and simmer on very low heat until meat is tender; moisten with a little water if necessary. Dry off all moisture except butter and juices by stirring continuously over high heat. Place the casserole in a moderate oven for 30 minutes. Serve with a scattering of finely chopped chives.

Lamb and Turnips

Lamb cooked with baby turnips is another popular dish. The technique is the same as above. The turnips should be on the point of disintegration though still in one piece. The meat must be fried well, and onions made a cinnabar red. Paprika is used to render the sauce a ruby red. A generous amount – $\frac{1}{4}$ lb. or more – of butter is needed. The finished preparation has a rich sauce, composed of butter, juices, aromatics, and thickened yoghourt residue. All moisture is dried off, and only enough used to tenderize the meat. This type of preparation is delicious but not heavy. It is customary to serve very light accompaniments such as unbuttered Indian bread and crisp salads.

Subh Degh ('The Felicitous Pot')

2 lb. boned shoulder lamb	4 medium courgettes (*tinda*)
2 cloves garlic	Grain of asafoetida
Lime juice	6 large onions
1 medium cucumber	8 peppercorns
$\frac{1}{2}$ lb. pumpkin, marrow, or	2 crushed red chillies
squash	4 oz. clarified butter

2 tablespoons ground
coriander seed
4 tablespoons parched and
ground sesame seed
10 fl. oz. yoghourt
1 lb. baby turnips
½ lb. baby carrots (or large
ones cut 2½ inches long)

¼ pint akni (see p. 253)
½ teaspoon ground saffron
strands
2 teaspoons ground black
cumin
¾ teaspoon salt
½ teaspoon mace

Parch or roast, pound, chop, etc., all aromatics. This is a dish traditionally made on feast days. Cube half the lamb and gash it with a sharp knife point; rub it with half the garlic ground down with a little lime juice. Reserve. Peel cucumber and marrow, halve courgettes, and steep these for 30 minutes in salted water aromatized with a large grain of asafoetida. Separate 3 onions layer by layer and steep in same water. Mince the remaining lamb and mix with freshly ground peppercorns, a little garlic, 1 grated onion, salt and a pinch of crushed chilli. Shape into kofta. Thinly slice remaining onions, heat the butter and fry until dark brown. Remove and add the cubed lamb to the same butter. Stir and cook over very high heat for ¼ minute then on medium heat until butter separates. Add coriander, chilli and sesame. Mix well and cook on low heat for 3 minutes. Enrich with three-quarters of the whipped and strained yoghourt, adding it 3 tablespoonsful at a time until it is well blended. When the liquid has dried and butter separates again, add the turnips and carrots. Moisten with ¼ pint akni and simmer until meat is tender and turnips are quite soft. Remove vegetables from brine and cut into thick slices. Arrange the kofta on the cubed lamb, then make a dome of the brined vegetables. Take the remaining yoghourt, mix with saffron and cumin and pour on top of the raw vegetables. Add salt and mace. Seal pan and place for 1½ minutes on very high heat, then give it a dum in a gentle oven for about 15 minutes. Shake the casserole sideways and up and down before opening, and serve. The vegetables should be crisp; the cooked turnips buttery; the two kinds of meats give two different tastes, and the aromatics at the base are different from those on top. A beguiling culinary experience.

Korma Dil-Pasand (Braised Lamb and Vegetables)

This recipe uses a mellow garlic sauce like the aïoli sauce from Provence. It is one of the very few Indian food preparations which make a feature of garlic rather than blending it with other flavours.

2 lb. boned leg lamb
5 oz. clarified butter
2 inches fresh ginger
2¼ tablespoons ground coriander seed
½ teaspoon salt
1 egg white
1 lb. carrots
Good pinch ground mace
2½ tablespoons finely minced or pounded garlic

Rice water or ½–¾ tablespoon cornflour
10 fl. oz. yoghourt
1 inch stick cinnamon, pounded
1 teaspoon turmeric
2 teaspoons chopped chives
¼ teaspoon black pepper
2 fl. oz. double cream

Prepare the aromatics as listed above. Take three-quarters of the meat and cut into almond-sized pieces. Heat 4 oz. butter and put in ginger cut in julienne strips. When crisped add the meat over high heat. Draw away from heat, and add coriander and half the salt. Cover the pan and, shaking it continuously, replace it on high heat. Lower heat and leave pan for 2 minutes, shaking it four or five times. Uncover, season with rest of salt and cover with water. Simmer until meat is tender and moisture is dried out. Meanwhile simmer remaining meat in water until half cooked, about 35–40 minutes. Mince it finely, pound into it 1 oz. of the clarified butter (or suet), and amalgamate with the egg white. Knead the mixture and reserve. Split carrots lengthwise and cut into pieces about 2 inches long. Form a coating of the meat paste round the carrots, by rolling between the wetted palms of the hands. Fry gently in half remaining butter. Lift out carefully when crusty brown. Sprinkle with mace and keep hot.

Take the garlic and mix with a little water from boiled rice or ½–¾ tablespoons cornflour. Add moisture-free yoghourt and beat the mixture. Heat rest of butter, gently fry the cinnamon and then pour in the yoghourt. Mix well and add turmeric, chives and freshly ground black pepper. Add the cream little by little, and reduce until it is a thick liquid.

Arrange the meat on one side of a dish and the carrots on the other. Pour garlic sauce over and serve. It is usual to serve more sauce separately. The forcemeat is sometimes used to coat cooked beetroot, or poached aubergine.

Magazh Korma (Braised Brains)

Prepare the lambs' or calves' brains as for *Talawa Magazh* (p. 29), drain, cool and cut in ½-inch slices. Make a sauce of 5 fl. oz. yoghourt and 2 fl. oz. double cream, aromatized with a pinch of turmeric, ¼ teaspoon black pepper, a pinch of salt, 2 teaspoons each very fresh parsley, chives and mint all chopped fine. Simmer the sauce until reduced by half. Put in the brains and spoon sauce on top; heat gently or place in the oven until brains have taken the flavour of the sauce – about 7–10 minutes. Serve hot.

*

Doh-Peeazah. Doh-peeazah preparations achieve their singular flavour by using onions twice during cooking, and, traditionally, in quantities double that of the meat. The style has been explained in Chapter Three (p. 25): there is, however, no need to be rigid about the quantity of onions used.

Doh-Peeazah Dumwurdhi (Carbonnade of Pork)

1½ lb. boned loin of pork
2¾ lb. small onions
2 oz. clarified butter
2 tablespoons fresh lime or
    lemon juice
½ teaspoon salt (preferably
    rock salt)
2 teaspoons ground aniseed
5 fl. oz. moisture-free
    yoghourt (see p. 250)

Good pinch saffron strands
    or 1 teaspoon turmeric
    ground with 4 tablespoons
    water
¼–½ lb. blanched almonds
5 fl. oz. double cream
1 teaspoon freshly ground
    black pepper

Prepare the aromatics as listed above. Make onion paste: take

¾ lb. onions and cut into very thin rings. Fry in a little butter without stirring until dark gold. Add about 2 tablespoons lime juice and cook until dry. Continue frying until rich brown. Remove and pound or use blender. Reserve.

Peel rest of onions, keep them whole and prick deeply with a large sharp fork or with a meat skewer. Rub with salt and aniseed. Reserve.

Slice meat very thinly; moisten with half the yoghourt. Aromatize with half the saffron infusion. Fry the meat until yoghourt is dry. Continue to fry, stirring well, until meat is a dark gold. Moisten with the remaining yoghourt, and boil briskly until all yoghourt is dry. Enrich with almonds ground down with cream. Add the whole onions. Cover, simmer to reduce sauce, then leave over low heat until meat is cooked, about 30 minutes. Add rest of saffron and reserved onion paste. Aromatize with black pepper and salt. Seal pan and give it a dum in a moderate oven for 30 minutes, and serve.

Doh-Peeazah Massalam (*Spiced Carbonnade of Lamb*)

12 loin lamb chops
1 tablespoon cumin
4 red or dried chillies
Juice of 2 limes or 1 large lemon
3 oz. clarified butter
1 lb. minced onions
1 grated green pimento
2 inches grated fresh ginger
2 teaspoons ground fenugreek seed
1 lb. finely sliced onions
4 tablespoons minced mint leaves

2 tablespoons ground coriander seed
3 teaspoons turmeric
3 tablespoons finely ground pomegranate seed
1 tablespoon kari phulia leaves (if available)
Salt
2 teaspoons garam masala (see p. 249)
4 green chilli peppers
2 tablespoons chopped parsley

Pound, chop, grate, etc., all aromatic ingredients before beginning the cooking. For a milder dish use less chillies and seed them. Make a paste of cumin and red chillies pulverized with a little lime juice. Rub over the chops and marinate ½ hour. Meanwhile heat the butter and fry the minced onions, green pimento and ginger until dry, stirring well. Then cook without burning until a dark brown; sprinkle with a tablespoon of water, and repeat three times, cooking the onions to a dark cinnabar shade. Strain off the butter, cool and pound the onions (or use blender), reserving both butter and onions.

Heat the drained butter and add meat. Fry until dry, aromatize with fenugreek, fry 1 minute, then stir in the sliced onions and the mint leaves. Cook until dry, then add the coriander and $\frac{1}{4}$ cup water. Simmer until dry. Aromatize with turmeric, add pomegranate seeds and kari phulia leaves. Season with salt and add $\frac{1}{2}$ cup water. Boil once and then simmer on very low heat until dry. Meanwhile slit green chillies into 4 and fry. Sprinkle the doh-peeazah with garam masala, the fried chillies and chopped parsley. Cover and leave on low heat for 7 minutes. Add reserved onions, place in a slow oven for 15 minutes and serve.

Now we come to recipes where meat is combined with lentils and dried beans, and sometimes with dumplings. They are similar to the French *cassoulet* and should be cooked in an earthenware or stoneware casserole. A heavy old-fashioned metal casserole is a fair substitute.

Degh Fasli (*Harvest Cassoulet*)

$1\frac{1}{2}$ lb. breast of lamb
4 oz. black-eyed peas
4 oz. dried white beans
4 oz. kidney or red beans
5 oz. split green peas
Onion juice
1 cup milk
$\frac{1}{2}$ teaspoon salt
2 large green pimentos – one chopped, one cut in fine shreds
4 medium tomatoes

$1\frac{1}{2}$ teaspoons turmeric
Good pinch lovage seed
6 lime-tree leaves (or 1 teaspoon chopped lime or lemon peel)
$\frac{1}{2}$ teaspoon freshly ground black pepper
$2\frac{1}{2}$ oz. clarified butter
$\frac{1}{2}$ teaspoon ground basil
Good pinch ground mace
2 bay leaves

Soak overnight the black-eyed peas, white beans, kidney or red beans and split green peas. Make onion juice by pounding 2 medium onions with 2 tablespoons water, and squeezing the liquor through a muslin bag. Wipe meat with a damp cloth, dry, cut into large cubes and roll in the onion juice. Grind, pound, etc., the aromatic ingredients as far as possible beforehand, similarly prepare vegetables. Drain the legumes and keep them separate. Put the milk in a casserole with the salt. Add the red beans and split peas, the chopped pimento, and skinned, seeded and sieved tomatoes. Bring to the boil and add meat. Simmer until tender. Meanwhile cook black-eyed peas and white beans in water aromatized with turmeric, lovage seed, lime-tree leaves and a good pinch of pepper. Simmer on low heat for about 2 hours, until tender.

Remove meat from first casserole, drain and dry. Fry meat in butter with basil and a little sprinkling of cooking liquor to prevent the herb scorching. Sieve the split peas, red beans, etc., from the meat casserole, and add to the meat. Aromatize with the remaining black pepper, add shredded pimento, whole cooked black-eyed peas, and white beans. Strain liquor, reduce by half, and add to casserole. Aromatize with mace. Take a wooden stick or twig, and tie two bay leaves to it. Place in the casserole so leaves are above the sauce. Rub the bay leaves with a little butter, set fire to them, cover well, and let them scent the sauce. Remove bay leaves, and pick out any charred pieces. Serve.

If you grill the meat instead of frying, and dispense with the butter, this dish can be served chilled.

Degh Bhurta Mhaans (*Lamb Cassoulet with Dumplings*)

1½ lb. lean lamb
4 oz. chick-peas
1½ lb. masoor or 'pink' lentils
8 dumplings made from quantity given on p. 256
2½ oz. clarified butter
4 crushed cloves garlic
2 red chilli peppers
2 inches splintered cinnamon
1 small tin or 3 medium fresh red pimentos

1 teaspoon paprika
6 pounded cardamoms
10 fl. oz. yoghourt
4 tablespoons akni (see p. 253)
3 onions sliced in thin rings
1 tablespoon chopped chives
1 teaspoon turmeric
1¾ teaspoons salt
6 tablespoons chopped coriander leaves or parsley

Soak chick-peas overnight in cold unsalted water to cover well. Soak lentils half an hour in plain cold water to cover, then add the turmeric, 1 teaspoon salt and bring just to boiling point, remove from heat and leave to absorb the water and flavouring.

Make the dumpling paste, press out thinly to an oblong and cut into 2½ inch squares. Lay the squares out on a floured board or plate to dry out a little, but they must be kept covered and in a warm atmosphere so they remain pliable.

Mince half the meat and the pimento and fry in ¾ oz. butter. Season with half the paprika and cardamom. When meat is brown put a small portion on one angle of each dumpling square, damp edges, fold over and pinch to make triangular dumplings. Fry in ½ oz. butter until crisp and golden on each side. Heat yoghourt with akni, mixing smooth, season lightly with salt and pepper and poach dumplings in this sauce for 12 minutes. Cover and keep in low oven.

Slice remaining meat into large almond-sized pieces. Heat half remaining butter in heavy casserole (for preference) and fry 1 clove crushed garlic, 1 chilli (seeded for a milder dish) and the cinnamon until turning colour. Add meat and continue frying, adding a sprinkling of water to prevent aromatics burning. Repeat this sprinkling five times, frying until butter separates. Remove and keep hot.

Heat remaining butter and crisp onion rings, aromatizing with remaining cardamom, chilli, paprika and the chive. Cook 30 seconds only, then sprinkle with water. Repeat three times, drying water each time. When butter separates add meat, chick-peas and lentils. Aromatize with remaining salt, garlic and coriander leaves. Bring to simmering point and cook until meat is tender and lentils reduced to a purée – 30–45 minutes. Add dumplings. Cover closely and give the pot a dum for 20 minutes in a low oven or on asbestos mat on low heat. Serve hot.

Another way of preparing meat with lentils or dried beans is to use the korma sadah or simple braised mutton recipe on p. 53. When meat is almost tender, add white Urd lentils, previously soaked overnight (4 oz. to every 1 lb. meat). Then add a little extra butter (1–3 tablespoons), yoghourt and water, barely to cover, close lid, then simmer; reduce all moisture. Place in warm oven for 30 minutes, and serve. When cooked, the Urd lentil is a large grain, the size of a medium grain of rice. It should be kept whole and not reduced to a purée.

CHASNIDARH, INDIAN SWEET AND SOUR DISHES

These preparations involve steeping in a *chasni* or syrup of sugar and lime or lemon juice or vinegar. Pork, lamb and veal can be used. Vegetables for the most part are cut small and kept crisp, even half raw. The meat should be very tender. The *chasnidarh* or sweet-and-sour style uses meat, poultry or fish with vegetables (or sometimes vegetables on their own), and these may be combined with the leguminous or pulse vegetables, and fruits such as pineapple, banana or mango. Sweet vegetables such as carrots, beetroot and squash come naturally into use. Crisp vegetables like cabbage, celery, cucumber, fresh or dried mushrooms, leeks, cauliflower and large pieces of onion combine well with spinach and pimentos. The syrup must be tart, with the sugar taking the bite out of it, and the flavours should be delicate. Sometimes rice water or cornflour is used to produce a smooth translucent syrup; it can be thickened further by reducing. Alternatively essence of kewara can be used in these recipes. Traditionally, lime juice is used because it is cheap in India. Lemon or grapefruit juice or wine vinegar make acceptable substitutes.

Kofta Chasnidarh (Sweet and Sour Meat-Balls)

1½ lb. minced pork, lamb or veal
18 marble-sized dumplings (see p. 256)
About 2 pints akni (see p. 253)
2 teaspoons ground black cumin
¼ teaspoon paprika
½ teaspoon salt
½ cup sugar
1 tablespoon cornflour
½ cup sharp citrus juice or wine vinegar

2½ inches green ginger cut in fine shreds
1 small head cauliflower
2 large onions
Pinch saffron
1¼ teaspoons powdered fenugreek seed
Good pinch black pepper
2 teaspoons rose water
1½ oz. butter

Make dumplings, poach in akni. Reserve and keep warm. Knead minced meat with ground cumin and paprika, shape into marble-sized kofta, and fry in 1 oz. butter until crisp and brown. Reserve.

Make a syrup of sugar mixed with 1 tablespoon cornflour, ¼ teaspoon salt and the lime juice or vinegar. Simmer and reduce until thick. Place the kofta in this chasni. Sauté the ginger in ½ oz. butter and add to kofta with the raw cauliflower cut into small flowerets, and onions quartered, then halved and separated skin by skin. Add dumplings. Aromatize with saffron dissolved in a little of the chasni with fenugreek, black pepper, and rose water, and leave on dum for 35 minutes in a slow oven before serving.

Nargisi Chasnidarh (Sweet and Sour Pork with Egg)

Preparations using halved, hard-boiled eggs and green leaf vegetables are called nargisi (narcissus-like).

2 lb. loin of pork
½ lb. lentil or bean shoots
  (preferably green *moong*
  lentils, fresh or tinned,
  see p. 196)
6 hard-boiled eggs, halved
1½ teaspoons freshly ground
  black pepper
1 teaspoon ground aniseed,
  fennel or dill seed
3 oz. clarified butter
½ teaspoon salt
½ cup sharp citron juice or
  wine vinegar
½ cup sugar
1 tablespoon cornflour

8 kari phulia leaves
Good pinch ground saffron
¼ teaspoon grated nutmeg
2 oz. cucumber
4 oz. spinach leaves
4 oz. cooked white beans
2 shallots
1 stick celery
2 large onions
4 cloves
4 cardomoms
1 inch stick cinnamon
24 blanched almonds
3 tablespoons garlic liquor
  from 3 cloves

Those who prefer to sprout their own lentil shoots must start this recipe about a week in advance. Directions for sprouting are given on p. 194. Tinned bean or bamboo shoots may be used instead.

Pound, chop, mince, etc., all aromatic ingredients before beginning the cooking.

Cut pork from chine and bone; slice into very thin strips, about 1½ inches by ¾ inch each. Rub with half the black pepper, and then beat lightly with a kitchen mallet to press the pepper into the meat. Dust with half aniseed. Heat half the butter, and quickly sauté the pork. Stir and brown, but do not overcook. Salt, reserve and keep warm. Cut up or break the pork bones and fry them. When well browned, scrape the pan, moisten with ¼ cup water and strain the liquor. Reserve.

Make a chasni of sharp citrus juice or vinegar, sugar and cornflour beaten into the juice, and aromatize with rest of aniseed and black pepper and kari phulia leaves. Simmer until smooth and thick, then add saffron. Slice cucumber in thin rounds and steep ½ hour in salt water; sauté each spinach leaf for a few seconds in ½ oz. butter and remove; simmer cooked beans for 5 minutes in the liquor from the roasted bones; add grated shallots and garlic liquor; cook until moisture dries, then fry, using the remaining butter, without browning. Cut celery in slivers; separate onion layers; drain lentil sprouts. Mince cloves and cardamoms and splinter cinnamon.

Re-heat chasni, add lentil sprouts, cucumber slices, slivered celery, onions, beans and spinach leaves torn roughly with the fingers. Add the re-heated pork. Mix well and place the egg halves, with two blanched almonds stuck in each, in the syrup. Heat gently for five minutes before serving.

ROASTS AND KABABS

See Chapter Three, pp. 30–32

Here we have the dry cooked meats. These are true roasts done on the spit, or on a charcoal fire. Some of the preparations are roasted, then steamed with a little liquor or marinade; this is the dum-bhoona method. The tender meats cooked in a hermetically sealed casserole with only butter as moistening are called ard bhoona. Simple sautéed and grilled meats are called sukha bhoona. Tandoori roasts are done in a special oven, on long iron or steel spits, a method which can be duplicated on the modern revolving spit, or in the oven.

There are many kinds. For some, steamed meat is wrapped in a special batter and fried; other methods use batters to prepare the meat or to complete the cooking. The kababs are classified as follows: *shami* using forcemeat and lentils cooked in water and aromatics; round kofta kabab and long *seek* kabab with finely ground minced meat. There are slices of meat called *pursindah* or *pasendah*; then rolled slices, or even boned shoulder and leg of lamb, called *parcha*. Kabab *puksand* uses two pieces of meat tied together with string and then skewered; cheese and meat can be prepared in a similar way. The boti kabab is meat with bone on the spit; *barg* or *barra* kabab is fillet meat on skewers; *tikkah* kabab is cubed meat or liver on skewers. Kabab *darayhee* and *husainee*, indicate skewered meats and vegetables grilled, then simmered in a sauce; kabab *khatai* is acidulated; kabab malai uses cream, kabab *dehin* or jogurath, yoghourt; kabab *badam* is made with almonds; kabab nargisi with hard-boiled eggs. The kababs represent one of the high spots of the Indian cuisine.

Indian roasts and spitted meats can be very simple: lime juice and black or red pepper are the only aromatics or marinade used. As these are similar to roast meats everywhere, no recipes for them are given in this book.

Bhoona Pursindah (*Sautéed Lamb or Pork Chops*)

12 lamb or pork chops
4 pounded or minced green chilli peppers
1 minced green pimento
1 teaspoon ground black peppercorns
2 ground cloves

2½ fl. oz. moisture-free yoghourt (see p. 250)
½ teaspoon salt
2 oz. clarified butter
½ inch ground stick cinnamon
10 kari phulia leaves

Prepare the aromatics as listed above.

Wipe the chops with a damp cloth, then dry. Beat with the back of a heavy kitchen knife, lengthways and crossways, until meat is flattened and tender. Mix yoghourt with chilli, pimento, black pepper, clove and salt. Rub into meat, marinate 5 to

77

6 hours. Heat the butter in a heavy, wide frying pan. Aromatize with kari phulia leaves and cinnamon, leave on lowest heat for 1 minute shaking the pan a few times. Raise the heat high, and put in the chops. Cook rapidly, and turn. When chops are cooked and marinade is dry, serve at once.

Bhooni Kaleji (Sautéed Liver)

½ lb. lambs', calves' or chicken liver
½ tablespoon grated green ginger
¾ teaspoon fresh milled black pepper

1 teaspoon salt
½ teaspoon paprika
4 crushed cloves garlic
1 teaspoon lime juice
1–2 tablespoons clarified butter

Wash, clean and dry the liver, and cut into almond-sized pieces. Aromatize with all the ingredients pounded and mixed together. Mix well and leave to marinate for about 15–30 minutes. Heat a heavy 12-inch frying pan and add just enough butter to cover the bottom of the pan. When the butter begins to smoke, add the liver. Stir well and cook on high heat, so all sides of the liver are in contact with the heat. The liver will be ready in 60–70 seconds; overcooking will harden it. It should be crisp and very tender. Serves 2.

Bhoona Mhaans Massalam (Aromatic Sautéed Steak)

6 double lamb chops or fillet steaks
2 tablespoons peppercorns
2 tablespoons coriander seed
3 tablespoons lime juice

3 ozs. clarified butter
5 cardamoms
½ teaspoon paprika
¼ teaspoon basil
Good pinch salt

Crush peppercorns and coriander seeds, and beat into both sides of meat with a heavy kitchen mallet. Gash the meat, squeeze lime juice on both sides and stand on rack until perfectly dry. Heat butter, and when almost smoking hot, put in the meat, and sear on both sides. Then cook on low heat until done. Make a powder of cardamom seeds, paprika, basil and salt; dust one side of the meat and fry, then the other side until a light crust forms on the surface. Remove and serve at once.

Talawa Magazh (Fried Brains)

1¼ lb. lambs' or calves' brains
Special batter (see p. 255)
3 pints akni (see p. 253)

2 tablespoons shredded coriander leaves or parsley
2 tablespoons lime or lemon juice

Remove membrane and steep brains in salted water until they become almost white. Wash gently in three changes of running water. Heat the akni, and when it boils, put in the brains and barely simmer for 30 minutes. Gentle cooking is essential or the brains break up. Remove carefully, drain and cool. They should be firm and set. Moisten very lightly with a little lime or lemon juice, sprinkle with coarsely chopped parsley or coriander leaves. Cut the brains into medium-sized slices. Dip in batter, and fry in a shallow pan or deep fryer until batter is a rich gold. Remove, drain on absorbent paper, and serve.

Talawa Kabab (Batter-Fried Skewers of Meat)

Use skewers about 4½ inches long brushed with oil before use. Make the special batter (see p. 255), thickening it a little with extra bessan. Add 3 tablespoons double clotted cream or Indian malai (see p. 252) for every 8 oz. quantity of batter. Cool before use.

On each skewer thread some tender pork or lamb previously lightly cooked in a little akni. Roll each piece of meat in a little paprika. Sandwich between alternate pieces of a mushroom and onion, cut exactly to size: 1 inch in diameter and ⅓ inch thick. Dip skewers in the batter, filling the crevices. Smooth to a rounded shape. Dip in a very little flour and then in lightly beaten egg yolk. Deep fry in plenty of hot oil or fat – about 2 skewers at a time in the frying basket – and remove when the surface is crusty and dark gold. Drain and serve.

Mhaans Dumphoktai (Aromatic Mutton Pot-Roast)

2¼ lb. boned mutton
6 cloves garlic, crushed

7 tablespoons lime juice
1 tablespoon paprika

3 oz. each roasted, ground
  sesame, poppy and mustard
  seed and cashew nuts
1 teaspoon black pepper
¼ teaspoon salt

3 oz. clarified butter
4 green chilli peppers
1 tablespoon garam masala
  (see p. 249)

Parch or roast, pound, chop, etc., all aromatics. Take the mutton and remove as much fat, skin and sinews as possible. Beat all over with a kitchen mallet and trim off any ragged pieces. Gash surface with a sharp knife, and rub in half the crushed garlic. Then rub with 4 tablespoons lime juice mixed with 1 teaspoon paprika. Leave to marinate about 3 hours. Mix sesame, poppy and mustard seeds and cashews with rest of paprika, freshly milled black pepper and a little salt, and reserve. Melt butter in a very heavy casserole. When it is almost smoking hot, put in the meat. Sear all over, but do not let it burn. Lower heat and add seeded, slivered green chilli peppers. Aromatize with the garam masala, season with salt, and moisten with ¼ cup water mixed with remaining garlic. Cook over brisk heat until dry. Gently turn the meat without piercing the seared surface (use wooden spatula or tongs) and add 3 tablespoons lime juice. Cook over medium heat until dry. Now moisten with enough water to all but cover the meat. Boil once, then cook, covered, in a fairly low oven until dry. If the meat is not yet tender, repeat with a little more water, and dry off all moisture. Remove the mutton and let it cool a little. Meanwhile spread the ground aromatics on a piece of paper, or wooden board. Thump the meat hard on to the paper, pressing mixture on to all sides. Place under a very hot grill. When the aromatics form a crust, turn. Now moisten a little with butter, and again press aromatics into meat. Repeat three times. The meat should be golden and crusty. Sprinkle with salt and if necessary with melted butter. Serve by cutting slices slantwise.

Shahi Dumphokat Kabab (Royal Pot-Roast)

This is my own variation of the preceding recipe. The fillets should be a mixture of meats; for example pork, mutton, veal and beef, or pork, duck, chicken breasts and mutton.

1 piece each of filleted lamb, pork, veal, etc. (each about 1 lb. in weight and ½ inch thick). (Where poultry is used the layers will be made up of several pieces.)

4 tablespoons pounded mint leaves

3 ground bay leaves

1 tablespoon paprika

8 ground cardamoms

1¾ inches chopped green ginger

10 cloves garlic

2 oz. ground blanched almonds

1 teaspoon nutmeg

2 oz. ground pistachio nuts

2 oz. ground cashew nuts

3 oz. each ground poppy and sesame seed

2 oz. clarified butter

1 large grain of asafoetida

10 cassia leaves

1¼ teaspoons salt

6 cloves

1 tablespoon cumin

½ pint yoghourt

2 red peppers

2 teaspoons freshly ground black pepper

Pound, chop, grate, etc., all aromatic ingredients before beginning the cooking.

Wipe meat with a damp cloth, then dry. Beat each fillet well with a heavy kitchen mallet until the ½ inch thickness is reduced to ⅛ inch. Then place fillets one on top of another, and trim edges straight. Place each fillet on the table or cutting board and, with a very sharp knife, lightly score the surface diagonally, the cuts about ¾ inch apart. Aromatize the mutton with a little of the pounded mint leaf, a dusting of bay and paprika, a good pinch of cardamom, a little ginger, and crushed garlic; now sprinkle with the ground almonds, and a little nutmeg. Repeat the same aromatics for pork but finish with ground pistachio and nutmeg. For the third fillet the same aromatics with cashews, crushed red peppers and black pepper. For the fourth the aromatics with a mixture of ground poppy and sesame seeds. Press the fillets firmly together, roll up, and tie firmly with two or three strings.

Heat butter in a very heavy casserole, add the crushed asafoetida and brown the four-layered roll of meat on all sides without puncturing the aromatic crust. Put in the cassia leaves, salt, cloves and half the bruised cumin. Stir and fry for one minute on low heat. Add ¾ cup water, more salt, and boil briskly until dry. Add ½ cup water and cover well. Simmer very gently until dry. Repeat with 1 full cup water and simmer again.

Test with sharp needle which should meet little resistance.

When meat is tender, and dry, add well-whipped yoghourt, two tablespoons at a time; repeat until all yoghourt has dried up. During this time, roll the meat about so that yoghourt coats all surfaces. Now cook on fierce heat to let the juices glaze. When the meat begins to stick to the bottom of the pan, moisten with a little butter, and cook, covered, in a gentle oven for 20 minutes. To serve, cut into thin slices. All four layers, though distinct, should be fused together.

This four-layered kabab belongs to a type of cooking found all over India, and has a different name in each region. It is similar to a *roulade*. Some years ago, in an earlier cookery book, I used the word parcha or parchment (roll) for this method. Small parcha kababs are cooked in a casserole; the large one is cooked on the spit. Other methods of preparing parcha kababs with fish, poultry, and vegetables are given in the appropriate chapters.

Parcha Kabab Yakhni (Glazed Roulades of Mutton)

12 pieces fillet lamb or mutton 4 inches by 2½ inches	soaked several hours in lemon juice or wine vinegar
2 tablespoons minced coriander leaves or parsley	4 oz. clarified butter
10 blanched, roasted and pounded almonds	¼ teaspoon turmeric
	1½ inches green ginger
¾ tablespoon spiced salt (see p. 249)	1 tablespoon chopped chives
½ teaspoon black pepper	1 pint yakhni (see p. 253)
2 whole eggs	½ teaspoon nutmeg
1 tablespoon pomegranate seed, or minced raisins	2 tablespoons lime juice

Parch or roast, pound, chop, etc., all aromatics. Make an infusion of the chopped ginger in ¼ cup water, and the chopped chives in a separate ¼ cup water. Wipe the fillets with a damp cloth, then dry. Place on a board and flatten with a kitchen mallet or the back of a heavy kitchen knife. Trim the edges to make them regular in shape. Chop the trimmings and mix with coriander leaves, almonds, a good pinch of spiced salt, freshly ground black pepper and the pomegranate seeds. Fry in ½ oz. butter until pale gold. Heat further $\frac{1}{2}$ oz. butter, stir in turmeric and scramble eggs in this. Add to rest.

Put a portion of the spice and egg mixture on each piece of meat. Roll up, and tie each end with string or fix with poultry pins to hold stuffing. Heat the butter and put in the kababs. Fry over medium heat until the meat is dark brown on all sides, and the butter separates. Aromatize with spiced salt, and moisten with the ginger infusion. Cook until butter separates again. Raise heat and aromatize with the chive infusion. Stir on lower heat and cook until dry. Moisten with about $\frac{1}{4}$ cup of yakhni and repeat if necessary until tender. Test by piercing with a sharp, slim skewer. Now aromatize with grated nutmeg and shake the pan over low heat. Heat the lime juice in a frying pan or casserole and when scalding hot throw in the kababs. Cover and shake the pan. Leave on low heat for about 2 minutes and serve. The sauce consists of butter and natural juices from the meat.

Parcha Seekhi (Gigot of Lamb on the Spit)

3 lb. boned leg of lamb (or veal)	5 fl. oz. yoghourt
3 inches pounded green ginger	2 tablespoons lightly roasted cumin
$1\frac{1}{4}$ teaspoons salt	9 ground cloves
5 oz. clarified butter	2 inches ground stick cinnamon
$\frac{1}{2}$ lb. onions	9 ground cardamoms
2 tablespoons ground coriander	

Poach or roast, pound, chop, etc. all aromatics. Remove as much fat, sinews, gristle and connecting tissue as possible from the boned meat. Wipe with a damp cloth. Dry and prick all over with a sharp knife. Rub it well with green ginger and salt. Reserve for the moment.

Heat 1 oz. butter and fry grated onions with ground coriander, until onions are dark gold. Add a little water (about 5 tablespoons) and cook until mixture is dry. Place this mixture in the centre of the meat and roll it up, securing with string. Place on a greased revolving spit (if in oven use rack in tin, or oven-shelf with tin on shelf below, and turn meat from time to time) and cook at high heat (450° or Reg. 8–9) until browned, then lower heat to medium. As soon as the flesh looks dry, baste at once with butter mixed with whipped yoghourt, cumin, cloves, cinnamon, and ground cardamoms.

When the stuffed parcha is done – test with a sharp kitchen needle – collect all the drippings, mix with some water, reduce to a paste, and serve with the kabab.

PURSINDAH or ROAST FILLETS

Next comes a method called *pursindah*, or sometimes *pasendah*. Essentially it is the roasting of tender fillets of meat, first flattened out and beaten with a kitchen mallet, then skewered, or spitted if large enough, and cooked on charcoal. Some pursindah kababs are fried: sometimes a korma is made from them.

Pursindah Seekhi (*Lamb Fillets on Skewers*)

The traditional skewer or spit for the pursindah seekhi is a sword-shaped, flat blade of steel. No doubt at one time meat was actually cooked on the straight sword, but this is a method of cooking that belongs to the almost forgotten part of Indian haute cuisine. This kabab speciality was once popular all over north India. Variations of the pursindah seekhi will today be found in parts of Iran, Afghanistan, the Punjab and other widespread areas. It is made either from the lean taken from loin of lamb (or tenderloin of beef may be used), when the meat must be cut and flattened; or from the long flat strips of lean found in breast of lamb, when several breasts may be needed, and care must be taken to peel off the layers of thin tissue each side of the lean strips. With good quality meat and the fierce heat necessary, the cooking is very quick, particularly where a barbecue is used. This is a particularly good barbecue party dish.

Preparation, however, must be exact and this is by no means an easy recipe, especially without the proper apparatus. With a thin sword skewer, such as those found on some modern rotisseries, the metal running through the centre of the meat heats up and speeds the cooking, hence the need to beat the outer edges of the strips thin. Where the meat is looped on to a round skewer and is to be grilled, edges and centre of strip are better left an even thickness.

Three different ways of flavouring the kababs are given, and accompaniments are suggested that will do for all three. It is essential to get all accompaniments and the meat absolutely ready before starting the grilling, and the grill must be at its fiercest. Quantities are for ten.

Preparing the meat. Ten fillets of tender lamb prepared as follows if cut from thick portions of lean: each piece of meat should measure approximately 3 inches long, 2½ inches wide and ¾ inch deep. Prepare each fillet in the following manner to make them extremely long and thin: lay it on the table in front of you. With an exceptionally sharp knife, cut a ¼-inch layer from the top but *do not sever it completely*. Then turn it over and repeat this process starting from the opposite edge. This should produce a Z-shaped piece of meat which will be ¼ inch thick and about 9 inches from end to end when flattened. Fold back both strips and beat and flatten along the seams with a kitchen mallet. *Lightly* flatten the entire strip. Beat more strongly at the two long side edges to thin them slightly.

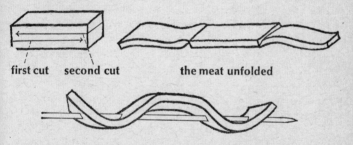

first cut   second cut   the meat unfolded

For breast fillets choose meaty *unchopped* breasts, carve out the long lean layers and cut or beat to the correct size and thickness.

If you are using a sword skewer the blade is now greased lightly and carefully pushed through the centre of the 9-inch long strip. For a round skewer, omit the beating of the edges and thread the strip in a series of short loops or S-curves along the greased skewer.

Flavourings. Some flavouring methods are carried out before, some after the skewering, as directed.

1. 1 large onion
    4 tablespoons water
    ½ teaspoon ground saffron

    strands (or 1 envelope powdered)
    2 oz. melted butter

Chop finely, then pound the onion with the water and squeeze the resulting liquor out through muslin. Put the liquor back on the onion and squeeze out again. Mix liquor and saffron and rub into the meat with the back of a wooden spoon. Grill first side, brushing with butter once meat has had 30 seconds or less under fierce heat. When first side has had total of about one minute's cooking, turn and repeat on other side. Serve at once.

2. ½ lb. green mango purée
    or ½ lb. seedless raisins
    minced and pounded
    into 3–4 tablespoons
    fresh lemon or lime
    juice

    ½ teaspoon saffron (as above)
    2 oz. melted butter

Mix saffron with purée and spread thinly on both sides of kababs. Leave for 4 hours. Skewer and grill as above.

3. ½ teaspoon saffron
    2½ fl. oz. moisture-free yoghourt (see p. 250)
    1 oz. each poppy and sesame seed
    1 tablespoon cumin
    1 teaspoon spiced salt (see p. 249)

    2 red chillies
    6 tablespoons minced pounded onion
    4 oz. butter
    Salt

Mix saffron with yoghourt, spread over kababs and leave 4–5 hours.

Grind the spices. When ready for grilling mix spices and onion and spread them on large sheet greaseproof paper. Grill the meat 30 seconds, brush with butter then 'thump' the skewers of meat lightly on to the spices to coat thinly. Grill, brush with butter, coat again, grill. Repeat until a crisp brown crust is formed and the spices are used up – about 3 times. Very lightly salt before serving.

Accompaniments: Rice. A selection of pickles and chutneys. The

Alu Bhoone potatoes (p. 175), the Mattar Sukhe peas (p. 177), or Cauliflower Purée (p. 184) with the Khumbi Sukhe mushrooms (p. 181) would all be suitable and provide substance.

Badam Pursindah (Lamb with Almonds)

1¼ lb. tender boned leg of lamb
4 oz. blanched almonds
8 fl. oz. moisture-free yoghourt (see p. 250)
2 tablespoons pounded mint leaves
6 cloves pounded garlic
¼ pint milk

1 red chilli
1 teaspoon paprika
4 oz. clarified butter
4 ground cardamoms
½ teaspoon spiced salt (see p. 249)
1½ teaspoons garam masala (see p. 249)

Pound, chop, grate, etc. all aromatic ingredients before beginning the cooking.

Keep the meat in one piece. Wipe with a damp cloth, dry, and remove as much fat, gristle and skin as possible. Use a trussing or larding needle, or the point of a sharp, narrow-bladed knife, and make deep incisions in the meat, inserting a blanched almond in each incision. Place meat on a board, and beat well with a kitchen mallet. The almonds will be bruised and splintered in the meat.

Spread yoghourt over the meat. Rub with half the mint leaves and a little crushed garlic, and leave to marinate for 4 hours. Meanwhile infuse crushed red chilli and rest of garlic in the milk.

Heat a saucepan and put in the meat taking care not to break it. Over brisk heat dry off all the marinade. When the meat begins to stick, turn it over, using a wooden spatula or two wooden ladles, and repeat with the other side. Strain the infusion of milk over the meat. Boil once, then simmer until milk is dry. Melt butter, add paprika and fry with remaining mint, without burning, until butter separates, stirring constantly. Aromatize with ground cardamom seed and spiced salt, and add enough water to half cover the meat. Simmer until reduced and the meat is tender, about 1 hour. Repeat moistening with a few tablespoons of water if necessary. Finally, dust with the garam masala. Cover the pan and shake it well. Replace on high heat, and after 15 seconds shake again. Give it a dum for 15

minutes in a gentle oven. Uncover and carefully remove the
meat in one piece. Cut slices slantwise and serve with some of the
juices scraped from the pan.

Kabab Puksand Paneeri
(Meat-Cheese Sandwich en Brochette)

Kabab puksand is made from tender slices of meat tied together
with a light filling and then skewered to cook *en brochette*. The
first recipe is for lamb with cheese.

1 lb. boneless lamb
1 lb. Indian cheese (see
  p. 251)
1 tablespoon cumin seed
Juice of 4 limes
2 oz. grated green ginger
1 minced onion
5 fl. oz. moisture-free
  yoghourt (see p. 250)

4 fl. oz. double cream
3 oz. clarified butter
4 oz. blanched ground
  almonds
1 tablespoon finely ground
  pomegranate seeds
½ teaspoon ground saffron
  strands

Prepare the aromatics as listed above. Grind the cumin with a
few drops of lime juice. Make a thick infusion of the ginger with
half the remaining juice, and a similar infusion of onion and
lime juice. Combine yoghourt and cream with half butter,
melted, and ground almonds.

Cut meat into 2 inch squares a little less than ¼ inch thick,
and cut cheese to the same size but a little thinner. Prick surface
of meat with a sharp fork and rub in the ginger infusion. Dip
cheese in onion infusion. Over each slice of meat spread a little
of the liquid from cream and almond mixture, pomegranate,
a very light sprinkling of saffron and the rest of the onion infusion. Place a piece of cheese on top, and tie with a thread. Run
a long oiled skewer through four or five of these 'open sand-
wiches' at a time. Place under grill. When dry baste with remaining almond marinade. Cook until a perfect russet brown
colour on all sides. Then rub with the remaining saffron mixed
with a little hot clarified butter. Crisp meat for another few
seconds only, remove threads, and serve.

There are many variations of the Kabab puksand. Try
brochettes of pork and lamb, with a sandwich filling of cooked

green sweet peppers with ground pistachio and basil. The pork is dipped in a paste of cinnamon and nutmeg, and the lamb in an infusion of powdered bay leaf and garlic. Baste with butter only.

Other variations will be found in the fish chapter. Always hold the meat or fish sandwich together with a thread, removing this before serving.

Barra (Barg) Kabab Massalam
(Spiced Skewered Meat on the Bone)

The taste of meat grilled on the bone, and of the meat in the various crevices of bone is so good it can leave you eating all but your own fingers; and you will certainly have to use your fingers if you want the last delicious morsel from the kabab.

1½–2 lb. leg of lamb	2 teaspoons cayenne
2 inches pounded green ginger	1½ tablespoons ground coriander seed
2 teaspoons turmeric	1½ teaspoons spiced salt (see
1¾ tablespoons poppy seed	p. 249)
1 large onion	Clarified butter for basting
4 tablespoons yoghourt	

Trim off fat and gristle and cut the meat into small cubes. Drop each piece of meat into boiling water for a few seconds. This seals the surface, and also drains off matter sticking to the bone. Drain and pat dry with kitchen paper. Grind the aromatics (except coriander and spiced salt) into a paste with the yoghourt and minced onion. Prick the meat with a sharp fork and rub with the paste. Keep in a cold place or in the refrigerator for at least 1 hour, or overnight if possible.

Skewer the cubed meat, grill over medium heat and when it dries baste with a little butter. When crisp and well browned, dust with ground coriander; crisp under the grill and dust with spiced salt. Cook briefly until salt sets into a crust. Then serve hot.

The plain boti kabab is meat marinated in lime juice and black pepper with paprika to add colour. Marinate for at least 6 hours and then skewer and grill, basting with clarified butter as it dries.

Boti Kabab (*Fillet of Lamb en Brochette*)

1 lb. boned leg or shoulder of lamb
10 ground cardamoms
2 ground red chillies
10 pounded cloves garlic
Juice of 3 limes or 2 small lemons

2 tablespoons minced coriander leaves or parsley
Clarified butter for basting (see p. 252)

Prepare the aromatics as listed above. Wipe the meat with a damp cloth, dry and cut into walnut-sized pieces. Prick all over with a sharp fork. Rub the meat with a paste made of cardamoms (including the skins), red chilli peppers and garlic, moistened with a little lime juice. Leave until marinade is dry. Then rub with a little paste made by grinding coriander leaves or parsley with the juice of one lime or lemon. Leave for at least one hour, but 4 to 5 hours if possible. Skewer the meat and grill. Baste with a little lime juice beaten with butter. Salt the skewered meat when crusty brown, and serve.

Other marinades can be made from green mango purée, or papaya purée, both sieved raw, or cream mixed with lime juice, pomegranate seed and black pepper.

Kabab Kaishghee (*Lacquered Pork Chops*)

12 small pork loin chops
Juice of 4 limes or 3 lemons
½ teaspoon grated nutmeg
1 inch ground stick cinnamon
1 teaspoon paprika
1½ oz. clarified butter
½ teaspoon salt

Sauce:
3 oz. tamarind
Scant ¼ pint water
2 oz. pounded pomegranate seed

6 tablespoons sieved raw (or canned) plums (about ½ lb. before stoning)

or
6 oz. plum jam
¼ pint lime or lemon juice
1 oz. cayenne pepper
6 tablespoons green ginger infusion
6 tablespoons onion infusion
Black pepper

Pound, chop, grate, etc. all aromatic ingredients before beginning the cooking.

The lacquered appearance of the chops results from the final operation of glazing the sauce. Marinate chops 4–6 hours in lime juice, nutmeg, cinnamon and paprika. Meanwhile make the sauce (the first is mild, the second hot and pungent): soak tamarind overnight in water, to cover well, to produce a 2 fl. oz. infusion. Add plums and pomegranate, beat well and reduce over heat to consistency of jam. Or mix jam, with lime, onion and ginger infusions, cayenne and black pepper. This alternative resembles an authentic Indian sauce made from various preserves acidulated with verjuice. Grill the marinated chops, basting with butter to prevent drying. When thoroughly cooked, salt lightly and rub sauce over each chop with back of wooden spoon. Return to fierce heat and grill until sauce is glossy and fused to chops. Serve at once.

Barra Kabab (*Marinated Saddle of Lamb*)

2 lb. boned saddle of lamb	1 teaspoon salt
4 tablespoons freshly ground black pepper	2 grains of asafoetida
	1 onion
5 fl. oz. moisture-free yoghourt (see p. 250)	4 fl. oz. double cream

Remove all connecting tissue, sinews and gristle from the meat. Wipe with a damp cloth, and dry. Cut into pieces 2 inches long, 1 inch wide and $\frac{1}{2}$ inch thick. Flatten each piece lightly and rub with 3 tablespoons of the pepper. Then flatten the edges hard. This ensures even cooking. Mix yoghourt with asafoetida, salt and the rest of the black pepper. Use to marinate meat for 24 hours in the refrigerator, turning every few hours to allow both sides to breathe.

Run the oiled skewer through the side of each piece of meat and grill. When well browned, rub a little grated onion over each piece. Baste with cream. Dry off under high heat. Season with salt first before serving.

Tikkah Kabab (*Liver Noisettes en Brochette*)

Traditionally, this skewered dish is made from lambs' liver but calves' liver will do as well. Tikkah means noisette, and the same method can be applied to lamb or game, or even to cubed chicken.

1 lb. lambs' liver
Juice of 3 limes or 2 lemons
4 inches pounded green
  ginger
3 minced onions
2 teaspoons freshly ground
  black pepper

2 tablespoons ground
  coriander leaves or parsley
1–1½ oz. butter
Salt
Bay leaves

Prepare the aromatics as listed above. Clean and wash liver, then dry it thoroughly. Rub with lime juice and leave to marinate for 1 hour. Cut into small noisettes 1 inch square and ¾ inch thick. Make a paste of the ginger, onions, black pepper and coriander leaves. Prick the liver with a sharp fork and rub in the paste. Leave to marinate for 3 hours. Put on small greased skewers with bay leaves and cook under a very hot grill. If the grill is gas, let the flame lick the skewers occasionally. Baste with butter to keep moist, for liver tends to dry up quickly. Do not allow it to overcook. Serve with a sprinkling of salt.

Gurdakupura Kabab *(Stuffed Kidneys en Brochette)*

1¼ lb. lambs' kidneys
Vinegared water
6 oz. pistachio butter: 4 oz.
  pistachio nuts to 1½ oz.
  salted dairy butter and
  1 teaspoon finely chopped
  chives

4 oz. salted dairy butter
1½ oz. clarified butter (see
  p. 252)
1 teaspoon spiced salt (see
  p. 249)

Remove the membrane and steep kidneys in lightly vinegared water for 1–6 hours. Make the pistachio butter (see below). Wash and dry well. Split each kidney, 'butter' it with salted butter and place on buttered skewers. Place under a very hot grill. Baste once or twice with clarified butter. When kidneys are browned and succulent, dust them with the spiced salt, and let it crust. Remove from skewers, and on each half place as much pistachio butter as it will hold. Serve at once.

The pistachio butter is made by first lightly roasting the nuts in a heavy frying pan, without letting them burn or singe. Remove, cool, and grind down with the butter and chopped chives. Mix and grind until perfectly blended. Store in cool place until wanted.

Seek Kabab (*Minced Meat Kabab on Skewers*)

These kababs are made of finely minced lamb or beef. The meat must be free of gristle and sinews. Use a skewer the size of a pencil, or the spit of a modern electric rotisserie. The minced meat is first flattened out into a rectangle about 3 inches by 2¼ inches, a depression is formed in the middle and the meat is shaped with the palm of the hand directly on to the greased spit. It is then revolved to make it smooth and firm. Seek kababs do not need much, if any, basting, because a little butter is mixed in when the meat is minced and kneaded. Keep your palm and fingers moistened with water in which a little bicarbonate of soda has been dissolved – this will prevent the meat sticking to your hands. The grilling must be done with very fierce heat; both inner and outer surfaces should cook simultaneously. Overcooking will destroy the juices and the succulence of these kababs and will make them hard. If no skewers are available the meat can be shaped into sausage-like croquettes and fried or sautéed quickly in a lightly buttered frying-pan.

Basic mixture

1½ lb. finely minced lamb or beef	1 tablespoon clarified butter
¼ teaspoon ground saffron strands steeped overnight in 1 tablespoon hot water	1 minced onion
	2 tablespoons chopped coriander leaves or parsley
	½ teaspoon salt

Mince the meat, and knead in saffron with the water, clarified butter, onion and coriander. Form into kababs over the spit as described above. As with all food cooked on skewers, the spit must first be buttered or oiled.

Cook the kababs under a very hot grill, add salt and serve.

Seek Kabab Khasa

1 lb. minced lamb or beef	3 pounded cloves garlic
4 ground cardamoms	Juice of 1 lime or ½ lemon
1 teaspoon freshly ground black pepper	6 tablespoons yoghurt
	½ tablespoon ground cumin
1 tablespoon ground green ginger	1 minced onion
	2 tablespoons clarified butter

Knead all ingredients until stiff. Then proceed as above.

Seek Kabab Massalam

1 lb. minced lamb or beef	1 teaspoon ginger powder
6 ground red chillies	6 ground cloves
1 teaspoon freshly ground black pepper	1 inch ground stick cinnamon
2 minced green chilli peppers	6 tablespoons pounded coriander leaves or parsley
2 strips of minced pimento	2 tablespoons chopped mint leaves
2 teaspoons ground cumin	
2 teaspoons ground coriander	1 teaspoon ground aniseed
1 teaspoon ground fenugreek seed	1 tablespoon poppy seed
	2 tablespoons sesame seed
4 pounded cloves garlic	1 tablespoon cashew or chirongi nuts
1 minced onion	
1 egg yolk	2 oz. clarified butter

Grind or pound together the sesame, poppy seed and cashew nuts with the butter, keep aside. Mix minced meat with all the ingredients except nut mixture. Shape the meat, cook on skewers, basting if necessary. When well browned, roll the kababs still on their skewers in the nut mixture, and moisten slightly with clarified butter. Roll the kababs again and grill. Repeat until you have built up a thick coating of aromatic crust. Take care not to overcook or burn the crust. This kabab is peppery hot on the tongue.

Shami Kabab (Croquettes of Meat and Lentils)

In the shami kabab, the meat is normally mixed with uncooked ground lentils and is always cooked with aromatics in water, sometimes with a little butter added to make it more pliant for shaping.

2 lb. minced lamb or beef	1 teaspoon chopped mint
2 oz. yellow split peas	½ tablespoon pounded green ginger
½ teaspoon salt	
¾ tablespoon ground coriander	Clarified butter
¾ tablespoon ground cumin	Slivers of thinly pared lemon peel (optional)
2 pounded cloves garlic	
1 minced onion	

Prepare the aromatics as listed above. Soak the split peas over-night, then drain. Boil them together with the meat, salt and all

94

the aromatics. Simmer until meat is done using just as much water as will be absorbed. Cool, put through mincer and then pound in pestle and mortar, or use a blender.

Shape the paste into flat circular croquettes, about $1\frac{1}{2}$ inches in diameter. Use a heavy pan and fry the shami kababs in clarified butter on both sides without breaking. A few shreds of lemon peel can be enclosed in the centre before shaping the kababs.

This is the classic shami kabab. The meat must be a proper forcemeat, and not just minced. Most cooks in India use more lentils than this recipe to ensure that the kababs do not crumble; however they are then much less delicate.

Shami Kabab Noor-Mahali (*Imperial Croquettes*)

$1\frac{1}{2}$ lb. minced lamb or beef
4 onions
4 oz. clarified butter
$\frac{1}{4}$ pint water
1 tablespoon coriander seed
2 inches pounded green ginger
$2\frac{1}{2}$ oz. lightly roasted and ground yellow split peas
$1\frac{1}{2}$ teaspoons salt
$\frac{1}{2}$ teaspoon each, ground cardamoms, cloves, cinnamon

1 teaspoon freshly ground black pepper
2 tablespoons ground aniseed
1 teaspoon ground kalonji (nigella indica)
$2\frac{1}{2}$ fl. oz. moisture-free yoghourt (see p. 250)
1 egg white
Chopped coriander leaves or parsley

Grind, pound, etc. the aromatic ingredients as far as possible beforehand, similarly prepare vegetables. Cut up and fry three onions in 1 oz. butter, pound them with meat and give the mixture a bhogar in the hot butter: close lid, draw away from heat and shake twice. Replace on low heat and uncover after 1 minute (or 2 minutes in a preheated oven). Add $\frac{1}{4}$ pint water to the meat, with the coriander seed. Continue to cook, and shake the pan frequently until all water has been absorbed. Add ginger, remaining minced onion, $1\frac{1}{2}$ oz. clarified butter, split peas, 1 teaspoon salt, cardamoms, cloves, cinnamon, black pepper, aniseed and kalonji. Beat in yoghourt and combine with white of egg. Knead well. The longer you knead the better. Then shape into flat circular croquettes, $1\frac{1}{2}$ inches in diameter, and less than $\frac{1}{2}$ inch thick. Fry gently in remaining clarified butter using a heavy frying pan or *sauteuse*. Serve with a sprinkling of chopped parsley or coriander leaves and dust with remaining salt.

Kofta-Kabab Khatai (Piquant Meat Balls)

1½ lb. minced shoulder of lamb
Milk or buttermilk
5 pounded cardamoms
¼ teaspoon ground saffron strands
½ teaspoon ground black pepper
4 fl. oz. moisture-free yoghourt (see p. 250)
6 fl. oz. double cream
4 oz. blanched and ground almonds

3 tablespoons minced pimento
Good pinch of asafoetida
1 tablespoon roasted and ground black cumin
½ teaspoon salt
1½ oz. clarified butter
Juice of 4 limes
A little chopped fresh herbs when available

Pound, chop, grate, etc. all aromatic ingredients before beginning the cooking. Boil minced meat in milk or buttermilk with cardamom for about 12 minutes. Mix well with saffron and black pepper. Mix together yoghourt and cream blending into minced meat. Add almonds and sweet pepper; aromatize with asafoetida, and black cumin. Knead well and salt. Shape the meat into walnut-sized koftas. Keep them in a cool place for ½ hour. Fry the koftas in butter until well browned. Place on a low heat. In a small saucepan heat the lime juice and, when bubbling, sprinkle it over the koftas. Cook a few seconds over high heat, shaking the pan to prevent koftas sticking. Serve with a sprinkling of chopped green herbs.

Kofta-Kabab Kasta (Crusty Pork Meat Balls)

1½ lb. lean pork
2 minced green chillies (seed for milder dish)
1 tablespoon grated lemon peel

4 tablespoons ground coriander or parsley
1 minced bay leaf (preferably fresh)

½ teaspoon ground basil
  (preferably fresh)
3 inches ground fresh ginger
4 tablespoons minced
  pimento
6 tablespoons chopped chives
5 crushed cloves garlic
About ½ lb. sieved green
  plums or gooseberries

4 oz. clarified butter
½ teaspoon spiced salt (see
  p. 249)
¾ pint rich meat stock
  (yakhni: see p. 253)
4 oz. cucumber
1 egg white

Prepare the aromatics as listed above. Parboil the meat for 12 minutes with one minced green chilli and the grated lemon peel using only as much water as can be absorbed. Mince the meat and make a fine forcemeat with all the ground ingredients, knead well and leave for ½ hour. Knead again and shape into small flat cakes. In the centre of each, place ½ teaspoon sieved plum. Moisten hands with warm water, in which ½ teaspoon bicarbonate is dissolved, and draw edges of meat cakes over fruit and fashion into koftas. Let them 'set' for ¼ hour. Heat the butter and fry the koftas until a rich dark brown on all sides. Salt. Scrape the juices from the bottom of the pan and moisten with 4 tablespoons rich stock or yakhni. Cook the koftas until dry. Moisten with another 4 tablespoons stock, and cook until dry again. Now cover with stock, and simmer covered until liquid is reduced to a few tablespoons. Now raise heat high and stir the koftas gently to ensure that the stock glazes the surface thoroughly. Serve with cucumber salted, drained, dried and cut into thin rounds, then dipped in lightly beaten egg white and quickly sautéed.

Nargisi Kofta Kabab (*Meat Balls with Eggs*)

1 lb. minced leg of lamb or
  beef
8 hard-boiled eggs
1 teaspoon freshly ground
  black pepper
2 tablespoons ground
  coriander
2 tablespoons ground cumin
¼ teaspoon grated nutmeg

½ teaspoon salt
2 tablespoons tomato paste
1 teaspoon paprika
½ teaspoon garam masala (see
  p. 249)
6 cloves garlic
2 onions
1 oz. butter
Beaten egg for frying

Prepare the aromatics as listed above. Shell the hard-boiled eggs. Mince the meat finely and mix with black pepper, coriander, cumin, nutmeg, salt, tomato paste, paprika and garam masala. Chop and fry the garlic and onion in the butter, pound down to a fine paste, and mix with the meat. Coat the eggs with this mixture. Put the koftas on a well-buttered dish to cool for ½ hour, then dip in beaten egg and deep fry, taking care not to crowd the pan. Remove when an amber colour. Drain and serve.

Kofta-Kabab Sheer-Mal (*Meat Balls in Milk*)

1½ lb. minced leg of lamb or beef

½ teaspoon each ground cardamom seed, cinnamon, nutmeg, cloves, black pepper

½ teaspoon ground dry ginger

Good pinch ground aniseed

2 teaspoons (about 6 cloves) ground garlic

½ teaspoon salt

1 ground bay leaf

3 oz. clarified butter

6 whole red chillies

1 pint milk

2 oz. chopped pistachio nuts

4 onions, cut in very thin rings and fried dark brown

Grind, pound etc. the aromatic ingredients as far as possible beforehand, similarly prepare vegetables. Make forcemeat of the lamb with all ground aromatics, except ½ teaspoon of the garlic, the chillies and pistachio. Knead well and shape into walnut-sized koftas.

Heat half the butter and fry the koftas until dark brown. Remove and reserve. Seed the chillies and mince finely. Fry in the butter in which the meatballs were cooked until it takes colour. Moisten with milk, add pistachios and simmer until liquid is reduced to ¼ cup. Strain and reserve.

Melt the rest of the butter and fry the koftas again, adding remaining garlic. Stir often and dry off on high heat. Make butter very hot and pour in the milk sauce. Stir and cook until reduced by half. Scatter with the fried onion rings, and serve.

Mhaans Kabab Machchi (*Lamb Masquerading as Fish*)

$1\frac{1}{2}$ lb. lean lamb
$\frac{1}{4}$ teaspoon freshly ground
    black pepper
6 shallots grated
2 large onions, grated
Salt
2 tablespoons roasted, husked
    and ground coriander
    seed
2 ground cardamoms

$2\frac{1}{2}$ oz. clarified butter or
    frying fat
$\frac{1}{4}$ cup bessan (chick-pea flour)
10 cloves crushed garlic
$\frac{1}{2}$ teaspoon ground aniseed,
    dill or fennel seed
1 crushed bay leaf
$2\frac{1}{2}$ inches grated green ginger,
    or $\frac{1}{2}$ teaspoon ground
    ginger
Lime juice

Prepare the aromatics as listed above. Cut all connecting tissue and gristle from meat. Make a fine forcemeat by first mincing, then pounding in a mortar or blender. Aromatize the forcemeat with black pepper, shallots, onions, salt, half the coriander and the cardamoms.

Shape forcemeat to form one large, or several sardine-size 'fish'. Place in a heavy pan with 1 oz. butter and as much water as will be absorbed in 10 to 12 minutes of boiling. Remove the 'fish' and dredge with bessan, then rub in half the garlic. Gently press in the rest of the coriander, bay leaf and ginger. Melt remaining butter and fry 'fish' on both sides. Prepare a liquor of remaining garlic with $\frac{1}{4}$ cup water and a little lime juice. Immerse the fried 'fish' on both sides successively until it has absorbed the garlic liquor. Then remove and cool for about $1\frac{1}{2}$ hours. Remove and discard the chick-pea crust, chill the 'fish' a little, garnish with raw chopped vegetables and serve with a salad.

CHAPTER SEVEN

Poultry and Game

MOST of the recipes in this section are for poultry birds reared for the table: capons, pullets, cockerels, plump hens. The very young *poussin* is used for skewered or spitted preparations. Curries often make use of older birds of various species, such as boiling fowl, or casserole pigeons. Such birds have more flavour, which is extracted by the long cooking. But in recipes for roasting, sautéeing, or quick cooking use only young roasting birds. Older birds will be tough and so spoil the dish.

Chicken or white meat cooking is somewhat different from red or dark meat cooking. All chicken is gelatinous, and contains albumen. Even slight overcooking (which will not affect dark meats, like mutton, lamb and beef), dehydrates chicken and nothing can then restore its lost juices and latent succulence. Most of the fibrous quality of chicken is due to overcooking. More than dark or red meats, chicken and white meats require frequent basting or moistening, to prevent dryness: this also prevents the escape of natural juices.

The initial browning, which is so essential for dark meats, in order to crust the surface and seal in the juices, is not necessary when frying white meats. Roasting or frying can be started over a moderate heat. Albumen, unlike the concentrated juices of red meat, reacts best to gentle, even heat. To see if chicken is done, insert the sharp point of a knife or a skewer – if the juice that rises to the cut surface is colourless, the chicken is ready.

Poultry used for Indian cooking is invariably skinned to allow the aromatics to do their work.

Murgh Sadah (*Simple Chicken Curry*)

3 lb. boiling fowl	1 teaspoon paprika
1½ oz. clarified butter	½ teaspoon salt
2½ teaspoons turmeric	Coriander leaves or parsley
Good pinch cayenne	for garnish

Wash and dry the fowl, skin and cut into 12 pieces. Heat the butter in a heavy casserole and fry the chicken over moderate heat for 2 minutes. Then aromatize with 1¾ teaspoons turmeric and fry again, stirring frequently, until the chicken is well browned. Season with cayenne and fry another ½ minute. Then add the paprika and 5 tablespoons water, stirring all the time. Boil until dry. Season with salt and moisten with 1 pint water. Bring to the boil, then lower heat and cover to simmer gently for 1½ hours to 2 hours. The liquor should reduce by half, and the flesh will be tender if lightly pressed. Now add remaining turmeric, and put the casserole in a slow oven for 30 minutes so that when served the chicken is easily taken from the bone. Serve with a scattering of finely chopped coriander leaves or parsley.

Murghi Molee (Chicken with Coconut Sauce)

3 lb. boiling fowl
2 pints coconut milk (see p. 252)
10 kari phulia leaves or 4 bay leaves
4 whole roasted red chillies
½ lb. 'button' onions
5 tablespoons cooking oil
5 cloves garlic
2 tablespoons minced onion
1 tablespoon turmeric

2 teaspoons ground cumin
2 teaspoons roasted and ground coriander seed
2½ fl. oz. lime juice
1 teaspoon ground fenugreek seeds
1 teaspoon freshly milled black pepper
1 tablespoon lightly roasted sesame seeds

Wash and dry the chicken, skin and then cut into 12 portions. Simmer in 1½ pints coconut milk with the kari phulia leaves until half cooked (about 50 minutes). Remove and drain the chicken. Reserve the liquor. Prepare the aromatics.

Peel the button onions but leave whole, heat the oil and brown them all over, remove and reserve. Fry the garlic cut in thick slivers, remove, crumble or pound and reserve. Fry the minced onion until dark brown, add the chicken, stir and cook for five minutes until the oil separates. Season with turmeric, cumin and coriander. Stir and fry for another 2 minutes on low heat. Aromatize with the garlic. Mix ½ pint reserved liquor with lime juice. Add the fenugreek, chillies and small onions.

Cook over gentle heat until very tender. Use remaining liquor and rest of coconut milk as more moisture is required, for the liquid must constantly be kept about $1\frac{1}{2}$ inches above the surface of the chicken. Just before serving, season with black pepper, scatter sesame seeds on top.

Murghi Khasa (*Special Chicken Curry*)

3 lb. boiling fowl	2 tablespoons cashew nuts
2 inches fresh ginger	2 black cardamoms
1 tablespoon turmeric	1 teaspoon cumin
8 cloves	2 grains lovage seed
1 teaspoon sesame seed	4 oz. clarified butter
1 tablespoon poppy seed	4 onions
$\frac{1}{2}$ teaspoon salt	

Wash and dry the chicken. Bone, and cut the flesh into small pieces. Crack the round, larger bones, and fry them in a little butter. When these are dark brown and crusty, pound in a large mortar, or in several folds of greaseproof paper with weight or hammer. Scrape and collect all the juices in the pan, combine with crushed bones and pour $\frac{1}{4}$ pint hot water over. Strain the liquor and reserve. Simmer the rest of the carcass, broken up somewhat in a covered pan, over very low heat, for 1 hour using scant $\frac{1}{2}$ pint water, then strain the liquor into the first stock. Reserve.

Grind all the aromatics and divide into two equal parts: make a paste of one part with a little water, and leave the other in powder form. Rub the chicken with almost all the paste. Chop or grate onions, fry brown in half the butter, remove and reserve. Add rest of butter to frying pan, add chicken and fry over a moderate heat for 10 minutes. Stir often, and turn. When the butter separates add $\frac{3}{4}$ pint water, salt, and aromatize with a little more paste. Boil up then simmer covered, over very gentle heat until the chicken is tender, about 2–3 hours according to age of bird. Mix in rest of the powdered aromatics, the onions, and give the casserole a dum in a slow oven for 20 minutes. Serve.

Murghi Doh-Peeazah (Chicken Carbonnade)

4–5 lb. capon
1½ inches fresh grated ginger
10 pounded cardamoms
¼ teaspoon cayenne
2 tablespoons grated or
minced onions
4 crushed cloves garlic
4 lb. onions
5 oz. clarified butter
2 tablespoons ground
coriander seed

3 ground bay leaves
½ teaspoon salt
7 fl. oz. moisture-free
yoghourt (see p. 250)
1 teaspoon freshly ground
black pepper
½ teaspoon ground saffron
strands
½ teaspoon nutmeg

Pound or grind all the spices. Those which are used together may be pounded together. Wash and dry the chicken. Joint it and prick it all over with a sharp pronged fork. Moisten ginger, half the cardamom, cayenne, the 2 tablespoons minced onion and garlic with a little yoghourt and rub into the chicken, and marinate for 2 hours.

Take half the onions, and mince finely. Melt one third of the butter and fry these onions until a dark golden brown. Remove, pound (or use blender) and reserve. Add half the remaining butter to that in the pan, and heat. Fry chicken over moderate heat for about 10 minutes and wait until the butter separates. Then aromatize with coriander, bay leaves and remaining cardamom. Cook for 1 minute, add salt then moisten with 3 tablespoons of yoghourt at a time, repeating only when all moisture has dried up and all yoghourt is used up. Add the rest of the butter, cut remaining onions very thin, add them and cook until well browned and the butter separates. Moisten with ¼ pint water and cook until dry and chicken is tender, about 15–20 minutes. Moisten again if necessary. Add the first lot of minced, fried onions, some black pepper, and cook until everything is blended. Aromatize with saffron mixed with nutmeg in a very little hot water. Close lid, and raise heat. Place for 15 minutes in a slow to moderate oven, and serve.

Murgh Badam Sheer-Jogurath (*Almond Cream Chicken*)

3½ lb. roasting chicken
1¼ teaspoons powdered ginger
¾ teaspoon freshly ground
   black pepper
4 oz. clarified butter
15 fl. oz. yoghourt

10 lovage seeds
¼ pint double cream
4 oz. blanched almonds
¾ teaspoon salt
¼ teaspoon cayenne

Prepare the aromatics. Skin the bird and wipe it inside and out with a clean damp cloth. Prick it all over with a very sharp knife point and rub both inside and out with a mixture of black pepper and ginger. Heat 3 oz. butter in a heavy frying pan large enough just to take the chicken comfortably. When the butter is hot put in the chicken, and baste. After 5 minutes add the well beaten yoghourt and the lovage seeds and bring to a simmer. Continue to cook the chicken on all sides constantly basting the part not immersed in the sauce. After about 35 minutes, add the cream and slivered almonds together with remaining butter if needed, salt and cayenne. Continue cooking about 35–40 minutes when bird should be tender and the sauce dry. Test bird by running skewer into thigh meat, when it should draw out easily. If sauce is not dry, raise heat, and cook until the sauce just begins to stick. Scrape up sauce and dish over the chicken.

Kookarh Korma (*Chicken Korma*)

3 lb. roasting chicken
5 fl. oz. moisture-free
   yoghourt (see p. 250)
5 cloves garlic
3 onions
½ teaspoon salt
1 teaspoon paprika
1 tablespoon grated green
   ginger
3 oz. clarified butter
2 tablespoons minced
   coriander leaves or parsley
2 tablespoons minced mint
   leaves

1 tablespoon turmeric
2 teaspoons cumin
2 teaspoons roasted mustard
   seed
1 tablespoon ground poppy
   seed
2 ground cardamoms
1 ground bay leaf
1 teaspoon freshly milled
   black pepper
1 inch piece green ginger

Skin and wipe the bird and cut into 12 pieces. Make small incisions all over with a sharp knife point and steep 1 hour in a marinade made from yoghourt, garlic minced with 1 onion, salt, paprika and the grated ginger.

Slice one onion into very thin rings and fry in 1 oz. butter. Reserve. To the same butter, add the ground coriander leaves and the mint. Fry until dry, then add turmeric, cumin, and roasted mustard seeds, all ground down with $\frac{1}{2}$ oz. butter. Cook for 1 minute over low heat. Remove. Add chicken to butter (adding a little more butter if necessary) and sear the meat, shaking the pan often to prevent burning. When the marinade has dried, add the fried aromatics with 2–3 fl. oz. water. Mix, stir and dry off. Add the third onion, minced or grated, and cook until brown and the butter separates. Add ground poppy seeds, and fry for a few seconds. Moisten with enough water (3–4 teaspoons at a time) to cook the chicken until tender, about 20–25 minutes.

Aromatize with ground cardamoms, ground bay leaf and black pepper. Cover well and place the casserole in a slow to moderate oven for 25 minutes. Meanwhile, cut the piece of ginger into julienne strips and sauté in remaining butter. When well crisped add the fried onion rings. Scatter these on the chicken, give them time to warm through, then serve.

Murgh Dumphokat (*Chicken in a Pot*)

2$\frac{1}{2}$ lb. roasting chicken	Good pinch salt
1 oz. clarified butter	Good pinch cayenne
4 crushed cardamoms	1 teaspoon chopped parsley
2 crushed cloves garlic	

Wash and dry the chicken and divide into four parts. Fry in butter one or two pieces at a time. Do not crowd the pan. When well browned, aromatize with cardamoms, garlic, salt, cayenne, and parsley. Moisten with enough water almost to cover the chicken. Bring liquor to the boil. Seal the pan well, shake and place in a moderate oven for about 55 minutes. Remove, and uncover. If any moisture remains, dry it off on high heat. Then, on very high heat, fry, stirring continuously, scraping the bottom of the pan. When the chicken is well glazed with the last drop of juices and butter, serve at once.

Murgh Masthana (*Chicken with Dumplings*)

2½ lb. roasting chicken
12 dumplings (see p. 256)
Akni (see p. 253)
¼ lb. chick-peas soaked
 overnight
5 fl. oz. moisture-free
 yoghourt (see p. 250)
½ teaspoon ground saffron

½ teaspoon salt
4 crushed cloves garlic
4 oz. clarified butter
2 grains asafoetida
4 ground cardamoms
2 teaspoons ground cumin
4 tablespoons chopped chives

Prepare the aromatics as listed. Make dumplings and keep them warm in akni or water. Cook chick-peas (see p. 193) and reserve. Wash, clean and dry the chicken. Place in a heated saucepan without butter. Let it draw until juices come to the surface. Remove chicken and scrapings from the pan and wipe dry. Cut into four parts (or eight if smaller servings are required).

Cook the chicken in a little water until almost tender. Take moisture-free yoghourt and add to the chicken with ground saffron and garlic. Cook and stir for a minute, then add the chickpeas and salt. Cook until yoghourt is dry. Now enrich with butter and mix well, frying over medium heat. Aromatize with asafoetida, cardamoms, and black cumin. Stir well, and moisten with ¼ cup water. Add the dumplings. Mix together and then place the casserole in a moderate oven for 30 minutes. Serve with a sprinkling of chives.

Murghi Brabarr (*Two Chickens in One*)

2 2-lb. roasting chickens
8 shallots
4 oz. clarified butter
Good pinch ground mace or
 nutmeg
2 tablespoons minced parsley
½ teaspoon black pepper
½ teaspoon spiced salt (see
 p. 249)

1 minced pimento
2 tablespoons ground poppy
 seed
4 tablespoons yoghourt
1 egg
1 crumbled bay leaf
½ cup akni (see p. 253)

Spice mixture: a generous pinch each of cayenne, cumin, cardamom, garlic and spiced salts ground together with a few grains of asafoetida.

Clean, wash and dry the chickens. Carefully remove the skin of each so as not to puncture or tear them. Bone the birds and crack the bones and carcass. Fry them in $\frac{1}{2}$ oz. butter, and simmer with 6 pints water for 1 hour, then boil fast until reduced to about $\frac{3}{4}$ pint. Reserve liquor. Brown the shallots in $\frac{1}{2}$ oz. butter and mince them. Mince the meat from both chickens, making a forcemeat, and aromatize with the mace, black pepper, salt, pimento, parsley, poppy seed, minced shallots and yoghourt. Knead the mixture with the egg, to make it pliable but firm. Leave for $\frac{1}{2}$ hour, then form into a large roll. Place this in the centre of the better of the two chicken skins and fold it neatly over the minced mixture making a large sausage. Secure by sewing, or with several poultry pins. Alternatively, tie the roll at about $2\frac{1}{2}$ inch intervals with thin string.

Heat remaining butter, and turn the roll in it until it is crisp and mottled red and brown. Aromatize with crumbled bay leaf, and moisten with $\frac{1}{4}$ cup akni, cooking this dry, and moistening again with rest of akni and a scant $\frac{1}{4}$ pint of the broth from the chicken bones. Simmer covered, turning once, until the force-meat is set firm, about 20 minutes. Test with a thin skewer. Remove, then reduce the liquor until only a few tablespoonfuls remain. Put back the roll and spoon the liquor on to it. Aromatize with the spice mixture. Close and leave in a moderate oven for 15 minutes. To serve, cut slices straight across with a sharp knife dipped in hot water.

Murgh Bhogar (*Chicken in Scrambled Egg*)

2 lb. roasting chicken
2 inches green ginger
6 onions
$2\frac{1}{2}$ oz. clarified butter
$\frac{1}{4}$ inch stick cinnamon
$\frac{1}{4}$ teaspoon black pepper
7 eggs
$\frac{1}{4}$ teaspoon turmeric
$\frac{1}{2}$ teaspoon salt
4 oz. thickly sliced bamboo shoots or mushrooms or lotus root (bhasenda) sliced paper thin
Generous pinch paprika

Mince the ginger with 3 onions, and make an infusion with 5 tablespoons water. Strain after 1 hour. Meanwhile skin and bone the chicken, cut into thin slices and rub with the infusion. Marinate for 1 hour. Break up bones, grill them and make a broth by simmering in $\frac{1}{4}$ pint water for 1 hour. Strain and reserve.

Cut remaining three onions very fine, and fry them in 1 oz. butter. When medium brown, remove, chop and pound with 4 tablespoons water. Strain and reserve the liquor. Heat remaining butter, and sauté the chicken pieces until tender, about 7 minutes. Reserve. Reduce the fried onion liquor until 2 tablespoons remain. Add to sautéed chicken and warm through. Meanwhile grind the cinnamon and black pepper, and mix with turmeric and salt. Beat the eggs and mix them in a saucepan with the chicken and juices. Add bamboo shoots. Moisten with reserved broth, stir and cook over medium heat. After 5 minutes add the ground aromatics. Cook, and stir continuously until the mixture sets. Sprinkle with paprika, and give it a dum in a moderate oven until the mixture is firm and smooth. Serve hot.

Murgh Makhni (*Buttered Chicken*)

2½ lb. roasting chicken	½ teaspoon salt
5 bay leaves	¼ teaspoon freshly ground
2½ oz. clarified butter	black pepper
6 tablespoons yoghourt	

Skin chicken and roast with a bay leaf in the cavity, and with four bay leaves on the chicken breast, two on each side, tied down with a string. Baste with clarified butter while it roasts on medium heat. Cook the chicken on a revolving spit if possible. (The basis of this recipe is the tandoori or spitted chicken grilled in the tandoor – a man-high clay oven.)

When the chicken is cooked, remove the bay leaves, and cut the chicken into eight pieces. Heat the butter without letting it brown. Mix into it beaten yoghourt. When blended add the chicken. Cover well and give it a dum in a moderate oven for 15 minutes. Serve with a sprinkling of salt and black pepper.

Murghi Dehin (*Chicken in Yoghourt*)

3 lb. roasting chicken	1 large pimento
12 fl. oz. yoghourt	2 inches grated green ginger

2–3 crushed green chillies	5 tablespoons minced parsley
16 large crushed cloves garlic	or coriander leaves
1 teaspoon salt	2 oz. clarified butter
1 teaspoon paprika	

Wash and dry the chicken, skin and joint it. Prick all over with a very sharp fork. Beat the yoghourt and make a marinade with grated or pounded pimento, paprika, green ginger, chillies, garlic and salt. The garlic is not excessive; yoghourt takes care of its pungency. Marinate chicken for 10–12 hours in cold place or in refrigerator, turning from time to time. Heat a heavy saucepan till the metal is very hot. Almost throw in the chicken and marinade so that it makes a slight splash, producing steam. Stir in the parsley, cover immediately. Cook on high heat for 5 minutes; then on medium heat till the yoghourt is all dry except a tablespoon or two at the bottom. Do not let this get brown. Stir the chicken to coat it evenly. If you prefer a lighter dish, serve at this point. Otherwise continue as follows: Draw the pan half off the heat, and ladle all the sauce onto the chicken, pushing all contents to one side of pan. Melt butter and roll chicken in it gently without browning. Serve hot with all the scrapings from the pan.

Murgh Massalam (*Spiced Baked Chicken*)

There are two methods for this recipe. In one, the chicken is cooked whole; in another it is cut into eight pieces. Both use ard-bhoona or pot-roasting techniques: the chicken is cooked with butter only, and almost no liquid is used. For the murgh massalam whole, a yoghourt marinade is used to flavour the chicken. But this is almost dry by the time cooking starts. The ard-bhoona is done by the dum method (see p. 27).

For the marinade:

1 tablespoon roasted	2 minced onions
coriander seed	1 red pimento
4 tablespoons yoghourt	2 green chillies

Pound together (or put in blender) the yoghourt, onion and all the spices. Remove seeds from chillies unless a very hot 'bite' is liked.

For the casserole:

2–2½ lb. roasting chicken
5 oz. clarified butter
½ lb. spring onions minced
½ lb. spring onions cut
thinly into rings
4 cloves garlic crushed under
salt
6 crushed cardamoms
1 inch pounded cinnamon
stick
6 pounded cloves
½ teaspoon salt
Good pinch grated nutmeg
1 tablespoon minced mint
leaves

2 inches grated green ginger
½ teaspoon freshly ground
black pepper
16 raisins soaked in warm
water
½ teaspoon spiced salt (see
p. 249)
6 almonds blanched, pounded
and infused for ½ an hour in
2 tablespoons kewara
essence (rose water)
½ teaspoon ground saffron
heated with ¼ oz. butter

Skin bird. Make incisions with sharp knife point all over it and spread marinade over it. Leave for a minimum of 5 hours, but overnight if possible. Prepare aromatics. The marinade will dry somewhat. Heat 3½ oz. butter in heavy casserole and put in bird with marinade. Fry on all sides for 15 minutes, basting well. Lift out and add minced onions in thick bed covering the bottom of pot, return bird. Aromatize with garlic, cardamom, cinnamon, cloves, salt and nutmeg. Top with the onion rings, and strew them with ginger, mint, pepper and raisins. Lastly add the spiced salt, and sprinkle with saffron-butter and the liquor from the infusion of almonds and rose water. Dot top with remaining butter. Seal pot and put on high heat until contents are heard simmering. Leave 1 minute on this heat, shaking pot 3–4 times. Put in moderate oven (370°F; gas 5) for about 30–40 minutes, shaking pot 3 times during this cooking. Bird should be tender and the rest crisp. Unseal and serve. The aromatic steam released when first uncovering the pot is delectable. Some gourmets use more butter in this recipe, making a still richer dish.

Murgh Khara Massaledarh (Chicken with Whole Spices)

2 lb. roasting chicken
2½ oz. clarified butter
5 white onions
2 teaspoons turmeric
¼ teaspoon ground ginger
2 crushed cloves garlic
4 crushed cardamoms
½ inch splintered cinnamon stick

3 ground cloves
Good pinch ground mace
Good pinch cayenne
¼ teaspoon black pepper
½ teaspoon salt
½ crumbled bay leaf
1 teaspoon ground mustard seed

An easy dish to prepare. Crush or grind spices. Wash and dry the chicken, and skin and cut into 10–12 small pieces. Cut the onions medium thick. Heat half the butter, and put in the chicken pieces. Aromatize with turmeric and ginger. Shake and fry for 1 minute. Turn over and fry for another minute. Cook and stir over a gentle heat until the butter separates. Take care not to burn the spices, or let the chicken overbrown.

Scatter onion over chicken with garlic, cardamom seeds, cinnamon, cloves and mace. Season with cayenne, freshly ground black pepper, salt, bay leaf and mustard seed. Dot with the remaining butter. Close lid and seal, preferably with a ribbon of paste or dough. Raise the heat very high. When you can hear the contents of the casserole bubbling, shake and replace over heat. Lift again and shake lightly. Now place the casserole in a moderately hot oven (about 375°F; gas 5) for about 45 minutes. To ensure that the chicken is totally dry of all moisture except the residue of butter and juices, place on top of stove on high heat and allow to dry while you shake the pan now and then. Then open the casserole and serve amidst a cloud of aromatic steam.

The dish can also be cooked on top of the stove if the casserole is heavy enough, and the lid sealed to prevent any loss of steam.

Murghi Sabz (Chicken with Green Herbs)

2 lb. roasting chicken
½ teaspoon salt

1½ oz. clarified butter
2 tablespoons chopped chives

2 teaspoons chopped
  coriander leaves or
  parsley

1–2 chopped, seeded green
  chillies
3 tablespoons yoghourt

Skin, wash, and dry the chicken. Cut into 4 pieces, place in pan, and add just enough boiling salted water to come ⅔ way up. Season with salt, enrich with 1 tablespoon butter, and simmer over a low heat until chicken is tender, about 1 hour. Meanwhile prepare the aromatics. Uncover, and drain any liquor, reserving it for later use.

Dry off chicken completely. Heat the remaining butter, and put in the chicken. Aromatize with herbs and spices. Cook without browning for 10 minutes, then cover and leave on low heat for 15 minutes. Now enrich with beaten yoghourt and remaining liquor. Cook over moderate heat, stirring the chicken, or shaking the casserole, until the butter sauce is reduced to three or four tablespoons, and serve very hot.

Murgh Talawa Kasta (Batter-fried Chicken)

2½ lb. roasting chicken
¾ pint akni (see p. 253)

For the batter:

2 cups bessan
Good pinch saffron
¼ teaspoon black pepper
2 teaspoons coriander leaves
  or parsley

7 fl. oz. yoghourt
4 cardamoms
¼ teaspoon paprika
2 teaspoons chopped pimento
2 cloves
1 tablespoon chopped chives
¾ teaspoon salt

Make the batter, using the yoghourt instead of water, and aromatize with other ingredients ground very finely together. Leave to stand.

Meanwhile simmer or steam chicken about 1 hour in akni, drain, dry and cut into 8 pieces. Season a little with salt, then coat with the batter and deep-fry, or shallow-fry in a heavy frying pan in 2 inches of cooking fat. When dark amber, remove, and drain before serving.

This batter is unique, and superior to ordinary batter made with flour, or with bessan alone without the aromatics. However, the addition of yoghourt will not give a crusting as crisp as ordinary batter; the yoghourt makes the batter more pliable and velvety. While ordinary batter should never be cooked darker than deep gold, the aromatics in this special batter will always produce a brownish red.

Murgh Keema Kabab Dumphokat (*Boned Chicken in Muslin*)

2½ lb. chicken	2 minced shallots
1 pint chicken stock	Yolks of 4 hard-boiled eggs
Almond milk from 2 oz. almonds (see below)	Pinch ground saffron
Pinch of nutmeg	Salt
4 oz. chicken livers (including liver taken from bird in recipe)	2 crushed cloves garlic

Pound the almonds and cover them with a little warm water, or milk and water. Leave 1 hour. Bone the chicken, reserving the bones and giblets. Set aside about 2 oz. of the breast meat. Mince rest of meat, cut the 2 oz. of breast meat into fine slivers. Knead the minced meat with nutmeg. Cover all meat to prevent drying, and put in cold place to firm up the mince. Cover bones and giblets (except the liver) with about 1 pint water, salted and lightly flavoured with a little onion, thyme, parsley and peppercorns. Simmer about 1 hour. Meanwhile quickly sear livers, brown shallots well, and put all through the mincer. Chop yolks and mix with liver and shallot, the saffron and a good pinch salt. Spread a large square of muslin on the table (an old, clean tea towel would do, scalded first in plain water). On this press out the minced chicken. Put liver mixture in centre of this, scatter breast-meat shreds on top, and mould forcemeat to a large cylindrical shape about 8 inches long (or to fit pan to be used). Wrap muslin round twice to keep shape. In India they sometimes hold such moulded meat in shape with 'splints' of thin bamboo placed round the cloth and secured with string. The splints also serve to keep the meat from direct contact with the bottom of the pot, thus precluding any risk of burning. Strain the stock into a large stew pan. Strain the almond infusion into the stock, and add garlic and pinch salt. Immerse the meat roll as soon as stock reaches boiling point, and turn it once to wet on all sides. For preference stand it on a shallow grid or place a few skewers on the bottom of the pot to keep the roll from direct contact with the base. Simmer very gently 45–50 minutes, turning once or twice to ensure even cooking. Serve hot as it is; or allow to cool, and roll in beaten egg lightly flavoured with saffron, and fry in clarified butter. It may also be cooled, sliced and fried in this way.

Murgh Ghilafi (Chicken Boiled or Baked Dumpling-Fashion)

This is a special method of 'boiling chicken without boiling it', that is without any liquid coming into direct contact with it. Another version of this technique is to bake the bird (or meat or fish may be similarly treated) in a casing of wet clay or earth. For the latter the meat is first wrapped securely in buttered paper or foil, enclosed in wet clay and thrust into a very fierce fire. Many camp-fire cooks employ the method and, at a pinch, an open grate could be used. It can be adapted to the modern oven by using the pastry casing of the boiling method described below, and this method of baking will be familiar to Western cooks, many of whom bake ham in paste casings. The flour-and-water paste hardens on cooking, and the meat inside is sealed. Its natural juices then provide the necessary steam and moisture for the cooking. The method takes about half as long again as the standard time, while, if stuffings are used, about 15 minutes should be added to the total time. Although goose and duck may be cooked by the method, they should be given a slight roasting first at a high temperature, the skins pricked to drain off some fat, and then enclosed in the paste. Even so, a crisp result is not to be expected. Cooked completely plainly, fowl boiled in this way is excellent for invalids as no nourishment is lost. Needless to say any sauces may be served other than the simple butter filling used here. Note that, while the inside of the bird may be lightly seasoned, salt should not be applied outside as salt causes juices to liquefy, when they would merely be blotted up by the paste and lost.

4 lb. roasting chicken	3 teaspoons grated lemon
¾–1 lb. flour	rind
1 blade mace	4 oz. clarified butter
¾ teaspoon spiced salt	

Cream butter with rind and salt. Push the mace into the centre and form up the butter into a rough cylinder of a size that will be easy to put inside the bird without much handling. Put the butter to chill. Add water to flour by tablespoons and knead well to form a pliable but neither soft nor sticky dough. With only light flouring of pin and rolling area, roll out this dough to a thick sheet large enough easily to enclose the bird without stretching or breaking. (Have the bird to hand so that you can try out the sheet as you roll.) Insert the flavoured butter in the bird and sew up the flap of skin at neck end, and the vent, so butter cannot run out as it melts. Truss bird compactly and avoid protruding bone ends which would pierce casing. Fold bird in dough, damping and pressing edges to seal. Lower into boiling salted water and cook about $2\frac{1}{2}$–3 hours (4 hours for large boiling fowl). Leave to drain well in colander before removing dough, which should be done in the serving dish to avoid loss of juices. Discard dough and clean up dish before serving. Flavour is much superior to that of ordinary boiled chicken. Accompany with a simple dish of rice and a vegetable chosen from Chapter Ten.

Murgh Yakhni (Chicken en Daube)

Preparations of this kind are usually made in a *handi* or earthenware *daubière* which is sealed with a ribbon of paste and cooked in a low oven. The handi imparts a distinctive quality to the food, although you may of course use a metal casserole.

3 lb. roasting chicken	$\frac{1}{2}$ teaspoon dry fenugreek leaves or thyme
8 minced onions	
1 tablespoon ground coriander seeds	2 red or dried chillies (seeded for milder dish)
2 bay leaves	4 oz. clarified butter
3 ground cardamoms	1 lb. minced mutton or lamb
5 tablespoons jellied stock	$\frac{1}{4}$ teaspoon nutmeg
$\frac{1}{4}$ teaspoon ground saffron	2 teaspoons salt
$\frac{1}{2}$ teaspoon powdered ginger	

Skin the chicken and wash in running water until the water runs clear. Drain and pat dry. Make a paste of ginger, a little salt, and seven of the onions. Rub this over the chicken; then make small incisions with a very sharp knife point, and rub the paste in again. Allow to stand for 2 hours.

Meanwhile make a forcemeat of the minced meat as follows: fry remaining onion in half the butter; when golden, raise heat, add meat; close lid, and shake the pan a few times, leave on low heat for 2 minutes; uncover, fry until well browned; aromatize with coriander, fenugreek leaves, salt and 1 bay leaf, crumbled, and moisten with just enough water half to cover the mixture; boil to dry off all moisture. Stuff chicken with the forcemeat, truss the bird, and rub with saffron and cardamom mixed together. Place in an earthenware pot or casserole, together with the marinade paste. Drench with remaining butter. Add whole chillies (for flavouring only) and remaining bay leaf. Dust with nutmeg, season with salt, and moisten with the jellied stock. Cover and seal pot. Place on heat with asbestos mat underneath when using earthenware. When you hear the liquor beginning to boil, put in slow oven. Cook for about 4 hours, shaking once or twice to moisten the chicken. Unseal and serve very hot. It is more attractive to wrap older, much-used vessels in a napkin before taking to the table.

MURGH BHOONA (SAUTÉED CHICKEN)

There are many ways to flavour the chicken for this quick, simple cooking method. By 'quick' I mean the cooking itself, rather than the preparation, which may require marination. Even so, the marinades are simple, and the chicken can be left in them all day while the cook is occupied with other things or overnight. Notice the double frying technique. Joint the chicken and, for greater speed if the bird is large, bone the joints and divide the meat into pieces. Three slightly different methods are outlined below, followed by a detailed recipe for each.

1. Marinate the chicken in lemon, lime, yoghourt, etc. as below. Sauté briskly in butter until brown, lower heat and cook through. Put in hot dish. Boil some good stock or lemon juice in the pan, pour over chicken. Repeat with some butter. Serve hot. Alternatively, marinate in oil, spices and garlic.

2. Season 2–3 tablespoons lemon juice with spices to choice. Marinate the chicken for a minimum 1 hour, turning at least once. Pat dry, fry in butter, 'thump' in ground spices to choice – some should be different from those in the marinade – fry to brown the coating.

3. Mix yoghourt, cream or a little strong stock with melted butter and seasonings. Marinate the chicken 1 hour or more. Heat a pan, put in chicken with marinade and cook briskly until marinade dries out. Add butter to pan and fry again until chicken is well browned. Extra spices may be added with butter.

Method 1: *Murghi Bhooni Khumbidarh* (*Chicken Sautéed with Mushrooms*)

2 lb. grilling chicken
¼ lb. button mushrooms
Good pinch turmeric
2 cloves garlic
¼ teaspoon paprika
2 tablespoons butter

2 tablespoons lime or lemon juice
3 crushed cardamoms
¼ teaspoon salt
1 tablespoon chives

Thinly slice mushrooms and just cover with water coloured with the turmeric. Pound the garlic and steep in 3 tablespoons water. Mix the paprika with lime juice. Cut the chicken into four or six pieces, sauté in 1 oz. butter in a heavy frying pan, preferably a proper sauteuse. Indians use a large *karahi* which is like a round bottomed sauteuse. Add cardamoms after 10 minutes, then cook further 10–15 minutes.

Remove the chicken, salt it, and keep hot. Drain and gently sauté the sliced mushrooms adding a very little butter if necessary. Add the chicken and turn about in the pan for ½ minute. Strain the garlic water into another pan and when it boils splash over the chicken. Boil lime juice and paprika and splash this also on the chicken. The chicken should be on a very high heat so the moisture dries within a few seconds. Finally, heat remaining butter until it becomes nutty brown and no more, mix with finely chopped chives and spoon over the chicken. Mix, and serve hot.

Method 2: Murghi Bhoona Massalam
(Spiced Fried Chicken)

1 2-lb. broiler chicken	¼ teaspoon ground dry
Juice of 2 lemons	saffron
½ teacup salt	5 ground cardamom seeds
2 teaspoons paprika	Black pepper
2 oz. clarified butter	

Skin and joint the broiler, and prick all over with a sharp knife point. Rub well with the lemon juice, salt and paprika. Leave overnight or at least 5 hours.

Heat a good ounce of clarified butter, and sauté chicken until it is tender and surface is gilded. Mix together the saffron, cardamom seeds and a good pinch of black pepper and press over the chicken. Sauté again briefly. When the seasonings are sticking firmly to the chicken, enrich with more butter to taste, heating it thoroughly and spooning over the chicken while doing so. Serve hot.

Method 3: Murghi Bhoona Kheera
(Fried Chicken with Cucumber)

1. Heat 6 tablespoons good stock (can be made from chicken carcass and giblets) very gently with 5 tablespoons cream. Add good pinch each powdered cinnamon, black pepper, nutmeg, anise or fennel seed, 1 tablespoon minced mint. Simmer, to reduce to half, on low heat.

2. Cut up cucumber into almond-sized pieces, to the weight of half that of the chicken, drain on kitchen paper.

3. Joint the chicken, skin and fry in clarified butter until browned and tender, about 20–25 minutes. As soon as it is in the pan crush up coarsely 2 teaspoons cumin seed, and add to pan, mixing well.

4. Dip the drained cucumber in beaten egg-white, which may be lightly flavoured with garlic and salt, and either fry or grill it.

5. As soon as any one of the above are done, they should be kept warm.

6. Add the cream sauce to the chicken, and barely simmer for 5 minutes. Add the cucumber. Serve hot.

There should be no more than 1–2 tablespoons of sauce at the end. This small amount of liquor is a characteristic of all bhoona dishes, and there should be merely about a teaspoonful per person.

TANDOORI

The recipes that follow are for whole grilled chicken. Some are cooked on the spit in the *tandoor* (see p. 30); others are cooked over charcoal. The modern revolving spit or rotisserie is excellent for all these preparations. Failing a spit, the cooking should be done in a fairly fierce oven.

Chirga (Roasted Whole Chicken)

2½–3 lb. chicken
¼ teaspoon cayenne
1 teaspoon paprika
Juice of 2 limes or 1 large
    lemon
8 tablespoons wine vinegar
1 tablespoon pounded green
    ginger

1 minced onion
Good pinch salt
1 fresh or tinned red pimento
8 fl. oz. yoghourt
2 oz. clarified butter

Wash, dry and skin chicken. Prick it all over with a sharp knife point. Mix cayenne and paprika with lime juice, some salt, and vinegar and rub into chicken. Leave for 1 hour. Then rub with a paste made from green ginger, onion, salt and pimento all minced together with well beaten yoghourt.

Roast the chicken in a moderate oven (375°F; gas 5).

As it dries, baste with clarified butter; repeat until the chicken is done. Then raise heat very high, and let the chicken redden, basting it well. Or finish under the grill, turning to redden both sides. Using a rotisserie I have found that by stopping the motor, and turning the chicken very slowly by hand, it will crust and redden well. Remove, sprinkle with a little salt and serve.

Tandoori Murgh (*Whole Roast Chicken with Almonds*)

2½–3 lb. chicken
4 onions
3 oz. clarified butter
¼ teaspoon ground saffron
5 tablespoons yoghourt
½ pint double cream
4 oz. almonds
2 oz. raisins

1 tablespoon roasted coriander seeds
1 teaspoon freshly ground black pepper
2 inches green ginger
5 cardamoms
8 cloves
1 teaspoon salt

Fry onions golden-brown, pound with the butter and saffron and mix with yoghourt and cream. Blanch and slice almonds, chop washed raisins, and combine with heated onion mixture. Reserve. Clean, wash and dry the skinned chicken. Prick all over. Grind roasted coriander seeds with black pepper, green ginger, cardamoms, cloves and salt. Rub the chicken with this, and begin to roast or cook under the grill or on the rotisserie. As it dries, baste with the aromatic cream sauce. When done, scrape and collect all the drippings, including the almonds and raisins. Mix with a little extra hot butter, and serve with the roasted chicken.

Murgh Kabab Seekhi (*Whole Stuffed Chicken on the Spit*)

2 lb. chicken
½ lb. minced lean meat (pork, lamb, or veal)
5 tablespoons yoghourt
1 teaspoon minced fenugreek leaves or thyme
½ teaspoon paprika
5 minced onions

4 oz. clarified butter
1 teaspoon salt
2 tablespoons roasted ground coriander seeds
3 ground cardamoms
3 pounded cloves garlic
1½ tablespoons garam masala (see p. 249)

Prepare all the aromatics as directed above. Wash, dry and skin the bird, prick all over with a fork or knife point. Mix half the yoghourt with fenugreek leaves, half the paprika and onion. Rub into chicken, and marinate for several hours, or overnight.

Heat butter, and brown the meat in it, add salt, and aromatize with coriander. Moisten with ¼ cup water and cook until moisture has been absorbed. Dry by mixing and turning the forcemeat over a high heat. Stuff the chicken with the prepared forcemeat, and truss for roasting. Set oven at 375°F; gas 5. Mix remaining yoghourt with butter, rest of paprika, cardamoms and garlic (optional). Baste bird with this and put in oven. When the chicken is done (about 1 hour) rub it with the garam masala. Replace in hot oven (425°F; gas 7) or under grill, and let the seasoning cook until it crisps. Baste again and serve.

For simple *chicken on the spit* make cuts on the chicken (after cleaning and skinning). Then rub with a marinade of lime juice, cayenne and paprika. Allow to stand for 12 hours. It may then be spitted (or cooked in the oven).

Here is a recipe for a slightly older bird which is first steamed or simmered in water.

Kookarh Tandoori (*Steamed Chicken on Spit*)

5 lb. boiling fowl
1 quart akni (see p. 253)
¼ pint garlic infusion (see below)
2 limes, or 1 large lemon
Good pinch turmeric
Good pinch cayenne

¼ teaspoon ground cardamom
¼ teaspoon freshly ground black pepper
2 bay leaves
Clarified butter
4 fl. oz. yoghourt

Simmer the skinned fowl in akni, until three-quarters cooked – about 2 hours. Meanwhile boil 12 cloves garlic for ½ hour in 1 pint water, reducing to ¼ pint at the end. Drain bird and allow to dry off in colander. Sprinkle it first with the garlic infusion, then with juice of 2 limes. Rub with mixture of turmeric, cayenne, cardamom and pepper, standing bird on rack over plate to catch drips. Tie bay leaves on the chicken breast.

Mix butter with surplus drippings of garlic infusion, lime juice and aromatics. Place bird in a hot oven and baste with this butter. When done – another 30–45 minutes – collect all the drippings, mix with an equal quantity of yoghourt, beat up, then boil until reduced to a quarter. Serve with the chicken.

Tandoori Murgh Massaledarh
(*Whole Spiced Chicken on Spit*)

2½–3 lb. chicken
1 teaspoon salt
1 tablespoon vinegar
6 minced cloves garlic
½ teaspoon onion salt
2 minced shallots
4 oz. sieved papaya (or plums)
4 minced, seeded green chillies
1¼ teaspoons turmeric
2 teaspoons ground fenugreek seeds
½ teaspoon ground black cumin
2 tablespoons roasted, ground mustard seed

4 tablespoons cream
4 tablespoons yoghurt
Juice of 2 limes or 1 large lemon
4 oz. clarified butter
2 inches green ginger
1 teaspoon paprika
1 teaspoon black pepper
¼ teaspoon ground aniseed, fennel or dill seed
1 inch cinnamon
4 tablespoons chives pounded with 1 tablespoon water
3 pounded bay leaves

Prepare the aromatics for the chicken and marinade. Skin, wash and dry the chicken, and prick all over with a very sharp knife point. Rub with salt, vinegar and minced garlic. Rub the cavity with onion salt. Leave for ½ hour.

Make a paste of shallots, papaya, chillies, turmeric, fenugreek seeds, cumin and mustard seeds. Rub this into the chicken and leave for 12 hours if possible. Next day prepare a basting sauce of whipped cream, yoghourt, lime juice and clarified butter. Combine with green ginger ground down with paprika. Prepare the rest of the aromatics.

Start to roast or cook the chicken for preference on charcoal or spit, otherwise in hot oven (425°F; gas 7). Baste frequently with the sauce whenever the chicken becomes dry. Collect all the drippings. As soon as the chicken is done (about 45 minutes) remove and rub in the following aromatics pounded to a paste (use the back of a wooden spoon): black pepper, aniseed, cinnamon, strained liquor from pounded chives, and bay leaves. Put back in hot oven or on the stationary spit. Let the fierce heat crust the surface of the chicken. Revolve it slowly by hand if using a rotisserie, or turn often under a hot grill. Rub with the drippings and serve.

These grills are adaptations of the whole spitted tandoori or roast poultry. Jointed chicken can be marinated briefly ($\frac{1}{2}$ hour) with a combination of the spices and cooked under the grill. For this style of cooking as well as for the whole spitted roast, it is necessary to use a young and tender chicken. Poussins will do well but if very small, 1 each or 1 between 2 are needed. If a poussin (*choussa* in India) is marinated overnight, it is possible to cook it in 20 minutes or less, as marination makes meat tender as well as aromatizing it, while the fierce heat cooks surface and inside simultaneously.

Here is a recipe for best quality capon or pullet. Pheasant, peacock, partridge, grouse, and other game birds can also be used.

Murghi Bhogar (*Chicken in the Bhogar Style*)

3 lb. chicken	$\frac{1}{2}$ pint buttermilk
1 inch green ginger	Juice of 2 limes or lemons
3 cardamoms	$\frac{1}{2}$ inch stick cinnamon
1 tablespoon chopped mint leaves	Pinch ground asafoetida
	6 lovage seeds
2$\frac{1}{2}$ tablespoons coriander seed	$\frac{1}{2}$ cup white meat stock
	4 oz. double cream
$\frac{1}{2}$ pint milk	$\frac{1}{2}$ teaspoon salt
4 oz. clarified butter	

Prepare all aromatics as described below and keep them separate for the various stages of the cooking. Wash, clean and dry the chicken. Cut into 10 or 12 pieces, then skin. Grind the ginger, cardamom seeds, mint leaves and half the coriander seeds. Mix with the milk and reserve.

Heat half the butter in a heavy pan, and fry the chicken for 2 minutes over high heat, stirring most of the time. Moisten with the aromatized milk. Simmer covered for 10 minutes. Remove chicken, and strain the milk, mixing it with buttermilk and lime juice. Reserve.

Heat the remaining butter in the same pan, add the splintered cinnamon and give it a bhogar (see p. 26). When the clarified butter is very hot add the chicken. Close the lid at once, and give it a good shake. Replace on very low heat for 1 minute. Now open the pan and, keeping one part of the pan on high heat, drain butter to that side and heat up. Add the asafoetida, again shake to mix with the chicken, and give it another bhogar. Repeat with a third bhogar, this time putting in the crushed lovage seed. Leave pan covered on lowest heat for about 3 minutes. Uncover and moisten with stock and salt; simmer until it dries. Cook the chicken until it just begins to stick to the pan. Now begin to moisten with a tablespoon at a time of the milk liquor which will be reduced to about ½ pint. Repeat this four times. Then cover with the remaining liquor and simmer until tender. Add rest of ground coriander seeds.

Uncover, and boil liquor down to about 3 tablespoonful. Mix in the cream. Give the whole a dum in a moderate oven for 2 minutes. Serve.

Murghabi Pistadarh (Duckling with Pistachio)

1 medium-sized duckling
4 oz. shelled and ground
    pistachio nuts
2 egg yolks (hard-boiled)
8 tablespoons yoghourt
3½ oz. clarified butter
1 teaspoon salt
1½ teaspoons bruised cumin
Pinch ground aniseed

6 ground lovage seeds
2 tablespoons rose water
About 1½ pints akni (see p. 253)
1 crushed, seeded green chilli
¼ lb. grated, raw carrot
¼ teaspoon spiced salt (see p. 249)
2 onions, browned and minced

Clean, wash and bone the duckling. (Your butcher may do this for you.) Make a stuffing from freshly ground pistachio, onion, yolks, yoghourt, half the butter, salt, cumin, aniseed, lovage seeds and rose water. Stuff the duckling, carefully plumping it out and reconstructing its shape as much as possible.

Roast for 15 minutes (browning the top by basting with butter), or brown in a heavy frying-pan. Then place duckling in a heavy casserole with enough akni to cover all but one-quarter. Add chilli and grated carrot. Simmer about 1 hour, until tender. When done remove duck and strain the liquor. Reduce to about 2 tablespoons. Spread this over the duckling.

Sprinkle with spiced salt and place in very hot oven until surface is glazed. Serve with a good rice pilau (see Chapter 9).

Murghabi Kashmiri (*Duck with Walnuts*)

1 large duck
1 lb. minced meat
1 lb. shelled walnuts
4 shallots
½ teaspoon black pepper
½ inch stick cinnamon
Clarified butter

5 tablespoons juice from fresh or dried pomegranates; or 3 oz. stoned morello cherries or figs crushed into juice of one lime or ½ lemon, and juice squeezed out in muslin

Place walnuts in a slow oven, until the skins are brittle. Rub skins and peel off. Mince all but 6 and reserve. Mince two shallots, mix with walnuts and a good pinch of freshly ground black pepper. Fry the mixture in butter over low heat for 2½ minutes, stirring all the time. Moisten with enough water just to cover and mix well; simmer on slow heat for ½ hour.

Mince the other two shallots, and mix with the minced meat. Aromatize with black pepper.

Take the duck, cleaned, washed, dried and cut into small pieces and brown well in butter. Add the walnut mixture, plus 6 walnuts in small pieces. Add minced meat and cook over a very low heat for about 50 minutes.

Flavour and moisten with either pomegranate juice, or cherries in lime juice, and ¼ cup water. Mix well and cook until juices become syrupy and the butter separates. Keep covered in a slow oven for 10 minutes, and serve.

Teetur Malai (*Partridge with Cream Sauce*)

6 partridges
1½ lb. stewing veal on the bone
Bessan
8 onions
1 inch stick cinnamon
1 inch green ginger, thinly sliced
1½ teaspoons salt

3 tablespoons ground coriander seed
4 oz. clarified butter
2 cloves
1 bay leaf
6 cloves garlic, crushed in 3 teaspoons water
Good pinch nutmeg
Lime or lemon juice

¼ teaspoon saffron
½ lb. blanched ground
  almonds

8 fl. oz. double cream
6 cardamoms

Split the partridges down the back. Wash, clean and dry well. Then rub them with the bessan. Leave for 15 minutes, then wash again. Spread with six onions pounded with cinnamon and leave for ½ hour. Scrape onion off birds into a stockpot, wash and dry the partridges.

Prepare a broth of the meat well covered with water, the chopped onion, ginger, salt and coriander. Cook until meat separates from the bone, about 2 hours, and only about ¾ pint of broth is left. The broth is then strained and given a bhogar as follows: heat 1 oz. butter with cloves and bay leaf and, when very hot, splash in the strained broth; cover, and leave 2 minutes over very low heat.

Next the partridges are also given a bhogar in the following manner: heat remaining butter with 2 minced onions and all but a teaspoon of the garlic infusion; when onions are pale gold, add the partridges; cover and place on low heat; shake two or three times.

Uncover, add nutmeg and moisten with ½ pint of the broth, cover, and cook about 45 minutes until no moisture remains and birds are tender. Stir and fry the partridges gently in this butter residue, moisten with lime juice and remaining teaspoon garlic infusion. Flavour the remaining ¼ pint of broth with saffron. While birds are frying, mix almonds with double cream and aromatize with cardamoms. Stir well and mix with the ¼ pint of broth. Pour over the cooked partridges, add salt, cover well, shake, and place in a slow oven for a dum of 20 minutes. Serve.

Khubab Hans (Roast Goose)

1 medium-sized goose
1 lb. minced meat
6 tablespoons ground aniseed
2 oz. ground coriander seed
½ lb. bessan
Few grains ground
  sandalwood (optional)
1½ inches grated green ginger

2 teaspoons black pepper
8 onions
Salt
3 oz. clarified butter
6 oz. seedless raisins soaked
  2 hours in water just to
  cover, then chopped

4 oz. blanched, roasted
    almonds
2 oz. roasted coriander seed
16 minced cloves garlic
2 teaspoons spiced salt (see
    p. 249)

1 cup cooked rice
1 tablespoon ground cinnamon
½ pint yoghourt
¼ teaspoon cayenne

Roast, grind and soak flavourings as in above list. Clean the goose, and wash in three changes of water. Then dip in very hot water for about 45 seconds. Remove and prick all over with a very sharp knife point. Rub aniseed and ground coriander into the goose. Moisten with a little water and leave the aromatics pasted on for 2 hours. Wash well. Rub with bessan, leave for 15 minutes and wash again. Mix the sandalwood in a little water and rub all but a few drops over the goose. Leave for another 2 hours; then wash. This is to sweeten the goose and rid it of excess fat.

In the meantime, prepare a stuffing of the minced meat, grated ginger, half the black pepper, onions and salt. Fry in 1 oz. butter until brown; add chopped raisins and a few drops of the sandalwood water. Stuff the goose and truss it well.

Simmer goose in water until half cooked, about 1½ hours. Remove and drain. Skim fat from cooking liquor, and reduce it to about ¼ pint. Grind together the almonds, roasted coriander, garlic, spiced salt, rice, cinnamon and remaining black pepper, and mix with 1 oz. butter and yoghourt, then with the cooking liquor. Roast the goose at 325°F; gas 3, basting with the spiced liquor until done, about 1½ hours. Baste finally with remaining butter and serve with drippings moistened with a little water and a dash of cayenne as a sauce.

〜〜〜〜〜〜〜〜〜〜〜〜〜〜〜〜〜〜〜〜〜〜〜〜

CHAPTER EIGHT

Fish and Shell-fish

THERE are more than two thousand varieties of fish in India and the result is a culinary repertoire of great subtlety. Coastal areas use fish daily and are fortunate too in having some of the finest prawns, lobsters and crayfish. The largest of these prawns (now quick-frozen and exported) weigh one pound apiece after cleaning. Their flavour is superb and they make fine grills. In Malabar they are aromatized very lightly and wrapped in banana leaves to bake under a hot fire. Oysters from some of the world's most extensive and ancient beds, range from thumb-nail size to full plate size.

It is impossible to deal with all the different ways of preparing fish, but these recipes will give a sample of the best Indian dishes.

Methods of cooking are the same as for other foods, with the dum technique predominating. Fish is also grilled, baked, roasted, poached, braised and steamed. The simple method of steaming fish over an akni or Indian court-bouillon is best, though if you live in the country and have access to fragrant grasses, herbs or aromatic woods these can be arranged as a bed over the perforations in the bottom of the steamer. The fish is placed on top and the steam rises through this herbiage imparting an especially delicate flavour to the fish. Batter-fried fish is an Indian speciality, the various batters giving a parti-cularly crisp and tasty finish. Even large steaks from the popular *mahseer*, a fish which can reach a weight of 140 lb., are batter-fried. A 2 lb. steak may be rubbed with pomegranate, coated in a batter made from bessan or other lentil flour, and fried – preferably in mustard or sesame oil, though any good oil will do. Fish cooked on the spit is incomparable; the outside is crisp, the interior moist and flaky. As the flesh of fish is more tender than meat, intense heat can be used in conjunction with careful basting.

In these recipes, stress is laid on repeated washing of the fish in various waters. Bessan (or refined white flour as a substitute) is used as a coating, and acts like blotting paper, sucking up the surplus oils and absorbing various odours. In this way the fish is made sweet while still retaining its natural flavour.

Myhee Molee (Fish with Coconut)

2 lb. white fish, filleted
4 oz. coconut
2 cloves garlic
2 onions
2 oz. clarified butter
2 teaspoons ground rice, cornflour or bessan

1 teaspoon turmeric
4 green chillies seeded and minced
½ teaspoon salt
1 teaspoon mustard seed
Juice of 1 lemon

Skin and wash the fish in three changes of water, then under running water for 5 minutes. Drain and dry. Make an extract of the coconut by grating it, and mixing with 4 tablespoons boiling water: leave 15 minutes and strain. Repeat twice more to give a total of 12 tablespoons liquor. Add 1 clove of crushed garlic to this liquor and reserve. Slice and fry the onions and remaining clove garlic until golden, in ½ oz. butter. Crumble the garlic. Add the coconut milk, ground rice, turmeric, garlic, chillies and salt. Cook the mustard seed in a very little butter and when they begin to pop, add to the mixture. Enrich with remaining butter. Add lemon juice, stir, and allow the mixture to thicken. Put in the fish, uncooked, or lightly fried, and poach gently, uncovered, until done, about 8 minutes if in pieces; about 10–12 minutes if in two large fillets. Take care to baste well. Serve.

Myhee Turrcarri Khasa (Fish with Nuts and Spices)

2 lb. white fish
1 tablespoon ground coriander seed
1 dried chilli (seeded for milder dish)
Juice of 1 lime
2 oz. shelled cashew nuts

3 oz. shelled chirongi or brazil nuts
4 onions
1 oz. grated coconut
1 teaspoon turmeric
1 large pinch of asafoetida
½ teaspoon salt

9 cloves

12 kari phulia leaves (or 2 bay leaves)

3 oz. clarified butter

1 tablespoon roasted ground fenugreek seed

½ teaspoon powdered ginger

4 oz. blanched, slivered almonds

2 tablespoons roasted poppy seed

Salt

Prepare the aromatics and nuts. Wash fish in running water. Prick all over with a sharp fork or knife point. Rub with salt and wash; rub with ground coriander, leave for 30 minutes, wash again, then dry. Crush chilli and make an infusion by soaking it in 4 tablespoons water and the juice of a lime for one hour. Make a paste of the cashew and chirongi nuts with a few drops of water, and reserve. Slice and fry onions, then crumble or pound them. Mix coconut with sufficient water to poach the fish, about ½ pint. Add turmeric, asafoetida, salt, cloves, kari phulia or bay leaves and onions, and put this into a pan or oven dish. Lay the fish on top, cover, and poach until tender either in the oven or on top of stove. Remove and drain fish. Reduce contents of pan to about one eighth, strain off resulting liquor through muslin and reserve.

Heat butter and put in fish with the fenugreek seeds. Turn once and lightly brown on both sides. Add the nut paste and cook until pale gold. Add the ground ginger and moisten with the chilli infusion. Salt and steam for 5 minutes. Moisten again with strained cooking liquor. Keep on a dum, to steam for a further 5 minutes. Add almonds and poppy seeds and serve.

Machchi Turrcarri Sadah (Simple Fish Curry)

1½ lb. haddock, turbot or brill

2 crushed cloves garlic

1 teaspoon crushed fennel or aniseed

3 oz. clarified butter

3 sliced onions

1 crushed green chilli (seeded for milder dish)

½ red or green pimento seeded and minced

½ teaspoon turmeric

1 teaspoon ground cumin

1 tablespoon ground coriander seed

1 teaspoon paprika

½ teaspoon salt

Good pinch mace

1 tablespoon parsley

1 teaspoon garam masala (see p. 249) optional

Skin, wash and dry fish. Rub with flour and allow to stand for ½ hour. Wash well and dry. Make incisions with a sharp knife and rub with garlic and aniseed. Leave for ½ hour, then wash well and dry. Prepare the remaining aromatics as listed.

Heat the butter in a pan and fry the fish until firm on both sides. Remove and keep warm.

Fry the onions until a dark even brown; moisten during the last few minutes of the browning with a light sprinkling of water; repeat when absorbed to keep the onions from burning. Remove and reserve, leaving as much butter in the pan as possible. Add chilli, pimento, turmeric, cumin and coriander. Stir and cook on a very gentle heat for 2 minutes. Add paprika, stir and cook for ¼ minute. Put back the onions, add salt, and moisten with 1½ cups water. Boil, then simmer until reduced by a third. Put in the fried fish and mace and simmer until tender. Add chopped parsley. Keep on lowest possible heat for 10 minutes, then serve. Garam masala is optional; if you want to make the dish more spiced, add it with the fish.

Myhee Joguranth (Sole Poached in Saffron Juice)

1½ lb. sole, filleted
1 teaspoon lime juice
½ tablespoon salt
Good pinch paprika
¾ pint yoghourt
Good pinch ground saffron
strands
8 crushed lovage seeds
1 tablespoon pounded fennel
leaves (or 1 teaspoon ground
fennel seed)

2 tablespoons chopped
pimento
2 tablespoons ground rice
(or ½ teaspoon cornflour)
5 crushed cloves garlic
1 tablespoon chopped chives
or parsley
1 teaspoon freshly ground
black pepper

Skin, wash and dry the fish. Rub with a little lime juice, salt and paprika and put aside for 1 hour. Prepare the aromatics.

Place the whipped yoghourt in a heavy saucepan and heat; add saffron, lovage seed, fennel and pimento. Stir in the ground rice or cornflour and cook until the mixture is smooth and velvety.

Aromatize the sauce with garlic. Cook another 5 minutes and add the fish. Poach without simmering or boiling, until fish is tender. Test with a sharp knife point (it should meet no resistance). Serve with a scattering of chopped chives, parsley or coriander leaves.

Khabab Myhee Bheykar
(*Fish in the Fashion Called Useless*)

The word 'useless' is a sarcasm. The fish can be steamed, fried, buttered or made sweet and pungent:

2 lb. white fish	2½ tablespoons roasted anise
6 oz. bessan	flour (ground aniseed, dill
	or fennel seed)

Make a fairly stiff dough or paste with 6 oz. bessan, and the anise flour and water. Wash the fish well and then dry. Wrap the fish in a ¼ to ½ inch thick covering of dough and bake in a medium oven until the casing is well browned. Remove and cool slightly. Break the casing, extract the fish, skin and bone it as necessary. The dish can now be finished in four different ways.

1. Take 2 oz. bessan and mix with the flaked fish. Grind pinch ground saffron, 8 cardamoms, 6 cloves, ¼ inch cinnamon, 2 tablespoons coriander together with 1 teaspoon anise flour, salt and enough yoghourt or 1 egg to make a firm smooth paste. Shape into the form of a whole fish. Steam till set and serve.

2. After baking, fry lightly in clarified butter until crisp and golden on both sides. Salt and serve.

3. Whip up 4 oz. butter with 5 tablespoons yoghourt and salt, and heat together without colouring. Stir well until smooth. Put in fish and aromatize with 2 tablespoons chopped parsley or coriander leaves. Keep covered for 7 minutes or so and then serve.

4. A chasnidarh (sweet-and-sour dish, see p. 33) is made with a syrup using lime juice or wine vinegar, sugar and corn-flour. The baked fish is dusted with pinch ground saffron and salt and steeped for 5 minutes in enough hot chasni to come

quarter-way or a little more up fish. Stand serving dish on asbestos mat over heat while steeping, and spoon the chasni over the fish a few times. Serve. Sometimes the chasni is tinted pink by boiling thin slices of beetroot with the syrup, discarding these before serving.

Machchi Dum (*Fish Steamed with Cucumbers*)

2 lb. white fish
4 fl. oz. good oil
2 tablespoons ground coriander seed
¼ lb. lightly roasted bessan
2 tablespoons ground aniseed or dill seed
½ pint yoghourt
1 inch grated green ginger
6 cardamoms
½ lb. onions sliced and fried

½ teaspoon ground saffron strands
1 tablespoon pounded mint leaves
1 small cucumber
½ teaspoon salt
½ inch stick splintered cinnamon
2 oz. clarified butter (optional)

Prepare above ingredients except mint leaves. Skin and cut fish into large pieces and wash. Rub with oil and ground coriander and leave for ½ hour. Wash well, then rub well with bessan mixed with aniseed. Leave 15 minutes. Wash well. Spread half the yoghourt all over the fish and leave for 1 hour. When the marinade is beginning to dry, rub with a paste made from the juice squeezed from the ginger pounded with the onions and cardamoms. Leave another ½ hour, meanwhile pounding mint.

Now rub with the remaining yoghourt mixed with saffron and mint leaves. Heat a heavy saucepan and put in the fish steaks with all the aromatized yoghourt. Add cucumber cut into pieces 1½ inches long and ½ inch thick. Season with salt and splintered cinnamon. Cook, turning once, until yoghourt is dry. Cover well and give it a dum for 15 minutes in a preheated medium oven.

Butter is optional in this recipe. It can be added after the yoghourt has dried. Crisp the fish on both sides and cook until it begins to stick to the pan. Then give it a dum before serving.

Machchi Khasa (Fish Favourite)

1½ lb. white fish (cod or haddock steaks; turbot or halibut slices)
½ pint milk
¼ lb. flour
¼ lb. bessan
Bunch lemon leaves or grated rind and pulp of 3 limes or lemons
1 tablespoon fennel seed
2 pounded bay leaves
1 teaspoon ground kalonji or 2 teaspoons chopped chives
1 teaspoon roasted, ground fenugreek seeds
8 pounded cardamoms
½ teaspoon mace
½ teaspoon salt
2 beaten eggs
3 oz. clarified butter
10 ground lovage seeds
¼ teaspoon cayenne

Cut fish in large slices. Steep in milk for ½ hour, then wash under running water. Rub with flour, leave for 5 minutes and wash well. Rub with bessan, leave ½ hour and wash again. During the waiting times grate lemons, roast and grind the aromatics as listed. Take roughly ground lemon leaves and rub over the fish. Wrap the slices of fish in muslin or double folds of cheese cloth. Heat a pan of salted water (barely to cover the fish), put in fish carefully and poach gently without boiling. Remove when three-quarters done, about 4 minutes. Unwrap the cloth and allow the fish to drain.

Mix the fennel, bay leaves, kalonji, fenugreek, cardamoms, half the mace, and salt, together with two beaten eggs. Coat the fish with this mixture and fry in butter until well crisped and golden. During the last minute of cooking aromatize with finely ground lovage seed, remaining mace and cayenne. Serve.

Myhee Mahali (Fish with Cream and Almonds)

1½ lb. good white fish
6 fl. oz. good salad oil
¼ lb. bessan
2½ fl. oz. yoghourt
¼ lb. grated onions
4 pounded cloves garlic
2 teaspoons black cumin
3 cloves
2 tablespoons coriander leaves or 1 tablespoon parsley
1 teaspoon turmeric
½ teaspoon salt
2 oz. clarified butter
4 fl. oz. double cream
4 oz. blanched almonds, slivered and roasted
8 kari phulia leaves or 4 small bay leaves

Skin and cut the fish into large pieces and wash well. Rub with oil and set aside for ½ hour. Prepare the almonds. Wash again, then rub with bessan; leave for 10 minutes, and wash well. Rub with half the yoghourt and leave for ¾ hour, meanwhile preparing onions and garlic. Wash again. Spread and press onions over fish, leaving for ½ hour before washing again. Then rub with garlic and leave for 10 minutes. Grind the cumin, cloves and coriander leaves, and mix to a paste with turmeric and salt. Fry the fish in butter with kari phulia or bay leaves until golden. Add a little yoghourt and boil it dry. Aromatize with the spice paste. Enrich with cream and roasted or fried slivered almonds. Keep on the dum in a preheated moderate oven for 5–10 minutes and serve.

Machchi Imlidarh (Fish with Tamarind)

If tamarind is not available, a substitute (giving a different but equally pleasant flavour) is provided by puréed tart rhubarb mixed with a little Worcester sauce (which is based on tamarind and garlic).

2 lb. fish fillets	½ lb. tamarind or tart rhubarb
½ lb. bessan	6 shallots
Salt	2 tablespoons ground
5 ground cloves garlic	coriander seed
Good pinch saffron	½ teaspoon black pepper
5 fl. oz. yoghourt	1 each green and red pimento
Vinegar or lemon juice	(fresh or tinned)
8 tablespoons oil or 2	Good pinch nutmeg
tablespoons oil and 3 oz.	4 crushed cardamoms
clarified butter	

Clean, skin and wash fillets and prick all over with a sharp fork. Paste with bessan, leave for 10 minutes, then wash. Rub all over with salt, ground garlic and saffron. Leave for 1 hour. Wash again. Rub the fish fillets with yoghourt and leave for 15 minutes. Then wash with vinegar, using just enough to remove the yoghourt. Rub with 2 tablespoons oil and put aside. Meanwhile prepare the tamarind by breaking up with the fingers and soaking in ½ cup water for 15 minutes, then straining the liquor through muslin. Reserve. Pound the shallots with coriander, black pepper, green and red pimentos, adding a few drops of water to make a paste. Wash the oil from the fish and rub on the aromatic paste. Heat the butter or remaining oil until very hot and put in the fish fillets, taking care to shake the pan to avoid burning. Lower heat and carefully turn the fish. Cook for 3 minutes. Scrape up any aromatics that stick to the pan and put on top of the fish. Now salt, and aromatize with nutmeg and cardamoms. Moisten with tamarind liquor or the rhubarb purée. Cover and cook until tender, about 15 minutes Do not overcook. Serve with remaining sauce.

Machchi Dumphokat (Fish Steamed with Black Mushrooms)

These black mushrooms are found in the Himalayas. Ordinary field mushrooms or *cèpes* may be substituted. Dried Indian black mushrooms (*guchi*) may be available, and they should be soaked overnight. Several changes of water are necessary to eliminate all grit. The mushrooms are sliced about ¼ inch thick, and cooked in just as much very lightly salted water as they will absorb, and set aside.

¼ lb. mushrooms (prepared as above) or thin cut fresh mushrooms	1 oz. clarified butter
	1½ teaspoons turmeric
	2 crushed cloves garlic
2 lb. fish (cod or halibut)	1 crushed red chilli
Bessan	½ teaspoon salt

Prepare mushrooms and aromatics as above. Skin, fillet, wash and dry fish. Rub with bessan then wash again. Dry thoroughly and cut into 2-inch squares. Heat butter in a heavy saucepan, add 1 teaspoon turmeric and cook for 10 seconds on a low heat. Add the fish, stir and cook until crisp all over. Add garlic, salt and chilli. Mix carefully without breaking the fish. Raise heat very high and sprinkle fish with about 1 tablespoon water. Cover immediately and lower the heat, or place casserole in a preheated medium oven (350°F; gas 4) for 15 minutes. Shake pan once or twice. If the fish is not quite ready, add a further ½ tablespoon water. Cover, shake pan, and steam until done. Uncover to release all steam. Add mushrooms and mix with fish. Add a modicum of turmeric and cover again. Leave on low heat or in a moderate oven for 5 minutes, then serve.

Machchi Talawi (Batter-Fried Fish)

2 lb. filleted fish
¾ teaspoon salt
Lemon juice or vinegar
½ teaspoon freshly ground black pepper
1 crushed clove garlic
1 tablespoon finely ground pomegranate seed

Fat or oil for deep frying
One of the batters in Appendix, p. 255, or any good frying-batter to choice

Skin, wash and dry fish. Cut into pieces about 3 inches by 2½. Make very small incisions with a sharp knife point. Rub with salt and lemon juice or vinegar mixed with black pepper and garlic. Leave to marinate for 1 to 2 hours. Remove from marinade and allow fish to dry for a few minutes. Meanwhile prepare the batter. Rub fish with pomegranate then dip in batter and deep fry. Do not overcrowd the pan, keep the fat almost smoking hot, and turn the fish over once or twice. Lift out, drain, then place for a few minutes on absorbent paper or towelling, and serve very hot. A perfect deep fried fish should be medium gold in colour. The special batter will produce a slightly darker colour.

Myhee Shahi Talawi (Batter-Fried Fish Royale)

The fish is cooked with batter as in the previous recipe, but two thinner fillets are used to make a sandwich with a filling between. This is often of dried pomegranate seeds or ground mint and parsley mixed with a little lime juice and a choice of mild aromatics, or a thin chutney (for example mint chutney p. 244). The filling is put between the fish fillets which are then pressed together and skewered with poultry pins. They are dipped in batter and deep fried.

A good filling for the fish sandwich is made with 1 teaspoon ground aniseed, 4 tablespoons ground mint, and equal quantities of fresh coriander or parsley, mixed with lime juice, 1 small seeded minced green chilli (optional) and 1 ground bay leaf.

Machchi Hazur Pasand (Fish Baked with Tomatoes)

2½ lb. whole fish or large piece
3 cloves garlic
1 inch green ginger
1 tablespoon coriander
1 tablespoon cumin
1 teaspoon paprika
½ lb. tomatoes
1½ teaspoons ground fenugreek seed
1 oz. clarified butter
1½ teaspoons turmeric
4 tablespoons double cream
½ pint yoghourt
1 teaspoon salt
¼ teaspoon cayenne
1 tablespoon vinegar
1 lemon or lime

Peel the garlic. Slice half very thinly, pound the rest. Thinly slice half the ginger, pound the rest. Grind the coriander, bruise the cumin. Roast the paprika. Skin, seed and sieve the tomatoes.

Fry the ground fenugreek seeds in butter over low heat, add sliced garlic and ginger, and when these are light gold, drain, remove and reserve. Add ground garlic and ginger to the left-over butter with ¾ pint water. Add the coriander, cumin, turmeric and tomatoes. Enrich with cream and yoghourt beaten well together, add the paprika. Put in the fried fenugreek, garlic and ginger. Bring just to the boil and simmer until reduced to a little less than half.

Meanwhile place the whole fish, minus head and tail, on a baking dish; dust with salt and cayenne and sprinkle with vinegar on both sides. Place in a hot oven (400°F; gas 6) until all moisture has evaporated, then pour the sauce over it. Cook in a medium (350°F; gas 4) oven until done, about 35 minutes. Now cut thin rounds of lime or lemon and decorate the fish. Put back in a very hot oven for a few minutes until the lemon slices have softened. Serve hot.

Machchi Jhal Frazi (*Fish with Sautéed Aromatics*)

1½ lb. cooked fish (steamed, roasted or baked)
3 oz. clarified butter
Pinch of asafoetida
¼ lb. green pimento seeded and sliced into thin rounds
1 red pimento cut into thick wedges

4 large onions, halved and layers separated
1 diced stalk celery
¼ lb. sliced mushrooms
½ teaspoon salt
About 20 chive blades
½ teaspoon coarsely broken black pepper

Remove any skin and cut the cooked fish into small cubes, and keep warm. Prepare vegetables and spices as above. Heat butter and add the asafoetida and fish, cooking and stirring gently over a high heat for 1 minute. Lower heat and add green and red pimento, onion, celery and mushrooms. Season with salt. Stir gently without breaking the fish and cook for another minute, then add chives cut into 1 inch lengths and the black pepper. Leave covered on a dum for 10 minutes or until fish is tender. Serve.

Machchi Seekhi (*Whole Fish on the Spit or Grilled*)

3 lb. whole fish, or 6 small whole fish
½ teaspoon paprika
4 tablespoons coriander seed
½ teaspoon salt
6 cardamoms
2 onions
2 cloves garlic
¼ teaspoon ground black pepper

1 tablespoon aniseed or dill
1 green pimento
2 tablespoons mint
4 tablespoons parsley
5 fl. oz. yoghourt
Juice of 1 lemon
2 oz. clarified butter

Lightly roast the paprika and coriander seed, then grind them with all the other aromatics, pimento and herbs. Use them to make a paste with the whipped yoghourt and lime or lemon juice. Wash fish in running water. Remove head and tail, clean and dry. Prick the fish all over and rub paste over the fish and in the cavity. Leave to stand for ½ to 1 hour.

Preheat the grill. Spit the fish as usual for a rotisserie; set grill pan at its highest. Cook until paste is drying without burning (about 15 minutes). Baste with the drippings and cook under slightly reduced heat until tender. A neat way to turn the fish, which must be done once if using grill, is to place a second grid on top of it, hold both racks firmly and turn them upside down, removing the first before replacing the fish. Test by piercing fish right through with a very sharp thin knife, skewer, or larding needle. When the surface is beginning to scorch, baste with butter. Raise heat again and let the fish-skin sear and crisp for another minute or so, then serve immediately.

Variations

1. Use a marinade of lime juice and butter combined with the same aromatics.

2. Or try 2 tablespoons black cumin, 1½ teaspoons onion salt, ¾ teaspoon garlic salt, 3 ground bay leaves, a few lovage seeds, 1 teaspoon cayenne and 8 cardamoms ground down with butter. In both these cases, prick the fish, rub with the paste, and cook as above.

3. Yet another version uses:

2 inches grated fresh ginger *or* ¾ teaspoon powdered dry ginger	2 large onions
	1 teaspoon freshly ground black pepper
7 fl. oz. yoghourt	Juice 2 limes
5 fl. oz. cream	Salt
20 ground cloves	4 oz. butter
¼ teaspoon ground mace	Bessan
8 ground cardamoms	

Rub prepared fish with salt, ginger, pepper and yoghourt. While fish marinates grate onions, and brown lightly in a little butter. Mix a little lime juice with half each of the ground cloves, cardamoms, mace and cream. Paste both onions and spiced cream on fish. Cook as above, and as the marinade dries, baste with butter. Repeat until done, turning once, and basting with the remainder of the cream. Dust with remaining aromatics and place under a fierce grill to gild the surface. Dust lightly with sieved bessan and let it crisp. Baste again with butter and serve.

Kabab Tikkah Machchi (Fish on Skewers)

2 lb. filleted fish
Cooking oil
Bessan
1 teaspoon powdered ginger
2 teaspoons ground aniseed
5 tablespoons yoghourt
2 teaspoons ground cumin

2 teaspoons freshly ground
  black pepper
8 ground cloves
1 teaspoon salt
4 small onions
4 oz. clarified butter

Skin and cut fish into small cubes, and rub with oil. Wash well and rub with bessan; wash again. Mix ginger with 6 tablespoons water, strain, and rub extracted juice over the fish together with whipped yoghourt, salt and all the ground spices. Marinate 1 hour. Slice onions in thick rounds and thread on skewers alternating with fish cubes. Dip in melted butter and place under grill until brown all over, basting frequently with drippings from grill-pan. Baste again with butter before serving.

Kofta Shami Machchi (Fish Croquettes)

2 lb. fish
6 tablespoons oil
Unroasted bessan for cleaning
  fish
3 oz. butter
5 tablespoons yoghourt
2 large onions minced
1 tablespoon ground
  coriander
1 teaspoon salt
1 teaspoon freshly ground
  black pepper

1½ oz. soaked green lentils or
  split peas, pounded to
  paste
1 oz. roasted bessan
3 tablespoons ground poppy
  seed
1 teaspoon ground aniseed or
  dill
4 ground cardamoms
½ inch ground stick cinnamon
1 egg white

Wash and clean fish, rub with oil and wash again. Rub with bessan and wash. Rub with half the yoghourt and allow to marinate for 2–3 hours. Grind, roast and chop the aromatics as listed. Wash fish to remove yoghourt, then dry. Put aside about 3 oz. uncooked fish and cut the rest into very small cubes. Heat butter and give the cubed fish a bhogar with the onions, coriander, salt and pepper. Fry on a high heat, then cover and leave for 1 minute over low heat, shaking pan well. Remove fish and aromatics and mince finely. Put aside.

Finely chop or mince the uncooked fish and mix with green lentil paste, roasted bessan, poppy seed, aniseed, cardamoms, cinnamon and egg white to make a sort of lentil and fish dough. Moisten with a little yoghurt. Form flattened croquettes by enclosing a little of the cooked fish in the casing of the spiced lentil and raw fish dough. Shallow fry until crisp on both sides.

These croquettes can also be fried on a griddle (tawa), or grilled in which case omit the aniseed, and chop or mince raw fish somewhat more coarsely.

To make a chasnidarh (sweet-and-sour) of the fish, boil sugar and water to produce a thick syrup and add enough lemon juice to give a tart flavour. Add 1 teaspoon each ground fenugreek, aniseed or dill, onion salt and paprika. Place fish in syrup and cook over a high heat until the syrup is sticky, but barely beginning to caramelize. Serve hot.

Machchi Bhurta (Fish Purée)

Take 1½ lb. fish, filleted and cooked in akni (see p. 253). Drain and cool, then chop finely or mince. Mix well with the following ingredients chopped and pounded together: 1 large onion, 2 green chillies, 2 cloves garlic, 1 bay leaf, 2 tablespoons mustard or olive oil. Add a good pinch each of mace, paprika and cayenne and 4 tablespoons yoghourt. Sieve this mixture and whip it up with a whisk. Chill before serving.

A fish *panna* is made by cooking the fish in akni and mixing it with half its weight each of shell-fish and another fish plus ⅛ its weight of coriander leaves or parsley, ¼ its weight of chopped hard-boiled eggs, a generous pinch of saffron ground down with oil, cayenne pepper, 2 tablespoons ground pomegranate or 1 tablespoon capers, and 1 teaspoon sugar, salt and other seasoning to taste. This mixture is also sieved, whipped and chilled.

The bhurta or the panna can be made with dried fish. This must first be soaked, and the water changed twice, then it is simmered until tender. Add oil to the mixture to counteract any dryness. Cream may be used in place of yoghourt, but should be thinned with lime juice then whipped and served.

SHELL-FISH

For the following recipes use uncooked prawns if possible, otherwise frozen or cooked ones. The latter should be well washed to remove brine and then dried thoroughly. Live shell-fish, according to their size, may be cooked tender by simmering anything from 3–5 minutes for shrimps or prawns, to 25 minutes for whole large lobsters, and 15 minutes per lb. for crab. If cooking continues after these times, the flesh tends to harden, but still further cooking renders it tender once again. When large raw shell-fish are grilled, the cooking is quicker than by simmering and they are done when the flesh is opaque right through or when a thin knife meets little or no resistance, as well as the outside turning the characteristic bright coral red. These points are important to remember in the currying of shell-fish, when 35 minutes at least should be allowed for the fish to simmer in the curry in order to ensure that it is tender.

Shell-fish can be used for many recipes given elsewhere in this book, such as the kormas, or various fried or sautéed dishes. For instance, pounded or ground, shell-fish other than lobster can be used to make forcemeat, as in the Lavta Kofta recipe given below (p. 145).

You can economize on some of the following recipes by buying tinned prawns from Indian grocers.

Jhinga Turrcarri (Prawn Curry)

1½ lb. prawns after shelling	2 tablespoons ground
½ medium sized onion	coriander seed
1½ oz. clarified butter	Good pinch cayenne
¼ teaspoon turmeric	½ teaspoon salt
Good pinch freshly ground	4 tablespoons yoghourt
black pepper	

Wash and dry prawns. Fry sliced onion in butter until deep gold. Add prawns, aromatize with turmeric and fry for 5 minutes over a medium heat, stirring often. Now add black pepper, coriander, cayenne and salt. Moisten with yoghourt, then add ½ cup water or akni; cover and bring to boil. Lower heat and simmer until tender. The sauce should barely cover the prawns. This curry is light and aromatic.

Jhinga Tandoori (Grilled Prawns)

2 lb. shelled prawns
¼ pint oil
1 teaspoon basil
4 cloves garlic, crushed
2 teaspoons paprika
½ teaspoon cayenne
2 teaspoons freshly ground
   black pepper
2 tablespoons minced mint
   leaves
¾ teaspoon salt
3 tablespoons vinegar
1 teaspoon onion salt
3 teaspoons turmeric

Wash prawns and dry thoroughly. Mix the oil and aromatics, score the prawns lightly with a sharp knife, place in the marinade and leave 8–10 hours in a refrigerator or cold place. Turn and stir the prawns several times during this period.

The prawns may be placed in the grill pan or on skewers. Sprinkle with half the marinade and start to cook under a medium grill. When the marinade has dried somewhat, add the remainder and turn up the heat. When the prawns are reddened and mottled with scorch marks, turn over and grill the other side, basting with marinade. Take care not to overcook. Serve with the residue of the marinade.

Kabab Jhinga (Prawns Grilled in their Shells)

The giant prawn from the Western coast of India is used for this recipe. Pacific prawns, or the largest Dublin Bay prawns may be substituted. A young lobster or crayfish can be prepared in the same way.

2 lb. giant prawns
3 ground bay leaves
1 tablespoon ground fennel
   or aniseed
12 crushed cloves garlic
½ teaspoon paprika
Good pinch cayenne
2 teaspoons salt
2 teaspoons onion salt
2 teaspoons ground kalonji
   seed
1 tablespoon turmeric
2 tablespoons ground
   coriander seed
10 cardamoms, crushed
4 oz. clarified butter
Juice of 4 limes

Wash and clean prawns. Loosen the shell on the underside, and score flesh with a fork. Make a paste of the aromatics together with the melted butter and lime juice. Rub this into the prawns and between the meat and the shell. Leave for 3–4 hours.

Rub some of the paste on to the shells, then place under a medium grill. Allow the shell to redden and scorch on one side (the meat will be coloured by the aromatics, not the heat) then turn and reduce heat. Turn again, keeping the grill low and serve when the centre of the meat is done.

Lavta Kofta (Lobster Quenelles)

1½ lb. cooked lobster or prawns (weighed after shelling)
1 oz. roasted shell (see below)
Good pinch each nutmeg, black pepper, paprika

¼ teaspoon spiced salt (see p. 249)
¼ lb. butter
2 pints akni (see below)
1 tablespoon roasted sesame seed

Make an akni by simmering 4 cloves of garlic, 3 cardamoms, 2 pounded bay leaves, ½ inch of cinnamon bark, 1 teaspoon cumin, large pinch asafoetida and 1 teaspoon salt in 2 pints water for 15 minutes.

Shell lobster or prawns and reserve meat. Lightly roast shells, pound them finely. Use 1 oz. of this in the mixture. Keep rest to flavour soups or sauces. Pound meat with all spices, adding butter gradually. Cover and chill for several hours.

Bring akni to simmering point. Shape chilled mixture into sausages or, using two dessertspoons, into eggs. Place on a buttered banana leaf or kitchen foil for a few minutes to lose chill, then slide gently into akni. Do not crowd the pan. Cover and poach until firm and slightly swollen. Lift carefully on perforated spoon, drain, and serve at once.

Note: Those who have had no experience in handling quenelles may like to bind the mixture with a little beaten egg. However, provided poaching is really gentle, this is unnecessary.

A very light chutney sauce is served with the quenelles and can be made by thinning a tart chutney with a little lemon juice and water, adding a teaspoon of rice flour or cornflour and cooking until the sauce becomes transparent. Serve hot, with steamed rice.

To make *Batter-Fried Prawn* or *Lobster Quenelles* the pounded meat is mixed with the yolks of two eggs. The shaped quenelles are dipped in beaten egg, then in flour or bessan batter, and deep fried in very hot fat or oil. After draining, these quenelles may be rolled in a little garam masala (see p. 249).

The batters suggested in the Appendix (p. 255) can be used for *Batter-Fried Prawns* and *Lobster Cubes*.

Spiced Shell-fish should first be cleaned, dried and split open, then rubbed with an aromatic paste, salt and lemon juice. Allow to marinate for several hours in a cool place or in the refrigerator. The batter used should be plain and un-flavoured.

Baked Shell-fish can be cooked in the shell or in a large banana leaf or kitchen foil. The meat is first ground down, bound with egg yolk, double cream, and yoghourt, then lightly aromatized with a ground bay leaf, a pinch of aniseed, nutmeg or mace, and paprika, and seasoned with salt, chives and green herbs.

For *Buttered Shell-fish* use small cooked shrimps, cooked diced prawns or any good quality firm fish. Clarified butter is essential. Use 2½ oz. for every 2 lb. shell-fish and 5 fl. oz. thick yoghourt. Heat these together in a pan without browning. Add the following aromatics, powdered and sifted to mix them: good pinch nutmeg, ½ teaspoon paprika, a very little cayenne, ¼ teaspoon black pepper, 2 cardamoms, 4 cloves, ¼ inch cinnamon. Add the shell-fish and stir for about 3 minutes. See that the butter and yoghourt *do not* bubble; the shell-fish must not fry. Add a little whipped cream, cover the pan and leave over a low heat for 5 minutes, shaking the pan occasionally. Serve.

Pakora (*Batter-Fried Vegetables and Shrimps*)

5 oz. bessan	¼ teaspoon turmeric
¾ pint water	1 teaspoon ground coriander
Large teaspoon salt	¼ teaspoon cayenne

Sift the flour, and slowly work in the water to make a thick pouring batter. Whip until perfectly smooth, and leave to stand for $\frac{1}{2}$ hour or more. Aromatize with turmeric, coriander, cayenne, and beat well for a minute or two before using. Dip vegetables into the batter, coating well, and deep fry in very hot fat. Remove when a light saffron colour, drain, and serve with a mint chutney (see p. 244). Use a selection of vegetables such as raw diced carrot, shredded spinach, cucumber rounds, sliced aubergine, cauliflower flowerets, small pieces of pimento, rounds of boiled potatoes or parsnip, slices of celery, and so on.

The pakoras can be three-quarters cooked, kept at room temperature, then fried again when ready to eat. They will be done in $\frac{1}{2}$ minute or so and the result will be a little crisper than usual.

For *Shrimp* or *Lobster Pakoras*, simmer fish, slightly under-cooking it, in a garlic infusion or akni. Cool and shell, cutting lobster into cubes or lengthwise slices; flatten shrimps lightly with a knife or mallet and slit down the centre without cutting through completely. Dust with aromatics and dip into batter.

Unlike plain flour, batter made with bessan produces a non-porous surface and no fat will penetrate to the food inside. Some people use aromatics with the batter, but I think this is over-doing the seasoning. For this most delicious of batter-fried food, the natural taste of meat, fish or vegetable should not be disguised.

CHAPTER NINE

Rice Cookery

WITH the many rice preparations – pilau, biriani, zarda, chawal – we come to the most subtle of all Indian food. The basis of this rice cookery is the best and longest grained rice. It is commonly called patna, but the best varieties come under different names such as basmati, almora, dehra dun. The finest of these has a delicate, crescent-shaped grain. It is often aged for fifteen years to give the special quality needed for the famous pilaus and sweet rice dishes of Indian cookery.

Rice preparations may be classed under the following headings:

Steamed and boiled rice where the grain should be dry, fluffy, separate and white.

Makhani or *buttered rice* which is made from cold steamed or boiled rice with the addition of butter and aromatics. It is given a dum until the rice is very hot and the butter has been absorbed.

Pilau or *baked rice* where the grain is completely transformed by absorbing more than its own weight of liquid. The rice is more flavoursome than the meat or vegetable, stock, cream, yoghourt, butter, aromatics, juices and essences used in the cooking. There are various styles of pilau: the sadah or plain pilau; yakhni pilau made with stock and jellied stock; massalam pilau made with certain aromatics and flavourings; korma pilau based on braised meat, chicken or fish; shahi or royale pilaus using almonds, cream, yoghourt, light spices and plenty of butter and stock; the shah degh pilau which is baked so that the outer surface is brown and crisp when the pilau is turned out of its mould or casserole; *zaraberian* or biriani pilau cooked with turmeric, saffron and aromatics like cumin, coriander, and so on. The sweet pilaus have their own style: *zarda* using saffron; *suffaida*, a sweet pilau cooked without saffron or colouring agent; *sheer bringh* or multi-coloured sweet pilau; the sheer or kheer, prototype of all rice puddings; chasnidarh or sweet and pungent pilau – the only sweet pilau using meat, fish or game. Finally, there are the rice desserts such as *fhirni* (p. 215) or jogurath that use some form of rice, usually ground.

The technique of cooking a pilau puts special emphasis on the dum which has been described in detail in previous chapters (see p. 27). Although the oven dum gives the most delicate finish, the pilau can also be finished on top of the stove by using an asbestos mat and (inverting the lid if necessary to make a flat surface) a bowl of boiling water can be placed on top, or, of course, charcoal where available.

Butter is used in every pilau recipe, but only a little liquid, and the heavy sealed pot is a feature of these dishes. In some, a good measure of cream and yoghourt helps to make this a nourishing and substantial dish that requires little in the way of side dishes, although garnishes are an important part of the pilau, and some recipes make use of a dozen or more. They may be almonds, blanched or fried, strips of ginger, pimento, green chilli, grilled tomatoes, boiled beetroot, cucumber dipped in egg white and fried, hard-boiled eggs, fried parsley and coriander leaves, chives, grilled or sautéed mushrooms, small fried onions, roasted red chillies, batter-fried slices of lime or lemon, raisins, sultanas, desiccated or grated coconut.

Most pilaus are improved by the addition of about 4 ground cardamoms (shell and seed), 8 whole cloves, a 1 inch splintered cinnamon stick, and a good pinch of nutmeg. These are standard spices that appear in most pilaus. They are scattered freely throughout the rice or placed in a small muslin bag and immersed in the rice during steaming.

During the initial browning or frying of the rice it is stirred constantly to prevent burning and to ensure that every grain is evenly saturated with butter. When it becomes translucent it has absorbed the butter and no good can come of further frying. A cold liquid is then added. It is brought to the boil, and the rice should be well stirred only once to prevent clotting or clumping of the grains. Thereafter, stirring is taboo except for the purpose of slipping in some ingredient. The casserole should be shaken occasionally to release steam and moisture. The finished pilau should be perfectly dry, each grain of rice separate, fluffy, wholly tender, yet in one undamaged piece and all juices, creams, etc. absorbed. There is nothing mystical about this. Reread this section carefully and follow the instructions for each recipe. Until you gain experience, add your liquid in two or three lots, stopping as soon as the rice is tender and dry. It is inundation with liquid that turns rice to porridge. Finally, always cook rice on the lowest possible heat, using an asbestos mat or an iron griddle. Rice cookery, especially the cooking of pilaus, is a matter of subtle persuasion.

Use an average of 2 oz. rice per person.

Chawal (Plain Rice)

Sometimes rice is soaked before boiling or steaming. The rice water can be used in other ways and fresh water used for cooking the rice, or, if the same water is used, it should be strained through muslin.

There are two main methods for cooking plain rice. I personally favour steamed rice using the minimum quantity of water.

Steamed Rice. The moistening will vary slightly according to the cooking vessel, the heat used, type of rice and even the time of year. Begin with salted water with a dash of lemon juice, rising 1–1¼ inches above the uncooked rice, though less for very small quantities. Boil, stirring for 1 minute, cover and reduce heat. When water has been absorbed, test rice by withdrawing a few grains from the centre, and if more cooking is necessary sprinkle in a tablespoon or so of water. Close lid and steam on a gentle heat, repeating until rice is tender. After a few sessions, you will be able to judge the amount of water needed. When done, place rice in a cool place for ten minutes before serving.

Boiled Rice. This method makes use of a generous quantity of water, and the rice is removed when done. Use a very large vessel and add washed or unwashed rice to boiling salted water, stirring well, and boiling briskly until done. Immediately rice is tender throw in a cup of cold water to halt the cooking process.

Drain in a colander and cover until dry. Serve in a heated dish. The water can be used as stock.

Rasadarh Chawal (*Flavoured Rice*)

Take enough rice for four people – about ½ lb. or more. Steam or boil, mixing in some tomato purée or sieved tomatoes and season with salt, black pepper or paprika. The flavouring can be varied according to choice: fish stock; pimento juice; beetroot purée; essences made by grinding parsley, coriander leaves, mint or chives and steeping in water, sieved celery, asparagus, artichokes, mushrooms and so on.

Makhani Chawal (*Buttered Rice*)

Use cooked rice which has been allowed to cool. Melt butter in heavy casserole but do not let it brown. Stir in the rice and mix well. Normally 1½ oz. butter will coat ½ lb. rice. The quantity of butter can be increased or cut down to suit personal taste. Add garnishing or flavouring as required and close the lid tightly. Place over gentle heat or in a slow oven. Shake the casserole. When rice is steaming hot, serve at once.

After the buttering you can add thinly sliced mushrooms, julienne strips of pimento, diced celery, sliced cucumber salted and drained, chopped parsley, or any cooked vegetable. Although mussels, scallops, flaked fish or chopped shell-fish may be added, dark meats are best avoided with buttered rice.

A variation is made by heating the butter and adding its weight in well whipped cream or yoghourt.

Sadah Pilau (*Plain Pilau*)

½ lb. rice	1 oz. almonds blanched and
2 oz. clarified butter	slivered
1 onion	2 oz. seedless raisins
½ teaspoon salt	¼ lb. shelled green peas

Cut onion into thin rings and fry in butter until browned. Do not stir. Remove, draining butter back into the pan. Keep onions warm.

Re-heat butter and add rice washed, or soaked for 2 to 4 hours and thoroughly drained. Stir well, cooking over medium heat. In 7 to 8 minutes, the rice will become translucent. Moisten with water and stir. Bring to the boil, season with salt and add almonds, raisins and green peas. Stir once and cover well. Lower heat and cook until rice is tender. Moisten if necessary. Sprinkle with fried onion rings before serving.

Green peas are a standard ingredient in the plain pilau, but grated carrots are just as good. With carrots use nutmeg in place of cloves.

Note: Western cooks should use caution in adding the chillies in the following recipes. To avoid all peppery bite, half to one seeded green or red pimento may be substituted for chillies. One seeded chilli will give a mild bite, two seeded chillies a moderate bite; leaving seeds in will produce a hotter dish, more so if the pod is broken, most if crushed or pulverized.

Massalam Pilau (*Savoury Pilau with Chicken*)

½ lb. rice
2 medium onions grated
3 oz. butter
2 lb. roasting chicken
1 inch grated green ginger
5 fl. oz. yoghourt
Salt
6–8 cloves garlic minced
1 teaspoon freshly ground black pepper
2 broken bay leaves
5 ground cardamoms
¼ teaspoon nutmeg
1 inch splintered stick cinnamon
1 large minced pimento
1 tablespoon chopped mint
1–2 dried or fresh red chillies lightly roasted and seeded

Soak the rice in cold water for 1 hour. Prepare spices, divide bird into 8 pieces. Drain rice and leave to dry. Brown the grated onions in butter until all moisture has dried. Put in the chicken and fry over medium heat. Add ginger and cook a further 5 minutes. Add a few tablespoons of yoghourt, season with salt and cook in or on low heat until the chicken is tender, about 35 minutes, and all moisture has dried.

Aromatize with garlic and moisten with more yoghourt. Add black pepper, bay leaves, cardamoms, cinnamon, nutmeg, pimento and mint. Put in the rice and fry for 5–6 minutes. Add water to cover the rice by 1¼ inches and stir well. Add broken chillies. Bring just to boiling point, then cook over lowest possible heat until rice is done. Give it a dum in low oven or over asbestos mat on top of stove for 12 minutes. Leave 5 minutes in a warm atmosphere, uncover and serve.

If the pilau is cooked in copper or metal ovenware, this can be brought straight to the table for serving. A gaily coloured cloth turbaned around the casserole will keep it warm and lend a note of colour to the table. Cast-iron enamelled ovenware is fairly satisfactory, although the rice tends to stick a little to the bottom.

Yakhni Pilau (Lamb Pilau with Double Stock)

¼ cup jellied stock
½ lb. rice
1¼ lb. cubed boned lamb
Juice of 2 limes
8 ground anise or fennel seeds
¼ pint lightly whipped double cream
5 fl. oz. yoghourt
4 oz. clarified butter

4 bruised cloves
7 bruised cardamoms
2 inches splintered stick cinnamon
2 tablespoons roasted, ground poppy seed
2 whole bay leaves
Salt
6 tablespoons chopped spinach or watercress

Prepare a heavy, clear, jellied stock from a little mutton and gelatinous bones like shin, knuckle and trotters. Clarify and remove all fat when cool. This stock can be made plain or with the addition of a few strips of lemon rind or a handful of lemon leaves, parsley or coriander leaves, 1 inch chopped green ginger, 2 inches splintered cinnamon, 1–2 green chillies or a green pimento, 1 teaspoon peppercorns and some chives (a most appetizing broth incidentally on a winter's day).

Soak the rice in cold water for 1 hour, and then drain.

Wipe the lamb, remove skin and dry thoroughly. Prick all over with a fork and rub with lime and aniseed. Moisten with the cream and yoghourt, lightly mixed, and set aside. Prepare the spices and flavourings as listed.

Heat a little butter and add cloves. Splash in stock and stir. Cover and leave on low heat for 5 minutes. Heat remaining butter in another pan, add cardamoms, cinnamon, poppy seed and bay leaves. Add rice and cook over medium heat, stirring

153

until rice becomes translucent – about 6 to 8 minutes. Then add cream-and-yoghourt sauce strained from the meat and enough stock to cover rice by 1¼ inches. Bring to the boil, add salt and chopped watercress or spinach. Steam until done.

Meanwhile, fry the cubed lamb and when crisp and well browned place inside the pilau. Cover and cook until almost done. Now give the pilau a dum in a low oven for 15 minutes. Leave in a warm atmosphere for 5 minutes before serving.

The pilau can be garnished with blanched almonds, slivered and fried; pimento rings, salted and then roasted or grilled; onion rings dipped in batter and fried; and raisins, soaked, drained and lightly fried.

Murgh Korma Pilau (Braised Chicken Pilau)

The korma pilau is made by using good braised meat but omitting saffron or turmeric from the recipe. Any of the chicken kormas given on page 100 ff. can be used. Make the korma in advance and keep in the refrigerator.

Alternatively, the following method can be used:

1 3 lb. chicken	2 tablespoons coriander
1 inch green ginger	2 tablespoons cumin
4 cardamoms	1 bay leaf
1 pimento	2 oz. almonds
4 cloves garlic	¼ lb. butter
3 grated onions	5 fl. oz. yoghourt
4 oz. minced onions	2–3 chillies or 1 red pimento
1 oz. minced raisins	Juice of 2 lemons

Skin, wash, clean and dry the chicken and prick all over. Grind the green ginger, cardamoms, pimento, garlic and onions into a paste and rub on to the chicken. Leave for ½ hour. Meanwhile grind or pound together the minced onions, raisins, coriander, cumin, bay leaf and almonds. Fry in the butter and when well browned and dry, add the yoghourt, 4 tablespoons at a time. Then add the chillies or red pimento seeded and coarsely chopped, and fry with the chicken for 3 to 4 minutes. Acidulate with the lemon juice. Add spice and almond paste to pan and cook until the meat is tender and the sauce velvety, adding water if necessary. Reserve for the pilau.

To prepare the pilau:

¾ lb. rice
2 oz. butter
8 bruised cardamoms
¼ teaspoon grated nutmeg
2 broken bay leaves
2 oz. washed sultanas
Salt

Meat stock
2 oz. blanched almonds
2 onions
Chopped parsley
1 teaspoon kewara essence or
    rose water

Soak rice for 1 hour and drain. Prepare the spices. Fry rice in 1½ oz. butter until translucent, then add cardamoms, nutmeg and bay leaves. Fry another minute. Heat the chicken korma and mix into the rice. Add sultanas, season with salt, and moisten with enough stock to cover rice by 1½ inches. Bring to the boil and cook over lowest possible heat until done, moistening with more stock or water if necessary. Cut almonds into slivers, thinly slice onions and fry both in remaining butter.

Open the casserole and sprinkle with almonds, onions and parsley. Sprinkle rose water over top, cover and place in a gentle oven (or put charcoal or hot water on the lid) for about 15 minutes.

Any lamb, mutton or pork korma can be used for a korma pilau, but always remember to omit the saffron and turmeric.

Dumnavardhi Pilau (*Chicken and Lamb Pilau*)

3–3½ lb. chicken
¾ lb. boned lamb
3 oz. bessan
3 oz. ground fennel or aniseed
1 whole bulb of garlic
    pounded to paste with 1
    teaspoon water
2½ tablespoons coriander
    seed
3 inches green ginger
8 oz. butter
¾ lb. onions
6 oz. almonds
3 oz. honey
3 oz. raisins

½ pint double cream
¾ pint yoghourt
Juice of 3 small limes or
    lemons
14 cardamoms
11 cloves
1½ inch stick cinnamon
3 teaspoons salt
Good pinch nutmeg
¾ pint milk
1 lb. rice
½ teaspoon saffron
1½ teaspoons freshly ground
    black pepper

Clean, skin and wash the chicken. Rub with bessan and wash. Prick all over with a sharp knife point, rub with most of the fennel, leave 10 minutes, wash again; rub with the garlic paste, leave for $\frac{1}{2}$ to 1 hour, wash and dry thoroughly; finally rub with coriander ground with $2\frac{1}{2}$ inches of the ginger. Reserve. During the waiting periods read the directions below, put lamb on to cook; prepare the various marinades and spices, keeping them in small covered basins; parboil rice 9 minutes.

Heat 3 oz. butter in a heavy saucepan and fry half the onions. When brown, mix with 3 oz. chopped blanched almonds, honey and raisins. Use to stuff the chicken. Truss and then roast in the oven or on the spit, basting with a marinade of 3 oz. blanched ground almonds, the cream, yoghourt, lime or lemon juice, and half of each of the given quantities of ground cardamoms, cloves and cinnamon – using a little water to make into a paste, finally mixing with 2 oz. melted butter.

During preparing and cooking bird, slice the lamb into thin strips and cook in just enough water to tenderize, about 15 minutes, aromatizing with $\frac{1}{2}$ inch green ginger, the remaining onions sliced very thinly and fried dark brown, and 1 teaspoon salt. Drain meat when done and reserve broth after straining. Fry meat in 2 oz. butter until crisp and browned. Give the broth a bhogar: heat 1 oz. butter in a pan, add a good pinch of ground cloves and splash in the broth. Stir and leave on very low heat for 1 minute. Repeat 3 times in all, using nutmeg for the second bhogar and a few grains of fennel or aniseed for the third. Add milk and boil together for 3 minutes.

Take rice and cook in the liquor until tender, about 7 minutes, then remove. If any liquor remains, reduce it to a few tablespoons and return to the rice.

Place the roasted chicken in a heavy casserole with all the scrapings of juices and marinade and sprinkle with the remaining nutmeg, cardamom, cinnamon and all the black pepper. Use saffron dissolved in a tablespoon of boiling water to colour one third of the cooked rice. Place on top of the chicken. Add the rest of rice and bury the crisp meat in the rice. Sprinkle remaining melted butter evenly on top. Shake the casserole and season with 2 teaspoons salt or to taste. Close lid tightly (preferably seal with a ribbon of paste or dough). Place over a hot fire for 2 minutes, then put in a moderate oven for $\frac{1}{2}$ hour. Leave to stand for about 7 minutes before unsealing. Carve the chicken and spoon out the stuffing with each helping of pilau.

Pilau Hazur Pasandh
(Festival Pilau with Meat, Fruit and Nuts)

$\frac{3}{4}$ lb. rice	Pinch mace
$\frac{3}{4}$ lb. boned lamb	Pinch ground saffron
6 eggs	8 cardamoms
4 oz. clarified butter	2 oz. shelled pistachio
5 minced onions	2 oz. chirongee or brazil nuts
1 tablespoon ground cumin	2 oz. cashew nuts
1 teaspoon salt	1 peeled sliced orange
10 peppercorns	4 oz. mango or peach (fresh
2 oz. raisins, washed and	or tinned)
soaked	4 oz. seeded grapes
2 oz. dried apricots	3 bay leaves
2 oz. blanched almonds	1 inch stick cinnamon

Prepare the aromatics, nuts, fruit; parboil rice 9 minutes; separate eggs. Mince $\frac{1}{4}$ lb. meat, put in saucepan with 1 oz. butter and water just to cover and cook 45–60 minutes leaving just a $\frac{1}{4}$ cup liquor. Meanwhile cut remaining meat into almond-sized pieces, mix with onion, a little cumin, $\frac{1}{2}$ teaspoon salt and 3 crushed peppercorns. Simmer (using only as much water as can be absorbed) until tender. When minced lamb is done, add raisins, chopped apricots, 1 oz. slivered almonds, mace and saffron. Mix with beaten egg whites and leave on low heat until set. Keep warm. Heat 1 oz. butter and fry the egg yolks. Keep these warm also. Strain the liquor from the cut lamb and reserve, giving this meat a bhogar in 1 oz. butter and 2 crushed cardamoms. Leave covered on a low heat for 1 minute, then uncover and fry until crisp and well browned. Sprinkle the meat with remaining cumin and keep warm.

Mix parboiled rice with the reserved liquor from the cut lamb. Simmer until rice is tender, about 7 minutes. Put the meat in a heavy saucepan, add the rice and sprinkle with sieved or chopped fried egg yolks. On top arrange slivered pistachio, the remaining almonds, brazil nuts, the cashew nuts, slices of orange, cubed peach or mango and halved grapes. Bury the bay leaves in the rice. Scatter with remaining whole pepper-corns, salt, broken cardamoms, cinnamon and remaining melted butter. Close lid tightly and give the pilau a dum in a slow oven for 35 minutes. Serve with the minced meat and the fruit in egg whites spooned over the top.

To make a chasnidarh pilau of the hazur pasandh pilau, make a syrup to which the juice of 1 lemon is added, and use ¾ of it with the rice while it is cooking in water. Add the remaining syrup to the minced meat before cooking it.

Memna Pilau (Favourite Pilau)

¾ lb. cubed lean lamb
6 onions
4 oz. clarified butter
3 inches fresh green ginger
1 teaspoon salt
5 oz. blanched almonds
1 teaspoon rose water
2 inches stick cinnamon
6 cardamoms
1 tablespoon cumin

4 oz. carrots
¾ lb. rice
½ pint yoghourt
¼ teaspoon cayenne
2 green chillies
1 teaspoon freshly ground
   black pepper
Fried cucumber slices
   (garnish)

Slice onions very thinly and brown them in 1 oz. butter. Pound half ginger. Cut meat into large dice and mix with onion, pounded ginger, salt and the butter that has been used for frying. Moisten with enough water to cover by 2 inches and simmer until tender about 1 hour. Meanwhile prepare the aromatics: pound half the almonds with rose water; splinter all but ¼ inch cinnamon; cut remaining ginger in julienne strips; toast remaining almonds and pound with cardamoms; pound cumin; chop chillies (remove seeds for mild result); grate carrots. Keep all separate.

Reserve meat, and dry. Strain liquor, and mix with the almonds and rose water. Heat ½ oz. butter and fry ¼ inch stick cinnamon for 1 minute, add half cayenne and splash in the liquor. Stir and boil for 1 minute, then reserve. Wash rice and put on to parboil 9 minutes in salted water.

Rub the meat with about 3 tablespoons yoghourt, then fry in 1 oz. butter with half nutmeg and half the ginger julienne until dry and well browned. Add cumin and cook the meat over gentle heat for 5 minutes, stirring well. Add browned almond and cardamom mixture. Fry together for a minute or two.

Place parboiled rice on top of meat and aromatize with chilli, black pepper and the remaining cayenne, nutmeg, cinnamon and ginger julienne. Add carrot, sprinkle with remaining melted butter and moisten with rest of yoghourt. Finally, sprinkle with the liquor (there should be about ½ cup). Cover tightly and place over high heat for 1½ minutes. Put in a moderate oven for 40 minutes. Garnish with fried cucumber slices.

Mutanjan Pilau (Pork Pilau with Coconut)

¾ lb. rice
¾ lb. pork fillet
Akni (see p. 253)
4 oz. butter
2 onions
7 fl. oz. yoghourt
6 cloves
6 crushed cardamoms
3 inches green ginger
1 complete bulb of garlic
4 oz. honey

1 oz. blanched halved almonds
¼ teaspoon ground nutmeg
1 oz. shelled pistachio
Pinch ground saffron
Pinch ground dill or aniseed
4 tablespoons grated or
  desiccated coconut
1 teaspoon salt
1 tablespoon aniseed (or
  fennel, etc.)
2 teaspoons black cumin

Soak rice for 1 hour then drain thoroughly. Heat the akni and put in the pork cut into 2 inch pieces. Simmer until tender, about 1–1½ hours.

Meanwhile in another saucepan, melt 1 oz. butter and fry the thinly sliced onions, add whipped yoghourt, cloves and crushed cardamoms. Remove pork when done and let dry. Pound together green ginger and garlic in ¼ cup water. Spread this over the meat, put in a casserole. Reduce pork liquor to ½ cup and reserve. Melt the honey with 1 tablespoon water and mix with halved almonds. Add to meat, and simmer 5 minutes. Remove from heat and arrange rice on top. Spoon reserved pork liquor over rice, but do not stir the mixture. Add nutmeg, and pistachio, sprinkle with saffron and dust with ground aniseed, and coconut. Then add cumin. Melt and add remaining butter. Close lid tightly and place over high heat for about 4 minutes. Put in a low oven (325°F.; gas 3) or put on an asbestos mat on top of the stove for 35 minutes. Then let it stand away from heat for 7 minutes, uncover, sprinkle lightly with salt, mix well and serve.

Teetur Pilau (Pilau with Game Bird and Meat Sauce)

3 small partridges (or 8 quails or 1 pheasant or grouse)
¾ lb. boned veal or lamb
½ lb. cooked chick-peas or white beans (see pp. 193, 198)
1 lb. rice
½ pint yoghourt
4 cloves pounded garlic
¼ teaspoon ground saffron
6 grated onions
4 oz. butter
2 tablespoons chopped mint
1 teaspoon black pepper

6 cloves
2 tablespoons chopped parsley
1 tablespoon roasted, ground poppy seed
2 inches splintered stick cinnamon
9 cardamoms
1 teaspoon salt
2 bay leaves
2½ tablespoons ground coriander seed
1 tablespoon sesame seed

Cook chick-peas or beans reserving the liquor. Clean the game birds, skin and split in half. Flatten with a heavy kitchen mallet so the smaller bones are broken and the portions lie flat. Prick all over with a sharp knife-point, then rub well with a paste made from whipped yoghourt, half saffron, garlic and onions. Marinate for 5 to 6 hours. Prepare aromatics.

Simmer the birds and meat in the reserved liquor. Remove each when tender (the meat should be falling apart). Mince the lamb then sieve it, or use a blender. Melt 1 oz. butter and add mint, black pepper and the meat. Fry and stir until dryish. Add rice to this mixture with enough water to cook it until tender.

Arrange a layer of about a third of rice mixture in a heavy casserole, dot with half the cloves, sprinkle with parsley, poppy seed, half the cardamoms, the chick-peas, a few pieces of cinnamon, salt and 1 bay leaf. Place birds on top. Melt remaining butter and spoon 2 tablespoons over birds. Aromatize with coriander and other remaining aromatics, then add another third of rice mixture and more melted butter. Dust with remaining saffron. Put in remaining rice and butter, cover well and place over high heat for 4 minutes. Put in a slow oven, or on top of stove on asbestos mat over low heat for 1 hour. Leave out of oven for 6 minutes before serving.

VEGETABLE PILAUS

For vegetable pilaus, the method is similar. The first recipe in this section gives the general directions. Mixed vegetables such as cauliflower, spinach, potatoes, tomatoes, squash, marrow and especially green beans, can be used in a pilau. Raw or fried vegetables can be added to the rice with the liquid or they can be fried and cooked in akni and added to the rice in the last 5 or 6 minutes.

Phalahar Pilau (Vegetable and Lentil Pilau)

3 oz. *channah* (yellow lentils) or chick-peas
¾ lb. rice
3 oz. *moong* (green lentils)
3 oz. *masoor* (red lentils)
2 tablespoons coriander seed
3 oz. butter
Large pinch of asafoetida
5 oz. spinach
2 beetroot
2 medium turnips
3 oz. carrots
2 inches green ginger
2 sticks celery
2 green chillies
1 teaspoon freshly ground black pepper

6 minced cloves garlic
4 cloves
8 crushed cardamoms
1 inch splintered stick cinnamon
Small bunch of chives chopped
1 teaspoon salt
2 bay leaves
4 oz. Indian cheese (*paneer*: see p. 251)
3 onions
¼ teaspoon sugar
Bunch of coriander leaves
Bunch of parsley
3 tomatoes

Soak chick-peas overnight, and begin cooking them in water well to cover, about 4 hours before lentils. Soak lentils for 1–2 hours, wash and drain them, and cook in water with coriander, salt and asafoetida until tender. Strain both liquors and reduce to about ½ cup. Prepare the aromatics.

Lightly fry the spinach, then shred and reserve. Wash and peel beetroot and cut into slices. Quarter the turnips, dice the carrots, slice the celery and add chopped chillies (seeded for milder dish) and black pepper. Cook with the garlic in sufficient water until tender, then strain. Give liquor a bhogar in a little butter with cloves; leave on very low heat for 5 minutes. Heat remaining butter in a heavy casserole and put in rice. Stir and cook over medium heat until the rice becomes translucent. Add crushed cardamoms, splintered cinnamon and chopped chives; stir and fry another minute. Season with salt and pour in the vegetable and lentil liquor. Aromatize with bay leaves. Bring to boil, then cover and steam on lowest heat until done (about 20 minutes). Meanwhile heat ½ oz. butter and fry the onions, cut in rings, with ¼ teaspoon sugar until well browned. Five minutes before the rice is ready put in the paneer, sliced thin and fried a rich brown, the vegetables and lentils lightly sautéed and the shredded spinach. Garnish with fried or grilled tomatoes, fried parsley and coriander leaves, fried onion rings and crisply fried slivers of ginger.

Kadoo Pilau (Pilau with Stuffed Marrow)

A small marrow, about ½ lb.
¼ lb. minced celery or water chestnut (*shringara*)
3 oz. butter
½ lb. rice
6 onions
1 teaspoon paprika
Juice of 1 lemon
Pinch saffron
2 tablespoons ground poppy seed

5 tablespoons milk
2 fl. oz. double cream
½ teaspoon salt
1 green pimento
5 crushed cardamoms
2 oz. sultanas
Good pinch ground mace
5 whole cloves
2 broken bay leaves
1 tablespoon cumin

Prepare the aromatics as indicated. Peel the marrow (cucumber can also be used), cut out a 'lid' (about a third), scoop out the seed pulp and reserve. Salt the inside and leave for 15 minutes. Drain and dry with kitchen paper. Meanwhile, chop seed pulp with celery or water chestnut, and sauté in ½ oz. butter with the paprika, a good pinch of saffron and the poppy seed. Stuff the marrow with this mixture and replace the lid. Secure with a string or cocktail sticks, and grill or fry, using about 1 oz. butter, browning well on all sides. Remove from pan and prick all over with a sharp silver fork and rub with lemon juice and a pinch of saffron soaked in a little water. Mix the scrapings of the pan with ½ oz. butter, then moisten with milk and cream. Add salt and heat for 30 seconds or so.

Heat remaining butter and add rice with cardamoms, sultanas, mace, cloves and bay leaves. Fry over medium heat, stirring all the time until grains become translucent. Place marrow in the centre, cover with rice, moisten with enough water and the pan scrapings to cover by 1¼ inches and bring just to the boil. Simmer over very low heat until done, about 1 hour. Five minutes before it is ready, add thin rings of green pimento and cumin to rice, mix carefully; finish cooking. Remove from heat 4–5 minutes before uncovering, and incorporate any liquor from the marrow as you serve.

This pilau can also be made by stuffing the marrow with minced meat, fish or shell-fish.

Kookurh Pilau
(Pilau with Chicken, Eggs and Fricadelles)

3 lb. chicken, or capon
1½ lb. boned lamb
5 eggs
1¼ lb. rice
5 oz. clarified butter
3 onions
4 tablespoons bessan
1 teaspoon freshly ground black pepper
2 bay leaves
4 tablespoons ground coriander seed
5 oz. blanched almonds

2 oz. shelled pistachio
2 oz. raisins
¼ pint yoghourt
1 teaspoon salt
9 cardamoms
¼ teaspoon saffron
3 inches green ginger
2 roasted, dried chillies (seeded for milder dish)
5 cloves
1½ inches splintered cinnamon
8 lovage seeds

Grate 1 onion, chop and fry rest. Prepare aromatics as indicated above and in recipe. Mince ¾ lb. of lamb.

Separate eggs using whites to bind the minced lamb with bessan, browned onion, black pepper, one ground bay leaf and half the coriander, then cook it in water. When tender remove and grind. Mince or pound the almonds, pistachio and raisins with a little yoghourt, salt and 4 crushed cardamoms and a pinch of saffron. Fold into the lamb and egg white forcemeat and shape into walnut-size balls. Fry these in 1 oz. butter until a rich brown.

Meanwhile, prepare the chicken: wash, skin and dry, then prick all over with sharp knife point. Rub in some pounded green ginger, grated onion and 4 pounded cardamoms. Stuff with the rest of the lamb cut into almond-size pieces and fried in 1 oz. butter with lovage seeds, salt and 1 broken chilli. Roast the chicken, basting with yoghourt until done, about 1 hour.

Heat all but ½ oz. of remaining butter and fry the rice with remaining broken cardamom, cloves and cinnamon. When translucent, add one powdered bay leaf, remaining green ginger, chopped fine, and rest of coriander seed. Take all the yoghourt bastings and drippings from the chicken, mix with 1 cup water and bring to the boil. Pour over the rice. Place the chicken in the middle and the meatballs on one side. Bring to the boil and then lower heat and cook until done. Place for 15 minutes in a gentle oven, or give it a dum with charcoal on lid on top of stove.

Meanwhile, beat egg yolks with ¼ teaspoon black pepper, salt, 1 crushed chilli and a pinch of saffron. Make an omelette from this with rest of butter just before the pilau is ready to serve. Before serving place it on the other side of the chicken. Serve each person a portion of omelette, capon with stuffing, meat fricadelles with the pilau spooned over.

Palak Pilau (Pilau with Spinach and Aubergine)

¾ lb. rice
4 oz. clarified butter
Small handful of minced parsley or coriander leaves
4 oz. desiccated coconut
12 cardamoms, bruised
12 cloves
1½ inches cinnamon, splintered
4 tablespoons white sesame seed lightly roasted

8 onions
12 kari phulia leaves
Pinch of asafoetida
1¾ teaspoons salt
1 lb. aubergine (baingan)
¼ cup thickened tamarind pulp (optional)
1½ lb. spinach
1 green pimento
2 cups of milk

8 red chillies, seeded,
roasted, and crushed (or
less if preferred)
2½ oz. bessan
1 egg (optional)

1 teaspoon black cumin
6 oz. cashew nuts
½ teaspoon sugar
12 peppercorns
4 oz. fresh coconut

Soak the rice for 4 hours, then drain. Heat a little butter and add some parsley or coriander leaves, desiccated coconut, half the bruised cardamoms, whole cloves and splintered cinnamon, the sesame seed, 2 chopped onions, kari phulia leaves and asafoetida. Brown, then remove and grind or pound to a paste with salt and some water. Cut the aubergines down the middle, prick all over and rub with some of the paste. Tie together again with string, then grill. When tender put aside. Mix remaining paste with the tamarind pulp.

Grind together the spinach and pimento. Cook in milk until only about 2 tablespoons liquid remains, then fry in butter, stirring in bessan, seasoning with salt, chillies and parsley. When dry, remove and cool a little, then shape into walnut-size balls adding an egg to bind if necessary. Fry until crisp and dust with half the ground black cumin. Reserve.

Heat butter and add ¼ teaspoon sugar, remaining cinnamon, cloves, cardamoms and peppercorns and fry for 3 minutes. Add rice and cook until translucent. Moisten with enough water to cover rice by 1½ inches. Place cooked aubergines on one side and spinach balls on the other. Bring to the boil then steam over lowest possible heat until done (about 18–20 minutes). Meanwhile fry slivered cashew nuts and reserve. Cut remaining onions into rings and fry until brown with ¼ teaspoon sugar, keep warm. Grate fresh coconut. Serve the pilau with hot onion rings, cashew nuts, remaining spice paste and fresh coconut.

Machachi Pilau Lowabdhar (Fish Pilau with Mushrooms)

2 lb. fish (salmon, halibut or
other firm-fleshed fish)
1 lb. rice
2–3 tablespoons oil
6 oz. butter
2 oz. bessan

1 tablespoon paprika
1 oz. garlic
Juice of 2 lemons or limes
Pinch of saffron
¼ lb. onions
8 fl. oz. yoghourt

2 teaspoons ground fennel
   seed
2 teaspoons salt
3 oz. blanched slivered
   almonds
½ lb. button mushrooms

Jellied chicken stock
8 crushed cardamoms
2 inches splintered stick
   cinnamon
¼ teaspoon nutmeg

Wash, clean and dry fish. Cut into large steaks and rub with oil. Leave ¼ hour, then wash off oil. Rub with bessan mixed with 1 tablespoon paprika. Leave 15 minutes and wash off. Prick all over with a sharp fork. Give a final wash with ¼ pint water mixed with 3 cloves garlic, minced or pounded. Rub the fish with lime juice mixed with saffron and reserve. While waiting between operations prepare the aromatics.

Brown the onions in 1 oz. butter with remaining garlic, 5 tablespoons yoghourt and fennel seed. Rub over the fish and leave to dry for 15 minutes. Now fry the coated fish until richly brown. Season with salt.

Slice mushrooms and fry with almonds in 1 oz. butter, moisten with water, and cook 15 minutes to make a sauce, reserve.

Half cook the rice, then mix with stock and 5 tablespoons yoghourt and cook until tender. Place the fish in a casserole, then the rice, and moisten with remaining yoghourt. Aromatize with cardamoms, cinnamon and nutmeg. Add the sauce. Spoon over remaining butter, melted, and season with salt. Leave on a high heat for 2 minutes, then give it a dum for 30 minutes. Leave aside for a few minutes before serving. It may be garnished with slices of cucumber, first salted and drained, then dipped in egg white and grilled or fried.

Lavata Pilau (Shell-fish Pilau)

This pilau can be made with prawns or lobsters, or a combination of both with some scallops and small oysters.

6 oz. lobster meat (1 small
   lobster)
2 oz. scallops
4 oz. shelled oysters
6 oz. shelled prawns
Saffron

2 teaspoons salt
3 bay leaves finely ground
1 tablespoon paprika
1 tablespoon onion seed or
   chives
1 tablespoon aniseed

10 cloves garlic
Juice of one lemon
1 lb. rice
¼ pint yoghourt
4 oz. butter
10 crushed cardamoms

2 inches minced green ginger
10 lovage seeds
3 oz. blanched slivered
  almonds
2 tablespoons chopped
  parsley

Dice the lobster meat, slit scallops through, beard and cut up oysters if large, or keep whole if small. Save any liquor from these, straining it through double muslin. Vein and shell the prawns, (slicing through the middle without severing if large) and flatten with a kitchen mallet. Rinse any sand from fish and dry carefully. Make a paste by pounding together saffron, some salt, the bay leaves, paprika, ground onion seed, ground aniseed and garlic. Rub into the shell-fish with some lemon juice and leave for 4 to 5 hours. Meanwhile steep rice in water for 1 hour, drain thoroughly. Rub shell-fish with half the yoghourt, then sauté in 2 oz. butter until the marinade is dry and the shell-fish crisp.

Heat remaining butter and fry rice with cardamoms, green ginger, lovage seeds, almonds and parsley. When translucent, season with salt and moisten with enough water to cover by 1¼ inches. Enrich with remaining yoghourt. As rice boils, stir once, and put in shell-fish together with the shell-fish liquor and any scrapings of the marinade. Cover and cook over lowest possible heat until done (about 20 minutes). Give it a dum for 12 minutes. Leave in a cool place for 5 minutes before serving.

BIRIANIS

The Zarebrian or biriani pilau is distinguished from other rice preparations in three ways. It is always flavoured and coloured by saffron or turmeric and has cumin and coriander seed, whole peppercorns and large black cardamoms. The other aromatics vary. It is usually richer than other pilaus because of the amount of butter used. Finally, there is sometimes twice as much meat or fish, as rice.

There are many kinds of biriani. The *pukki* biriani is made with cooked rice, the *kutchi* biriani with uncooked, and the *kutchi-pukki* biriani with parboiled rice. A slightly different technique is used for each one. The biriani is always a vividly coloured and substantially aromatized dish.

Biriani (*Lamb with Spiced Pilau*)

1½ lb. boned lamb, pork or beef	1 lb. rice
A small handful of parsley or coriander leaves	1 tablespoon turmeric
2 inches green ginger	3 tablespoons ground coriander seed
1 teaspoon salt	1 tablespoon ground cumin
3 inches stick cinnamon	½ teaspoon cayenne
1 green pimento	1 tablespoon whole peppercorns
2 green chillies	4 oz. washed raisins
8 large crushed cardamoms	10 crushed garlic cloves
10 cloves	6 large onions
4 oz. butter	2 oz. blanched almonds

Make a broth as follows from the meat, using a few bones as well: cover by about 4 inches with cold water and add shredded coriander leaves, chopped green ginger, salt, half the cinnamon, the pimento and chillies. Boil once, skim and simmer until meat is tender, 1–3 hours according to type, cut and size of meat, which may be cut into 2 inch pieces before or after cooking. Drain and dry meat; strain broth and reserve.

Place cardamoms, cloves and remaining cinnamon, splintered, in muslin. Heat some butter and fry the rice with ¾ each of the turmeric, coriander, cumin and cayenne. When translucent, add the muslin bag, the peppercorns, washed raisins, crushed garlic and enough water to cover by 1½ inches. Season with salt and bring to the boil. Lower heat and simmer.

Meanwhile, melt a little butter in a large frying pan and cook meat with remaining turmeric, coriander, cumin and cayenne until a rich brown. Quarter onions, separate into layers, and then fry fast so they are coloured but still crisp, i.e. slightly under-cooked. Add whole almonds, mix well and keep warm.

When rice is almost cooked, uncover and quickly add the contents of the frying pan, scraping up all the butter and crusty part. Mix rice and meat well and cover. Raise the heat very high for a few seconds, then give it a dum for 10 minutes in a moderate oven, leave aside for 3 or 4 minutes before serving.

Myhee Biriani Khasa (Biriani with Fish and Cheese)

2 lb. firm white fish
1 lb. rice
½ lb. Indian cheese (paneer: see p. 251)
Scant ¼ pint milk
8 oz. bessan
4 tablespoons oil
Pulp of 8 limes or 4 lemons
2 teaspoons salt
2 tablespoons each ground coriander, cumin and fennel or anise seed
2 eggs
1 teaspoon saffron or turmeric

Good pinch lovage seeds
4 tablespoons finely chopped or pounded mint
6 oz. clarified butter
½ pint whipped yoghourt
2 inches grated green ginger
9 crushed cardamoms
10 cloves
2 inches splintered stick cinnamon
18 peppercorns
Large grated carrot
2 broken bay leaves
8 onions

Cut fish into medium steaks and wash in running water until clean. Prick the steaks all over. Soak in milk. Leave for 15 minutes and then wash in water. Rub with bessan and wash. Dip in oil and wash again.

Heat enough water to cover the fish and add lemon pulp, 1 teaspoon salt and aniseed. Wrap steaks in muslin cloth and poach until done. Drain and dry. Dip steaks in beaten egg mixed with half the saffron, lovage seeds and mint, then fry in about 2 oz. butter (for unclarified butter, first heat a tablespoon oil). When crusty and well browned put aside. Enrich the scrapings of the frying pan with yoghourt.

Parboil rice in lightly salted water about 7 minutes. Arrange the fish in a casserole (Indian chefs use small bamboo splints to protect it from direct heat). Mix the rice with remaining saffron, cumin and coriander and fry gently in 1 oz. butter; add green ginger during the last few seconds. Place rice on top of fish and scatter with cardamoms, cloves, cinnamon, peppercorns, salt, carrot, and bay leaves. Drench with all but ½ oz. remaining butter, melted. Bring to the boil over a medium fire and then raise heat very high for 1 minute. Give it a dum for 35 minutes. Meanwhile, cut cheese in slices about 1½ inches square, cut onion in rings and fry until well browned. Scatter over pilau, cover and leave in oven another 3 minutes. Leave aside for a few minutes before serving.

Bhooni Kitcheri (*Kedgeree with Lentils*)

Kitcheri (which means 'a porridge' or colloquially, 'a bit of a mess') is the prototype of kedgeree. However in India, lentils are used and not fish. The idea is to keep the dish light and digestible. The *geeli*, or moist kitcheri, is given to invalids and children. Here is a recipe for *bhooni* or dry kitcheri.

½ lb. green or pink lentils	8 peppercorns
½ lb. rice	2 tablespoons chopped green
4 oz. butter	ginger (optional)
12 small onions	¾ teaspoon salt
3 bay leaves	

Wash and soak lentils and soak rice for 1 hour. Heat butter in a heavy casserole. Cut onions into thin slivers and fry pale gold. Press butter carefully from onions, running it back into pan. Reserve onions. Add drained lentils and rice to the casserole. Fry, stirring well, for about 8 to 10 minutes until the butter has been absorbed. Aromatize with bay leaves, peppercorns, green ginger and season with salt. Stir in enough water to cover the rice and lentils by 2 inches. Stir and boil for 1 minute, then cover tightly and cook. Lower the heat gradually as the water evaporates. The heat should be a mere whisper by the time the lentils are done, about 1 hour. Uncover, stir, and add the onions. Mix well before serving. The rice should be slightly overcooked and soft, and a little moist.

The geeli kitcheri is made without butter. The only seasoning used being bay leaf and peppercorns, and it is kept moister and softer than the bhooni kitcheri. Both dishes can be made with the rice and lentils cooked in milk. This will produce a richer result.

Now we come to the line of grand and noble pilaus, called Shahi or Royale.

Shah Degh Pilau (*Pilau in the Grand Manner*)

For the jellied stock:

Chicken carcass, bones from the loin, and soup bones and meat from butcher (note that many Indians would not use veal or beef), a pig's foot would be excellent among the bones

Parsley or coriander
8 lemon leaves
2 inches cinnamon stick
2 inches chopped green ginger
2 minced green pimentos

For the pilau:

12 cloves garlic
4 large onions
1 teaspoon sugar
6 oz. sultanas – cleaned and soaked 1–2 hours
5 oz. butter
1½ lb. boned loin of lamb
8 oz. blanched, ground or pounded almonds
Juice of 1 lime
10 fl. oz. yoghourt
1½ teaspoons salt
30 grains aniseed

1½ lb. rice
1 pint milk
4 bay leaves
3 inches stick cinnamon
Black treacle
½ pint double cream
12 ground cardamoms
20 bruised peppercorns
¼ teaspoon nutmeg
9 cloves
½ teaspoon black cumin
2 oz. blanched almonds, fried and salted

The stock. Make the jellied stock, 1–2 days ahead, from meat and bones with about 2 quarts salted water using a large fistful of coriander or parsley leaves, lemon leaves, stick cinnamon, green ginger and pimento. Strain, chill and remove fat. This jellied stock – *garhi yakhni* – requires about 12 to 16 hours slow extraction over constant gentle heat. Simmer gently on top of the stove with an asbestos mat, then give it some hours in low oven, then again place on stove for a few hours. (You will find, if you use the bones a second time, that a good amount of flavour and some nutritious gelatine can still be extracted.)

The pilau. Crush garlic and soak for 1 hour in 8 tablespoons water. Cut two onions into thin rings, fry with the sugar, and reserve. Drain sultanas, fry, and reserve.

Grate two onions finely, heat butter, fry, press all butter back into pan, and reserve onion. Cut the meat into almond-size pieces about ¼ inch thick, fry lightly and remove, taking care to drain back butter again. Add ground almonds, and moisten with lime juice.

In another frying pan, heat 1 oz. butter and add 2 tablespoons yoghourt, salt and aniseed. Put in the fried meat and cook on both sides till tender, about ½ hour, aromatizing with garlic infusion.

Cook the rice in stock and milk with 2 bay leaves and ½ inch splintered stick cinnamon so rice is slightly undercooked, about 9 minutes. Allow it to cool. Butter a 3½- or 4-inch deep rectangular dish, preferably Pyrex or earthenware. Coat the sides and the bottom with a layer of treacle. On it arrange a layer of rice, a thin layer of yoghourt, and cream, a layer of meat pieces, and dust the whole with ground cardamom, bruised peppercorns, nutmeg, cloves, broken bay leaf, and small flecks of the remaining ½-inch cinnamon. Dot with a little butter.

Arrange another layer of rice on which scatter some black cumin. Repeat the other layers. Put fried almonds, fried sultanas, grated fried onions, and fried onion rings on top. Cover and cook on very high heat for about 1½ minutes to glaze and harden the treacle on the outer coating of rice, forming a crust. Put the casserole in a slow oven, and cook covered for about 40 minutes.

To serve: tap the dish smartly on all sides, and with a knife dipped in boiling water, prise the glazed rice away from the sides of the buttered dish. Turn it out on to a serving dish. The pilau will come out in one piece with a firm well-browned crust and fluffy rice inside. Serve with a helping of the crust, not forgetting the lowest layer of sultanas, almonds, and sugared onion rings.

See Chapter 13, Sweets and Desserts, pp. 216–18 for sweet pilaus.

CHAPTER TEN

Vegetables and Pulses

VEGETABLES

BECAUSE of the great variety of vegetables available to the Indian cook, a vegetarian diet is not only possible, but positively pleasurable. Techniques of cooking and preparation, and the use of aromatics, produce dishes with a distinction of their own.

Two factors should guide the use of aromatics: if the vegetables are to be served with a strongly flavoured dish then the aromatics must be used with a light hand. If the meat dish is bland, then the aromatics used with vegetables can be stronger. With a vegetarian diet, some vegetables tend to be seasoned in a manner which suggests that they are substitutes for meat. Secondly, the season of the year determines the type of food: curries and stews are more favoured at one time, light steamed food at another. With rice, vegetables tend to be hotter and more spicy; with whole grain breads they are milder, and relatively lightly cooked. A hot spicy vegetable *bhujia* is best for those who eat simple one-dish meals.

The villages and farmlands all over India have an enviable skill in vegetable cooking. In the Punjab, in North India, even the lentils, or spinach, or turnip purée are cooked with an inherited skill that renders a dish substantial yet fragrant, and a pleasure to the eye. In the Bengal villages the concoctions of freshwater chestnuts or marrow in milk, like other common dishes, show a purist care of the techniques inherited and a genuine appreciation of the ingredients used. From Kashmir to Kerala the village and farm homestead tradition is the ground base on which is built classic vegetable cookery. Unhappily the combined braising-steaming method of cooking vegetables which produces light, crisp food, is gradually dying out in India.

The recipes in this chapter do not try to parallel those in the meat section. Anyone who has tried some of the meat and fish recipes, will find it easy to adapt them for vegetables. The concept here is: light, fragrant and digestible. We begin with the potato.

Alu Turrcarri (*Simple Potato Curry*)

1 lb. potatoes
1 oz. clarified butter
1 teaspoon turmeric
1 tablespoon ground coriander seed
½ teaspoon salt

1 teaspoon kalonji or chopped chive
Freshly ground black pepper
1 tablespoon chopped parsley
1 tablespoon chopped pimento

Peel, wash and dry the potatoes. Heat the butter, add a pinch of turmeric and the halved or quartered potatoes. Fry over medium heat for about 8 minutes, stirring continuously. Add the coriander seed, and cook over low heat for 1 minute. Moisten with 6 tablespoons water; add salt. Boil until dry. Fry another minute or so on high heat until potatoes are crusty. Aromatize with remaining turmeric, and fry for ½ minute over low heat. Now moisten with enough water to cover the potatoes by 1½ inches and aromatize with kalonji, black pepper, most of the parsley and ¾ tablespoon of pimento. Bring to the boil, then simmer until potatoes are tender. Scatter in the rest of the chopped parsley and pimento. Keep covered for 5 minutes over lowest possible heat, and serve. This curry has plenty of liquor – more than in an ordinary stew.

To make the curry hot, add between 1 and 3 chillies, seeded or otherwise (according to degree of heat preferred), finely ground or coarsely broken up. Add them raw or fried during the final frying.

To make the curry pungent, add 1½ teaspoons of ground fenugreek and up to 8 cloves of ground garlic to the coriander, fry gently until well browned and the butter separates from the aromatics.

To make a korma curry, add whipped yoghourt (about 5 fl. oz.) instead of the 6 tablespoons water. When this becomes stiff, but not dry, gradually add a little water, and stir to amalgamate. Then simmer until potatoes are tender.

Alu Bhoone (Sautéed Potatoes)

1½ lb. potatoes
1½ oz. clarified butter
1 teaspoon turmeric
1 large bay leaf
½–¾ teaspoon salt
½ teaspoon onion salt

½ teaspoon chilli powder or
  cayenne pepper
½–¾ tablespoon garam
  masala (see p. 249)
½ teaspoon black pepper

Peel, wash and dry the potatoes, then cut into 1 inch pieces. Heat butter in a large frying pan and put in the potatoes with turmeric and bay leaf. Stir and fry over medium heat for 5 minutes. Season with salt, onion salt and chilli powder. Fry again for another 5 minutes and dust with garam masala. Add a little more butter and stir. Cover the potatoes and leave a few minutes over very low heat. Shake the frying pan three or four times during this period. The potatoes should now be done. Uncover and let them crisp until the garam masala has formed a crusty coating. Add some freshly ground black pepper and serve.

The potatoes may first be boiled in their jackets, peeled and quickly sautéed as above. This is a much quicker method, but inevitably the potatoes will be more floury in texture.

A simpler sautéed potato (among many variations) can be made by sautéeing the potatoes with 1¼ tablespoons ground or chopped mint, ¼ teaspoon garlic salt, seeds of 1 cardamom, with a little parsley added during the last minute of cooking.

Alu Dum (Smothered Potatoes)

1½ lb. medium size potatoes
2 teaspoons turmeric
½ tablespoon garam masala
  (see p. 249)
7½ fl. oz. yoghourt
3 bay leaves

3 oz. butter
3 red chillies
Good pinch sugar
2 tablespoons minced
  parsley
1 tablespoon salt

Boil the potatoes until three-quarters done: they may be peeled before or after boiling. Prick with a sharp fork. Rub with a paste made from turmeric, garam masala, salt and whipped yoghourt. Cook the bay leaves in butter for a few seconds. Add the broken chillies and stir over medium heat until they become translucent, and the butter colours a little. Add sugar and stir until slightly caramelized. Now put in the potatoes, stir and add the minced parsley. Cover well, and leave in a preheated moderate oven for about 25 minutes. The yoghourt should form a dry thickened crusting. Serve hot.

Alu Badam Dum (Smothered Potatoes with Almonds)

1½ lb. potatoes	Oil for frying
2¼ oz. blanched almonds	Aromatics as in preceding recipe

Choose potatoes the size of an egg. Peel and wash them. Prick each potato with a thick pronged serving or carving fork, or a thick larding needle. See that the holes go through to the other side. Let them steep half an hour in salted water, meanwhile preparing aromatics as above. Remove and squeeze hard to expel all moisture inside the small cavities. Then dry the potatoes with a cloth or kitchen paper. Stand and let dry thoroughly. Stick slivers of blanched almonds into the cavities. Now deep fry the potatoes in aromatized fat till golden brown. Remove and drain. These are delicious as they are. Sprinkle with salt and serve.

For a still better result first fry the dried potatoes *without* the almonds, cool enough to handle, insert the almonds and fry just long enough to brown the nuts.

You may vary the basic process by preparing them in the dum style:

8 cloves garlic	2 teaspoons chopped mint
1¼ oz. butter	Good pinch nutmeg
1 teaspoon paprika	¼ teaspoon ginger powder
1 teaspoon ground sesame seed	Good pinch ground saffron
4 ground cardamoms	5 fl. oz. yoghourt

Grind the garlic in a few tablespoons of water. Press through a fine-mesh sieve or strainer over the fried potatoes. Heat the butter and colour with the paprika. Add sesame seed, cardamoms, mint, nutmeg, ginger, and saffron. Mix well, and add two tablespoons yoghourt. Cook until dried to a thick paste. Repeat with half the yoghourt. Place the potatoes in the pan, and moisten with the remainder of yoghourt and salt. Pour over the aromatic paste. Heat for a minute on top of the stove, then place in the oven (moderate heat) for about 30 minutes. Serve.

Alu Bhurta (*Purée of Potatoes*)

Take 1½ lb. boiled, peeled potatoes, and sieve or mash them with 2 tablespoons minced pimento, 2 tablespoons chopped chives, 2 tablespoons melted butter, 1 tablespoon chopped parsley or coriander leaves, ¼ ground bay leaf, salt, and 1 teaspoon freshly ground black pepper. A pinch saffron dissolved in a tablespoon of hot milk, may be added. Serve steaming hot, or chilled.

Mattar Sukhe (*Steamed Green Peas*)

1 lb. shelled green peas	6 bruised peppercorns
1 teaspoon turmeric	Good pinch cayenne
4 oz. clarified butter	½ teaspoon salt
2 teaspoons ground coriander seed	2 onions

Fry turmeric and peas in butter for 3 minutes over lowest heat. Cut the onions into large wedges, and separate into layers. Add coriander, peppercorns, cayenne and salt to peas, stir, and add the onions. Cook on low heat for 1 minute. Then sprinkle with a tablespoon of water. Cover well and steam for a few minutes until peas are cooked and all moisture has dried off.

To make a green pea curry, proceed as in the simple potato curry on p. 174, with the following modification. Take 3 large onions, mince fine and fry until they are a deep red-brown colour. Sprinkle with water to prevent them scorching. Remove the onions, sauté the peas; return onions to pan with the aromatics (as in the potato curry), plus 2 teaspoons ground cumin, 1 teaspoon ground garlic, 1 tablespoon minced chilli, 10 grains ground lovage seed, and water to cover by 1¼ inches. Simmer until butter separates and rises to the top to form a skin.

Mattar Paneer (Indian Cheese with Green Peas)

1 lb. shelled green peas	½ teaspoon cayenne
½ lb. paneer (see p. 251)	2 tablespoons chopped
3 oz. clarified butter	parsley
1 teaspoon turmeric	½ teaspoon salt

Make the paneer, turning it on to a sieve to drain. Meanwhile prepare aromatics. Heat the butter and add the peas with turmeric and cayenne. Stir and cook 3 minutes over medium heat. Add the cheese, which should resemble dry scrambled eggs. Mix well and cook together for 2 minutes. Add parsley and salt. Cover and leave on low heat for 10 minutes. Uncover, raise heat very high to dry off any remaining moisture. Serve.

Phali Dum (Steamed Green Beans)

¾ lb. french beans	¼ oz. butter
1 small onion	½ teaspoon salt
2 teaspoons chopped green	Good pinch ground fennel
ginger	seed

Slice the beans slantwise into ½ inch slivers. Cut onions the same size, and green ginger a little smaller. Boil a few tablespoons of water mixed with the butter. Add the beans, onions and ginger, season with salt and ground fennel seed. Mix well. Cover tightly and let the beans steam for 5 to 7 minutes. The moisture should have dried off; if not, raise the heat briefly and shake well. Serve very hot. Do not overcook the beans – they should be *al dente*.

Bhujia

This is a style of cooking vegetables, where the final 'tarka' or 'chamak' (p. 33) gives it its characteristic flavour and spicing. It is often stingingly hot and dry.

1 lb. french beans	1 teaspoon ground
¼ lb. small potatoes	fenugreek seeds
¼ lb. spinach	2 teaspoons paprika
1 teaspoon salt	1½ teaspoons cayenne
1¼ teaspoons turmeric	½ teaspoon fresh ground
1 tablespoon coriander	black pepper
1 tablespoon cumin	3 oz. clarified butter

8 onions – sliced thin
3 chopped green chillies (seed
for milder result)

2 inches green ginger cut in
julienne strips
10 minced cloves garlic

Cut the french beans into ½-inch pieces and halve potatoes, chop the spinach fine. Season with ½ teaspoon salt, and moisten with just enough water to tenderize the french beans and cook the potatoes, about 20 minutes. Meanwhile prepare aromatics. If any water remains when potatoes are cooked, drain. Dry the cooked vegetables, if necessary pressing gently to remove all moisture. Aromatize the vegetables with turmeric, coriander, cumin, fenugreek, paprika, cayenne, black pepper and remaining salt. Reserve and keep warm. In a heavy frying pan heat the butter, add onions, chillies, garlic, and green ginger. Fry and stir over high heat till well browned. Splash this chamak into the vegetables on the heat. Fry well – 4–5 minutes. Leave covered 5 minutes and serve.

Spinach. Many kinds of spinach are available in India. The preparation is usually simple, but, done with care and with some varieties – such as mustard spinach – it can be lengthy. *Sarson*, or mustard spinach, is invariably cooked in an earthenware crock. The green leaves take about 9 hours to develop their full flavour, but most people content themselves with only 3–4 hours, although fully cooked it is the most velvety, smooth dish imaginable. The same method can be adapted for spinach greens of many different kinds, found the whole world over. Spinach cooked in this particular fashion is not steamed, nor is it dry. It is a dish rich in butter, and provides either the main course of a meal, or is served in small quantities as an accompaniment to a main course.

Sagh (*Spinach*)

2 lb. spinach
1 oz. clarified butter
½ teaspoon salt

1 teaspoon ground ginger
powder
Pinch of sugar

Wash the spinach and shred it very fine. Put in a pan with the melted butter and less than 2 tablespoons of water, the salt, ginger and sugar. Mix well. Cover and leave on very high heat for 2 minutes, then on medium heat until soft, and all moisture has evaporated (about 25 to 30 minutes). Stir once or twice during this period. Uncover, mix well and leave uncovered on low heat for 3 minutes or so before serving.

Alu Sagh (Dry Spinach and Potatoes)

2½ lb. spinach	¼ teaspoon paprika
2 oz. clarified butter	1 minced green pimento
1 lb. potatoes	1 crushed cardamom
2 large onions sliced thin	1 inch green ginger cut in
1 crushed clove garlic	julienne strips
1 teaspoon coriander	¾ teaspoon salt

Wash the spinach. Boil, then simmer in a little salted water until tender, about 12 minutes. Peel, and cut potatoes in halves or quarters. Drain spinach well and chop fine. Reserve. Prepare the aromatics.

In a heavy saucepan heat the butter, add potatoes, onions, garlic, coriander, paprika, pimento and cardamom. Put ginger under rest of ingredients to crisp it. Leave without stirring for 1 minute. Stir lightly and leave for another minute. Then stir and fry till the potatoes are well browned. Raise the heat very high, add the cooked spinach, a pinch more of salt, and moisten with ½ pint of water. Stir over very high heat; close lid, and steam over low heat till potatoes are tender. Stir and dry off any remaining moisture, leaving the spinach and potatoes well buttered. This dish can also be made without potatoes.

Buttered Mustard Spinach

3 lb. mustard spinach, weighed after cleaning and washing	6 oz. butter
	1 green chilli
	4 small bay leaves
4 cloves garlic	4 fl. oz. yoghourt
4 inches green ginger	Salt

Clean and wash the spinach, leave to crisp in cold water for 3 hours. Make a garlic infusion: crush the garlic, steep it in 2 fl. oz. water for 2 hours, then strain through a muslin cloth. Drain the spinach and chop extremely finely. Heat an earthenware casserole and put in 2 tablespoons garlic infusion. Shred the green ginger, sauté in a little butter and add to the chopped or minced spinach with the butter, chilli and bay leaves. Enrich with whipped yoghourt. Cover with water, mix, and place on a high heat. Let the butter melt thoroughly, add salt to taste and place in a very low oven for about 4 hours, or cook on low heat over an asbestos mat, keeping the casserole tightly closed, until the spinach is creamy. Remember to shake the casserole from time to time, and stir twice for 2–3 minutes.

This dish is eaten with very plain Indian whole-wheat, maize or barley bread.

Khumbi Sukhe (Sautéed Mushrooms)

½ lb. white mushrooms
½ teaspoon onion salt
1 teaspoon freshly ground
  black pepper
¼ teaspoon basil
Juice of ½ lime
1 oz. butter

¼ teaspoon salt
Crushed seeds of 1
  cardamom
¼ teaspoon turmeric
  (optional)
1 teaspoon garlic salt or 1
  large clove garlic, minced

Wash and dry the mushrooms. Cut evenly into medium-thin slices. Spread out and dust with onion salt, black pepper, basil and lime juice. Mix well and marinate for 15 minutes. Heat the butter, and when it begins to smoke sauté the mushrooms with the marinade and other aromatics over high heat. Turn once, and see that no moisture accumulates during cooking. If the mushrooms are fresh, and thinly sliced, 1 minute sautéeing is sufficient. For tougher mushrooms sauté for 2 minutes, then sprinkle with 2 tablespoons water, salt, and cover well. Keep on medium heat. Steam for about 5 minutes more, uncover and serve.

An alternative mixture of aromatics for the same quantity of mushrooms is: 1½ crushed cloves garlic, ¾ teaspoon fresh milled black pepper, pinch of cayenne, 4–6 crushed cardamom seeds, ½ teaspoon salt, 1½ teaspoons lime juice, clarified butter. Mix the aromatics and lime juice well, marinate the mushrooms for 5 to 10 minutes. Heat a heavy frying pan and use just enough butter to coat ½ lb. thinly sliced mushrooms. When the butter smokes, throw in the mushrooms. Stir well, cook on high heat for a minute or so, till no moisture remains. Lower the heat. Cook for a further 15–20 seconds and serve hot. In both cases the remaining juices should be not more than a tablespoonful or so.

Makhani Khumbi (*Buttered Mushrooms*)

Take some mushrooms and grill them whole or halved. Baste or rub with a little butter and black pepper. In a saucepan, heat 1½ oz. butter for every pound of mushrooms, add 2 tablespoons minced chives, a good ½ teaspoon paprika, and seeds of 1 cardamom. Add the mushrooms, mix, and leave covered on a very low heat for 10 minutes. They must not brown, merely simmer in the butter and juices.

A mixture of 1½ oz. butter and 2 tablespoons whipped yoghourt is sometimes used, and the mushrooms rolled in it, then steamed for a few minutes. The initial grilling must be thorough, for the steaming merely impregnates the mushrooms with the butter and should not actually cook them.

Dhingri (*Dried Mushrooms in Cream*)

2 oz. dried mushrooms or black Himalayan mushrooms (guchi) (Italian dried *boleta* are a good substitute)
½ teaspoon salt
6 minced cloves garlic
¼ teaspoon crushed fennel or aniseed

1 oz. butter
1 tablespoon yoghourt
1 tablespoon double cream
Good pinch cayenne
Good pinch black pepper
Pinch black cumin

These dried mushrooms need soaking for at least 24 hours though most people soak them for 3 hours or so and then wonder why the texture is always a little rubbery. This applies more to the white cap mushroom than to the conical black guchi which is much thinner and softens more easily.

Soak mushrooms with a little salt, and change the water 2 or 3 times. Drain and wash. Heat a cupful or so of water and add 6 minced cloves garlic and ¼ teaspoon fennel or aniseed.

Add mushrooms and boil briefly, then simmer until very tender. Drain and dry. Slice into strips about ¼ inch wide and an inch long. Heat some butter and sauté the mushrooms for 1 minute, taking care to toss or turn them so that both sides are cooked. Moisten with a tablespoon of yoghourt whipped with cream or whipped malai (see p. 252). Stir on lowest heat. Aromatize with cumin, cayenne and black pepper, cover, place over an asbestos mat, and leave for 5 minutes. Serve hot.

Dried mushrooms are usually made into a curry, which in my opinion is the wrong way to deal with dried fungi.

Phul-Gobi (Braised Cauliflower)

1 large cauliflower	2 teaspoons cumin
1 oz. clarified butter	¼ teaspoon paprika
2 teaspoons yellow mustard seed	¼ teaspoon freshly ground black pepper
2 inches slivered green ginger	½ teaspoon salt
½ teaspoon turmeric	

Prepare the aromatics as listed. Wash, dry the cauliflower and cut into small flowerets. Heat the butter and add the mustard seed. When they begin to snap and pop, put in the ginger (½ teaspoon powdered ginger may be used as a substitute, but should be added with the cauliflower). Cook the ginger until sautéed on both sides. Add turmeric, and stir over low heat for ½ minute. Put in the cauliflower, stir and continue to cook on medium heat. Stir well and see that the turmeric colours all the flowerets. Aromatize with cumin, black pepper, and paprika. Cook for another minute, and season with salt. Sprinkle with about 1 tablespoon water. Cover instantly and cook on a very high heat for about 1 minute to build up steam. Then cook on very low heat. The cauliflower should be ready in about 8–10 minutes or less. Uncover to dry off any moisture, and stir the cauliflower before serving.

This preparation has no sauce or liquid, and only a suspicion of butter. The cauliflower is *al dente*. It is crisp but cooked, and never soggy. The colour is lightest gold. Shredded green or red pimento can be added for the last 5 minutes.

Cauliflower Purée

1 large cauliflower
½ lb. onions
3 oz. butter
1 teaspoon turmeric
1 tablespoon ground
  coriander
4 cloves crushed garlic
1 tablespoon powdered
  pomegranate seeds

3 teaspoons cumin
½ teaspoon powdered ginger
½ teaspoon fresh ground
  pepper
2 teaspoons ground yellow
  mustard seed
½ teaspoon paprika
½ teaspoon salt
2 fl. oz. yoghourt

Wash and dry the cauliflower, divide into flowerets, and slice these thinly. Mince the onions and fry with the cauliflower in the butter and aromatics. When the mixture is a good brown, moisten with 2 oz. whipped yoghourt. Stir and cook on high heat for 2 minutes. Moisten with a scant pint water. Simmer until cauliflower is very tender and velvety and all moisture except butter and juices are dried off. Serve hot.

Narayeal Saluna (Coconut Curry)

1 fresh coconut (flesh and
  liquor)
1 teaspoon lemon juice
2 tablespoons grated onions
4 onions sliced very thin
1½ oz. clarified butter

Good pinch ground saffron
2 teaspoons ground
  coriander seed
½ teaspoon paprika
½ teaspoon salt
5 sliced hard-boiled eggs

Prepare the aromatics. Grate the coconut and pound. Mix in the lemon juice. Fry the grated onion in butter with saffron, coriander and paprika. Add the coconut and stir well, frying on medium heat for 4 minutes. Add the sliced onion and cook for another 2 minutes. Now stir, add the coconut liquor gradually, the salt, and simmer until done – about 10 minutes. Arrange rounds of egg on a flat dish, top with the coconut, and serve.

Shalgam Bhurta (*Purée of Turnips*)

1 lb. turnips
1 small chopped onion
1 oz. clarified butter
2 teaspoons ground aniseed
6 grains lovage-seed
1 teaspoon ground fenugreek
   seed

¼ teaspoon freshly ground
   black pepper
½ teaspoon salt
1 tablespoon minced coriander
   or parsley

Peel, quarter and cook the turnips in salted water until thoroughly tender, 20–40 minutes. Prepare aromatics. When done, press all moisture from turnips and sieve. Fry onion in butter for 1 minute, then add aromatics and salt. Stir and fry for a few seconds. Add the turnip purée. Stir over medium heat for 5 to 7 minutes. Mix in the coriander and serve.

Korma Shalgam (*Braised Turnips*)

1½ lb. turnips
3 oz. clarified butter
½ lb. minced onions
2 tablespoons ground sesame
   seed
1 tablespoon poppy seed
¼ teaspoon ginger powder
¼ teaspoon cayenne
1 teaspoon turmeric
1 teaspoon ground cumin
1 tablespoon ground
   coriander seed

1 teaspoon salt
6 crushed cloves garlic infused
   in 5 tablespoons water
5 fl. oz. yoghourt
2 tablespoons chopped
   parsley or coriander
   leaves
2 broken bay leaves
4 tablespoons cream

First prepare all aromatics as listed. Heat 1 oz. butter and fry turnips pricked all over, left whole if small or cut in halves. Crisp them, and reserve. Melt the rest of the butter, and add onions, sesame, poppy seed, ginger powder, cayenne and turmeric. Stir for a few seconds and moisten with 5 tablespoons water. Simmer until dry. Add ¼ pint water and cook again until dry and the butter separates from the softened aromatics.

Add the fried turnips. Cook with the aromatics and ground cumin and coriander seed for 5 minutes. Then add salt, garlic infusion and 4 tablespoons yoghourt. Stir and cook until dry. Repeat with remaining yoghourt until it is used up. Add chopped coriander or parsley leaves and 2 broken bay leaves. Mix in the cream and place the pan in a moderate oven for 12 to 15 minutes. Serve.

Navrattan Sabzi Dum (*Mixed Steamed Vegetables*)

1 small peeled cucumber
½ lb. peeled courgettes
¼ lb. peeled squash or pumpkin
2 baby white cabbages
½ lb. large cap mushrooms
24 small pickling onions
1 small whole garlic bulb peeled
1 tablespoon turmeric

1 tablespoon ground kalonji or 1 teaspoon onion salt
3 tablespoons chopped mint leaves
Juice of 3 limes
5 tablespoons yoghourt
1 teaspoon salt
About 3 pints akni (see p. 253)
1 ground bay leaf

Prepare the aromatics as indicated, then the vegetables. Make a paste of the turmeric, kalonji, mint leaves, garlic, lime juice and yoghourt. Prick all the vegetables with a fork, rub with salt and then with the aromatic paste. Marinate for 3 to 4 hours.

Heat the akni in the steamer or pan, and arrange the vegetables in the following way either in the steamer or on a trivet, or other substitute for a steamer: halved courgettes, whole onions, halved cabbage (cut side down), whole mushrooms, wedges of squash and cucumber cut lengthwise. Seal pan with ribbon of paste, boil for 1 minute, then steam over medium heat for about 45 minutes. Uncover and serve with a mild, preferably fresh chutney.

Kheera Talawa (*Fried Cucumbers*)

1 lb. cucumbers
Salt
8 oz. bessan
3 fl. oz. yoghourt
½ teaspoon salt
4 cardamom seeds
1 tablespoon coriander seed

1 teaspoon cayenne
Good pinch ground saffron
¼ teaspoon freshly ground black pepper
Clarified butter or oil for frying

Peel, wash and prick the cucumbers all over. Rub with salt and leave for $\frac{1}{2}$ hour. Grind or pound aromatics finely together. Wash and dry cucumber thoroughly. Make a batter of bessan and yoghourt, with the aromatics and salt. Cucumber is halved and sliced into 3-inch lengths, or cut into $\frac{1}{2}$-inch-thick rings, dipped in the batter, deep-fried and drained. Serve hot.

Bharela Kheera (Stuffed Cucumber)

Salt and wash cucumber as before. Cut down the centre and take out seeds. Stuff the inside with chopped mushrooms sautéed with a very little garlic, a little saffron and seeds of 1 cardamom. Tie up cucumber with string, or fix with cocktail sticks. Rub with butter and paprika. Brush with egg white and bake in a very hot oven for 15 minutes or so. Serve.

Alternatively the cucumber may be braised. Heat $1\frac{1}{2}$ tablespoons butter, gently brown the cucumber, sprinkle with water and salt. Cover and cook until done.

Sabat Pahari Mirch (Stuffed Green Pimentos)

4 large pimentos	2 firm tomatoes, skinned and
Approx. $\frac{1}{2}$ lb. cooked rice	chopped
2 oz. clarified butter	9 ground lovage seeds
$\frac{1}{2}$ teaspoon turmeric	2 broken bay leaves
1 teaspoon freshly ground	2 tablespoons minced chives
black pepper	4 chopped hard-boiled eggs
$\frac{1}{2}$ teaspoon salt	

Prepare all the above. Wash pimentos, cut off the tops around the stem and remove all the seeds. Mix rice with melted butter, turmeric dissolved in 2 tablespoons water, black pepper, salt, tomato, lovage, bay leaves, chives, hard-boiled egg, and stuff the peppers with this mixture. Replace the stems and make sure filling cannot fall out. Rub with butter and place in a fairly hot oven for about 25 minutes. Serve hot.

Bhindi Massaledarh (Stuffed Okra)

1 lb. okra (lady's fingers)	1 ground bay leaf
4 tablespoons ground	1 tablespoon ground aniseed
pomegranate seed	or fennel seed

2 teaspoons turmeric

1 tablespoon ground
  coriander seed

½ oz. butter

½ teaspoon paprika

1 teaspoon salt

Take all the aromatics save paprika, grind them and make a paste using a little butter. If pomegranate seed is not available use dry mango powder (*amchoor*). Failing both of these mix 2 tablespoons lime juice with ½ teaspoon brown sugar and 4 tablespoons ground, tinned pimento. Split the okra down the centre and stuff. Place in a heavy saucepan with a little hot butter and fry, turning gently. Now season with salt and paprika. Sprinkle with a tablespoon or so of water. Cover and braise until soft. Dry off all moisture and serve.

Baingan Massaledarh (*Spiced Aubergine*)

1½ lb. small aubergine
  (about 4 inches long)

Akni (see p. 253)

1¼ oz. clarified butter

½ teaspoon salt

½ inch green ginger

1½ tablespoons coriander seed

½ teaspoon black pepper

¼ teaspoon paprika

2 tablespoons sesame seed

Pinch of asafoetida

2 tablespoons coriander
  leaves or parsley

1 tablespoon chives

Juice of 1 lime or lemon

The aubergine should be split into quarters held together at the stem. Bring akni to the boil and poach aubergines using about ½ pint akni to make them tender without leaving surplus liquid. Remove, drain and reserve. Meanwhile grind all aromatics and salt with lime juice to make a thick paste.

Melt the butter and carefully add the aubergines, fry on all sides for about 5 minutes. Add the aromatic paste, mix with the aubergines and fry for another few minutes on medium heat until the aromatics are dry and beginning to get crusty, and stick a little to the bottom of the pan. Serve at once.

Baingan Bhurta (*Purée of Aubergine*)

1 lb. aubergines

1½–2 tablespoons butter

2 tablespoons chopped onions

2 tablespoons ground
  coriander seed

2 teaspoons minced parsley

Paprika

Salt

1 teaspoon finely ground
  aniseed

Scorch the aubergines over the gas flame or on the electric plate (better still over charcoal), spiked on a cook's fork. Keep heat high, and turn the aubergines continuously. After about 10 minutes the pulp will be softened. Scrape off all the burnt and charred skin with the blunt edge of a knife. Do not worry if small specks of the charred skin remain – they will contribute to the smoky flavour of this dish. Mince or mash the aubergines. Now heat the butter. Add the onions and cook without browning. Moisten with a few drops of water. When onions are soft, add coriander seed, parsley, a little paprika, salt to taste, and aniseed. Put in the aubergine, fry and stir well. After 3 minutes cover and leave on lowest heat for 5 minutes. Serve.

Seekhi Baingan (*Aubergine on the Spit*)

This dish can also be baked in the oven. Cut a cap from the top and scoop out the flesh of a large plump aubergine. Mince this, and mix with a little minced meat, celery and mushrooms. Aromatize with a little turmeric, cayenne, ground cumin, salt and basil. Fry the mixture in the minimum of butter for about 3 minutes stirring well. Stuff the aubergine skin with the mixture. Fix on the cap with cocktail sticks and rub the aubergine with a little butter. Thread on a spit (or place in oven) and cook over a moderate heat, turning the aubergine and basting with a little butter until done. Salt and serve.

The aubergine may also be basted with yoghourt and butter, and a little ground garlic.

Tamattar Bhurta (*Purée of Scorched Tomatoes*)

Take 1 lb. of tomatoes and place on the top rack in a very hot oven (or grill or spike on cook's fork in high flame), until they begin to scorch and the skin cracks. Remove the skin and sieve the tomatoes. Melt 1 tablespoon butter and very gently fry ½ teaspoon basil, 1 tablespoon mint leaves ground down with 1 teaspoon freshly ground black pepper, and a good pinch of saffron. Add 10 chopped green kari phulia leaves or a pinch of thyme, and mix it all with 8 tablespoons double cream. Add to the sieved tomatoes. Serve hot or chilled.

Bandhgobi Turrcarri (Cabbage Curry)

2 lb. white or green cabbage
4 onions
1½ oz. clarified butter
1 teaspoon ground kalonji
  or 1 tablespoon chopped
  chives
¼ teaspoon cayenne
¼ pint buttermilk

2 ground bay leaves
1 teaspoon ground fennel or
  aniseed
2 tablespoons minced red or
  green pimento
Good pinch ground mace
1½ teaspoons turmeric
Juice of ½ lemon

Shred the cabbage and steep in salt water for 1 hour. Prepare the aromatics as above, fry onions in ½ oz. butter and reserve. Drain cabbage well and fry in pan with onions adding the remaining butter. Stir and cook for 6 minutes. Add cayenne and kalonji. Stir and cook on medium heat for another minute or so. Moisten with buttermilk, add bay leaves, fennel and pimento. Simmer until cabbage is soft. Dry off all moisture. Now aromatize with mace, turmeric and lemon juice. Stir well and cook until the butter separates. Season with salt and leave covered on lowest heat for 12 minutes before serving.

Bandhgobi Parcha (Cabbage Rolls with Mushrooms)

6 large white cabbage leaves
1 oz. butter for cooking the
  rolls
Good pinch turmeric
½ teaspoon spiced salt (see
  p. 249)
Akni (optional, see p. 253)

For the filling:

½ lb. potatoes
¼ lb. minced mushrooms
4 tablespoons double cream

2 oz. butter
2 tablespoons chopped
  chives
1 tablespoon shredded
  parsley or coriander leaves
2 oz. blanched, quartered
  almonds
Few grains lovage seed
1 tablespoon ground
  pomegranate seeds or
  capers

Blanch the cabbage leaves and leave to drain. Peel and boil the potatoes; make them into a purée with the cream and 2 oz. butter. Add the mushrooms, chives, coriander or parsley, almonds, lovage and pomegranate seed or capers and mix well.

Place some of this filling in the middle of each cabbage leaf, and wrap it up securely. Fix with cocktail sticks or tie with a thread. Heat the butter and put in the cabbage rolls. Cook over a high heat until the leaves colour and redden on all sides. Then dust with turmeric and spiced salt. Moisten with a few tablespoons of akni or water. Cover tightly and raise heat very high for 1 minute. Then steam over lowest heat until all the moisture has dried up. Uncover and continue cooking until cabbage leaves stick a little to the bottom of the pan. Serve.

Bandhgobi Tandoori (Baked Whole Red Cabbage)

4 very small red cabbages	$\frac{1}{4}$ teaspoon dried basil
3 oz. butter	6 cloves minced garlic
2 tablespoons sesame seed	10 tablespoons sieved papaya
2 tablespoons poppy seed	or sweet plums (skinned;
2 tablespoons minced chives	about 1 lb.)
2 tablespoons minced parsley	5 tablespoons yoghourt
or coriander leaves	$\frac{1}{4}$ cup double cream
3 oz. blanched ground	1 teaspoon paprika
almonds	Juice of 8 limes
1 ground bay leaf	$1\frac{1}{2}$ teaspoons salt

Mix well with softened butter all ingredients except cabbage and lime juice. Make a small cut in the top of each cabbage, so you can separate the leaves without breaking them from the stalk or destroying the shape. Place some aromatic mixture between the leaves, reshape the cabbage, and if necessary tie the top with string. Brush butter over the cabbages and either grill or bake in the oven until the outer leaves are wilting or turning colour. Put in a pan and sprinkle with half the lime juice and salt. Cover and either poach on asbestos mat on top of stove, or bake in low oven. When dry, moisten with remaining lime juice, cover and leave over medium heat until done, about 20 minutes. Now place in a hot oven for 10 to 15 minutes. Collect any drippings, spoon over the cabbages, and glaze at very high heat, serving at once.

Peeaz Sirkidarh (*Marinated Leeks*)

12 medium-size leeks	¼ teaspoon saffron
Akni (see p. 253)	Juice of three limes or 2
6 cloves crushed garlic	lemons
Good pinch nutmeg	¼ teaspoon black pepper
8 lemon leaves or 3–4 strips	Good pinch cayenne
lemon rind	4 tablespoons olive oil
¼ inch stick cinnamon	1½ teaspoons salt
2 bay leaves	

Wash and clean all the grit from leeks. Heat enough akni or water to cover the leeks, and add garlic, nutmeg, lemon leaves, cinnamon, bay leaves, 1 teaspoon salt and half the saffron. Cover and boil for 1 minute, then put in leeks. Cover and simmer until very tender, about 15 minutes. Drain carefully and press out liquor. Whip the remaining saffron with lime juice, black pepper, cayenne, ½ teaspoon salt and the olive oil. Prick the leeks all over and place in a shallow dish. Pour over the marinade, and if desired add a few chopped parsley or coriander leaves. Mix, and leave for 7 to 8 hours, or overnight before serving. Serve with a little of the marinade.

Yams and Sweet Potatoes. There are several kinds of vegetable that come under the loose heading of yam and sweet potato. The tuberous *arbi* or *arvi* for instance, although it is not sweet. It is cooked in water until tender but firm, then completed with a quick sauté. A light dusting with turmeric or a few grains of lovage seed is all that is necessary to bring out the flavour of this vegetable. The yam, which is called *soot'hnee* in India, and the red sweet yam called *guranthor alu* can both be cut to the size of an arbi (about 2 inches by 1 inch). Boil, drain, peel and cool slightly, then sauté with just enough butter to prevent sticking. Its colour should emerge a light gold, and not a dark messy brown as some cooks make it. Dust on some dried mango powder (amchoor) immediately before serving (this is optional).

Vegetable koftas or Fricadelles. Like the spinach koftas in the pilau on page 165 these are made by first cooking vegetables in akni (see p. 253). After draining carefully, sieve, and bind with an egg or a little bessan, according to the type of vegetable. Form into walnut- or egg-size balls, dip in beaten egg, and either deep-fry, or shallow-fry in butter until brown and crisp all over. Marrow, carrots, mushrooms, bamboo shoots, lotus root, parsnips, in fact all root vegetables and certain fruits like the banana, make good vegetable fricadelles.

Boiling vegetables tends to destroy some of their natural taste and aroma, so I usually add a minute quantity of the raw vegetable, finely minced, to the purée. Here is a recipe:

2 lb. marrow; akni (see p. 253); 2 tablespoons minced chives; 2 tablespoons minced parsley; 1 tablespoon minced pimento; 1 tablespoon minced and fried onion; 3 ground cardamoms; $\frac{3}{4}$ teaspoon salt; 1 tablespoon black cumin fried $\frac{1}{2}$ minute in $\frac{1}{4}$ oz. butter; 3 tablespoons bessan. Prepare the aromatics. Reserve 2 oz. raw marrow; grate this, simmer the rest in akni until tender. Drain, scrape from peel, chop finely, then pound, including seeds, squeezing out all moisture. Mix with the other ingredients including the cumin over low heat, finally adding the bessan and uncooked marrow. Shape into walnut-size balls. Dip in beaten egg and sauté in a little clarified butter. When crisped, dust with salt, drain, and serve hot.

DAHLS–PULSES

There are sixty varieties of lentil in India. The main ones are black and white *urd* or *maahn*; moong – green lentils, and the small yellow Moong lentils; *malika Masoor* – pink lentils; *Motth* – round brown lentils; channah – yellow ones; and split peas of various colours and flavours. There are the black-eyed peas of literature, and that favourite the chick-pea (the Spanish garbanzos). There are many ways to prepare them. Some dishes are served with wheat and rice. Many are savouries; others are marinated and served chilled. Some are cooked and finished with tamarind or other sauces. Lentils can be 'puffed', or dried after cooking; they can be roasted or deep fried as savoury snacks (and prepared this way will keep many months).

Lentils are usually simmered in water, with a few herbs,

and then given a tarka or chamak: that is, a few thin slices of onion fried in butter to a dark brown with aromatics like ginger, asafoetida or garlic; when the clarified butter is smoking hot and a deep golden brown, the lentils plus their liquid (which makes a lot of spluttering), are added and stirred well. Then a small dum is given to marry the flavours.

The long cooking necessary for most pulses tends to exhaust the flavour of seasonings and spices, so a tablespoon of the various fragrant seasonings should be reserved for the last 5 minutes of cooking. In this way, a smooth and fragrant dish is produced. Another good method is to cook the pulses in akni, then drain and sauté lightly with aromatics. Lentils can be cooked to a purée, or kept whole like steamed rice grains. Preliminary soaking for at least several hours, or preferably overnight, is necessary.

Sprouting Lentils. There is a simple but remarkable way of using lentils which seems unknown to many present-day Indians, though it belongs to Indian cookery, and was popular in the past. As no recipe is included in this book, here is a general description. The green or moong lentils are excellent for this.

Take ½ lb. of green moong lentils and place in a glass or Pyrex dish. Moisten with a sprinkling of water and put in a cool place. When dry, in a few hours, moisten again. The lentils will begin to swell and plump out. Continue for 2 days or more. The lentils will have sprouted. Drain away any water, and moisten afresh to avoid mustiness. In India the common way to make lentils sprout is to put them in a muslin bag, soak it and hang it up. The bag is moistened regularly. The lentils should begin to sprout on the first day and will be ready in 2–3 days.

The lentil sprouts will be crisp like celery, and very light. They can be eaten uncooked with a little lime juice and salt; shredded green ginger is sometimes added, but then they must marinate for some hours.

To cook the sprouting lentils, heat a little butter, add some light green herbs, such as parsley, coriander leaves or chives and freshly ground black pepper. Roll the sprouts in the butter without browning and sprinkle with a tablespoon or so of water, then steam under a tight cover for 2–3 minutes. Serve.

Sprouting lentils can be steamed with herbs and water or akni, omitting the butter, which in any case should be sufficient only to grease the pan. Sprouting lentils make one of the most delicious of all vegetable dishes.

Urd or *Maahn Dahl* (*Snow-white Lentils*)

½ lb. urd lentils
¼ teaspoon turmeric
1½ teaspoons salt
4 cardamoms
2 bay leaves
2 inches green ginger cut into julienne strips

Good pinch cayenne
2 tablespoons finely chopped parsley
2 oz. butter
1 clove garlic
Good pinch ground asafoetida
2 teaspoons black cumin

Wash the lentils well in a colander, then leave overnight to soak in cold water (cover by 2 to 3 inches). Drain and let them dry a little. Take a very heavy pan and heat enough water to cover the lentils by 2 inches. Bring them to the boil and place on the side of the fire to simmer. Remove any scum or foam that rises to the surface, meanwhile preparing other ingredients. When clear, aromatize with turmeric, 1 teaspoon salt, half the cardamoms crushed with skins, bay leaves, ginger, cayenne, parsley, and enrich with butter. Stir and bring to the boil. Simmer over lowest possible heat (use an asbestos mat or an iron griddle under the pan). This particular dish should be like a thick country soup, with the lentils very soft, but more or less whole. Add water as often as necessary to achieve this consistency. Now grind the garlic with asafoetida, remaining cardamoms, black cumin and mix in with the lentils. Leave covered on lowest heat for 5 to 7 minutes. Serve.

Khara Maahn or Urd

Take ½ lb. white urd lentils (there is also an unhusked black variety), wash, clean and soak them overnight, drain, then place in a very heavy pan and enrich with 2 oz. butter. Add 2 tablespoons coarsely chopped parsley, 4 crushed cardamoms, ½ teaspoon salt, a good pinch asafoetida, a few chopped mint leaves and ½ teaspoon freshly ground black pepper. Mix and then moisten with just enough water to cover. Mix again, and poach (as you would rice), using lowest possible heat. Moisten lightly as often as necessary, but do not inundate with water. Test by extracting a few grains from the centre with a perforated spoon. When these are tender but whole (like rice grains) the lentils are done. If desired add 6 tablespoons melted butter and some chopped chives. Serve hot.

Black or whole urd or maahn lentils are cooked in the same way, but enough water is added to produce the consistency of a thick purée. If the lentils are cooked with butter, long and slowly enough – about 4 hours or more – they will turn a pinkish grey. Use 4 oz. or more of butter for every half pound of lentils and the result will be the most velvety dish imaginable. For an even richer dish substitute milk for a portion of water, and add 2 tablespoons cream and a little yoghourt half an hour before the lentils are done.

The green moong lentil or dahl, used for sprouting lentils, can also be prepared in a similar way. The aromatics may be varied. Pimentos and fresh green chillies are cooked with the lentils to add flavour and then removed. Use red or dried chillies to make the dish hot. More turmeric (which is not used with all lentil preparations) and the addition of garlic, grated browned onions, or ground coriander seed, make the lentils more pungent. South Indian lentils are soup-like, and north Indian thicker. The Punjab lentil preparations (they have been eaten there from Vedic times or earlier) are smooth, thick and rich with butter, not excessively spiced, and bland enough to eat as a basic protein food. The village way of cooking them is considered superlative. They use great ancient iron, brass or copper stock pots. These are kept on hot ashes and near a fire but not on it. The pot is hermetically sealed, and the cooking may take 10 to 12 hours.

Yellow split-pea lentils are cooked so that the lentils retain their shape, but are soft as butter. The pink and brown lentils are cooked to a very smooth, though thinnish purée. But the beans and black-eyed peas, the haricot beans and chick-peas are always kept whole.

Channeh Sabat (Whole Chick-peas)

½ lb. chick-peas
8 crushed cloves garlic
2 red or dried, and 2 fresh green chillies
3 medium onions finely chopped
2 oz. clarified butter
Salt
1 teaspoon turmeric*
1 teaspoon paprika*
2 teaspoons fenugreek seed*
1 tablespoon cumin*
1 tablespoon coriander seed*
Good pinch asafoetida*
*all ground finely together

1–2 tablespoons chopped parsley
1 large peeled, seeded, sieved tomato
1 minced green pimento
1 tablespoon lime juice
3 cardamoms
1 inch cinnamon
2 tablespoons minced mint leaves
1 teaspoon garam masala (see p. 249)

Wash, clean and soak the chick-peas overnight. Drain and cook in salted water aromatized with a clove of garlic and the green chillies. Keep water level at a constant 4 inches above chick-peas. The cooking will take between 2–3 hours. When tender, drain chick-peas, reserve them and the liquor. Prepare the aromatics as directed, and set aside.

Heat butter and fry the onions until dark brown. When the butter separates, add ¼ cup chick-pea stock and cook until dry. Crush and add the red chillies (seeded for milder flavour), and fry on medium heat for 1 minute. Then aromatize with the mixture of finely ground spices. Stir on low heat for ½ minute, then add the chick-peas, stir and cook for 5 to 7 minutes. Moisten again with reserved liquor, season with about 1½ teaspoons salt, add parsley, tomato, pimento, the remaining crushed garlic dissolved in lime juice, cardamoms, cinnamon and mint leaves. Bring to the boil, then cover and simmer for 20 minutes. Uncover and add garam masala. Cover and place in a medium oven for 10 minutes. Serve.

Channeh. Dry chick-peas or Bengal gram are made by draining the peas when perfectly tender but still whole. Dry, and sauté in hot clarified butter with aromatics like saffron or turmeric, a little julienned green ginger, and your own choice of black or red pepper, or garam masala or perhaps just a hint of garlic and salt. To serve chick-peas as a cold vegetable toss in lime juice mixed with a little water, chopped chives, green herbs and salt – add cayenne if you want it hot.

Lobia Khattai (Black-Eyed Peas)

Take ½ lb. black-eyed peas and wash them. Soak overnight. Simmer in akni (see p. 253) with 2 tablespoons ground coriander seed and 2 broken red chillies. When tender (2–3 hours), drain and allow to dry. Whip up some yoghourt with 1 clove crushed garlic, ½ teaspoon black pepper and a little tamarind pulp (optional).

For a less hot dish, seed chillies.

To make dish more spicy, add 2 teaspoons garam masala (see p. 249), a pinch of roasted asafoetida, ½ teaspoon ground kalonji or ¼ teaspoon onion salt, a few kari phulia leaves and a few mint leaves.

A dressing of oil and vinegar with garlic, black pepper, paprika and salt, makes a good dish of black-eyed peas to serve chilled.

Tikki Channeh Dahl (Dried Split-pea Cakes)

Take ½ lb. yellow split peas (or black-eyed peas) and cook them in akni (see p. 253) until very soft (3–4 hours). Sieve them and add to the purée 2 oz. minced parsley, 1 inch green ginger, chopped, ½ teaspoon salt, 1 ground bay leaf and 1½ teaspoons crushed black cumin seed. Bind with egg and sauté in frying pan after forming into small croquettes.

Bhalle (Steamed Lentil Cakes)

1 lb. urd lentil or yellow split peas
½ teaspoon salt
¼ teaspoon each black or white cumin, freshly ground black pepper and paprika

2 teaspoons chopped mint leaves
¾ pint yoghourt

Soak the lentils overnight. Drain and place in blender, or grind, until smooth. Squeeze in clean cloth or muslin to expel surplus moisture. Season with salt and half the cumin, black pepper, paprika and mint leaves. Shape into flat circular croquettes, pressing gently again between muslin or kitchen paper to squeeze out any remaining water. Put in steamer over a large saucepan of akni or water. Steam and turn once. Remove and cool. Now marinate in whipped yoghourt mixed with 2 fl. oz. water, for 1 to 2 hours before serving. Scatter remaining paprika, crushed cumin, black pepper, chives and chopped green herbs on top. To make Dal Varra take the lentil cakes after shaping them and expelling surplus moisture. Omit the steaming and marinating. In the centre, cut a small hole with a biscuit cutter. The cakes should be the same size and general shape of an American doughnut. Sauté or deep-fry them and serve plain. They should be crisp and savoury.

CHAPTER ELEVEN

Eggs

Khagina (*Indian Spiced Omelette*)

6 eggs	4 ground cardamoms
5 tablespoons bessan	¼ teaspoon salt
¼ teaspoon freshly ground black pepper	4 tablespoons grated onion
¼ teaspoon ground coriander seed	2 teaspoons chopped chives
	4 oz. butter
	2 oz. yoghourt

Beat the eggs, mix in the bessan, all the aromatics and salt.
Melt butter in a heavy, wide frying pan, stir in yoghourt
adding a little more salt, then add the egg mixture. Cook until
almost set. Turn over once to make a 'half-moon' shape.
Turn again. Serve by cutting thick slantwise slices from the
khagina. The yoghourt may be incorporated with the eggs and
bessan if preferred.

Anda Dar-Behest (*Aromatic Soufflé Omelette*)

6 eggs	1 minced green chilli
½ teaspoon turmeric	½ teaspoon salt
3 tablespoons onion juice	½ oz. butter
1 tablespoon minced parsley	

Separate the eggs. Beat yolks until smooth; whip whites until
very stiff. Add onion juice, parsley, turmeric and chilli and
season with salt. Carefully fold in the egg whites. Butter a large
pan or round baking dish liberally, and spoon in the egg mixture.
Place the pan in a pre-heated medium oven and wait until the
omelette rises and is firm but fluffy. Serve immediately.

Khagina Turrcarri (Omelette Curry)

6 eggs
2 fl. oz. milk
1 pint stock
2 onions
1 stick celery
1 tomato
1 teaspoon turmeric
1 teaspoon ground coriander
   seed

¼ teaspoon freshly ground
   black pepper
½ teaspoon salt
Juice of ¼ lime
2 fl. oz. yoghourt
2 oz. butter

Heat milk and stock or akni and add thinly sliced onions and celery, chopped tomato, turmeric, coriander, pepper and salt. Simmer 15 minutes, then drain, reserving liquor. Make an omelette from the eggs in the usual way, taking care it is not overcooked, and fill it with the drained onion and celery mixture (reserve the liquor), pressing the edges together. Add lime juice and yoghourt to the liquor, boil until it thickens and spoon over the omelette. Place in a very hot oven or under the grill and serve when the sauce is beginning to glaze.

Anda Turrcarri (Whole-Egg Curry)

A whole-egg curry is made by rubbing an aromatic paste into hard-boiled eggs, then simmering them in a sauce similar to the one given above. Do not use onions and tomatoes as a base for the sauce though, as the authentic whole-egg curry should be sweet and sour. Here is a recipe:

8 hard-boiled eggs
3 oz. blanched slivered
   almonds
2 tablespoons ground saffron
2 tablespoons garlic salt
   moistened in lime juice
8 fl. oz. yoghourt
2 fl. oz. double cream

2 oz. poppy seed, roasted and
   ground
1 oz. sesame seed
1 teaspoon kalonji
1 ground bay leaf
2 ground red chillies
¾ teaspoon salt
2–3 fl. oz. stock (optional)

Prick the eggs all over and spike with almonds. Gash the eggs with a sharp knife in two or three places, cutting through to the yolk, but not any deeper. Dust with saffron and garlic salt moistened with lime juice. Heat together the yoghourt and double cream; add poppy seed, sesame seed, kalonji, bay leaf, chillies, and salt. Stir over heat until thick. Moisten with stock or water and add the eggs. Cook over medium heat until the sauce is much reduced. Serve.

Anda Kabab (Whole-Egg Kabab)

6 eggs	Ground seed of 3 cardamoms
½–¾ teaspoon turmeric	About ¼ lb. slack flour-and-
Salt	water dough
Pinch cayenne	3 oz. butter
¼ teaspoon paprika	3 fl. oz. double cream
¼ teaspoon freshly ground	2 teaspoons ground parsley
black pepper	4 oz. blanched and ground or
1½ tablespoons finely chopped	slivered almonds
mushrooms	

This dish is something of a *tour de force*. With a sharp knife, remove a neat cap from the top of each egg shell. Extract the egg and beat well with turmeric, salt, cayenne, paprika and black pepper, chopped mushrooms and ground cardamoms. If liked a little minced meat or fish may be added. Return to the egg shells (you will need an extra shell or two which can be kept in reserve), replace the cap and cover the top with a thick layer of dough pulled well down to seal the edges. Secure with string. Place the eggs upright in a pan of boiling water and cook for about 20 minutes, until well set. Cool and remove shells: the kababs are ready to be sautéed or grilled. They should be basted with butter, cream, parsley and ground or slivered almonds. (For a less rich sauce use only butter with minced chives.) Serve hot with the sauce.

Anda Dum Mahali (Steamed Egg Custard with Shell-fish)

8–10 egg yolks	Good pinch cayenne
1 fl. oz. double cream	2 teaspoon minced sweet
2 fl. oz. milk	pepper
¼ teaspoon ground saffron	4 minced mint leaves
Pinch ground bay leaf	1 teaspoon parsley
¼ teaspoon aniseed	8 oz. cooked shrimps
3 grains lovage seed	Butter

Beat the egg yolks well with the rest of the ingredients, adding lastly the shrimps, shelled and cut into thin slices. Pour into a well-buttered wide and shallow bowl or mould (if cooked in a high or conical mould, the shrimps and aromatics will sink to the bottom); cover and steam at least one hour or until the custard is set. Turn out carefully and serve at once.

CHAPTER TWELVE

Indian Breads

WITH one or two exceptions, Indian bread is unleavened. It is eaten hot, or within a few minutes of cooking. The flours used are unrefined, and many people grind them at home by hand. They are made from whole wheat, barley, millet and buckwheat. It is worth noting that wholemeal flour is not the same as whole-wheat, being more refined and not including the entire wheat grain. It can be substituted for whole-wheat flour, but the result will of course be slightly different.

Since they are unleavened, most Indian breads are flat, and they are usually circular in form, often resembling griddle scones or pancakes, the dough often being like very thick batter. There are many kinds: some fried, some cooked on a griddle, a few baked in the oven, some stuffed, and one speciality cooked in the tandoor. A heavy 'electric' base frying pan makes a good griddle. The nan is a leavened bread, $1-1\frac{1}{2}$ inches thick and made from refined or white flour. The *bhatura*, a 'chewy' whole-wheat bread, is only $\frac{1}{2}$ inch thick, and less if fried. The *feni* which is saucer-sized and resembles a flat, circular, shredded wheat-cake, is usually soaked in milk overnight when it turns to a creamy consistency, and is eaten with sugar. Best known is the *phulka* (which means blown-up), a light and airy bread that puffs up during the last stage of cooking. The chappati is a bigger and more substantial version of the phulka. It is eaten in the farming areas and suits rural appetites. The chappati needs thorough chewing which ensures sound teeth and helps promote good digestion. Chappati dough can be made and cooked within a few minutes, but personally I like to leave the dough overnight in the refrigerator, covered with a damp muslin cloth. If the dough is kept for seven hours or more a substance called phythin is released which makes the whole-wheat flour more easily digestible, and also makes the bread more pliable.

The sieved phulka dough is also used to cook a very light,

pliant chappati on the reversed griddle. This is the *roomali roti*, the roomali being a thin, chiffon-like scarf. The *warki* roti and the warki *paratha* consist of many layers of gossamer-thin dough, deep-fried to bind the dough together. The dry, souffléed, crisp yet pliant phulka or its thicker variety the chappati are the favourite bread and a good standby.

Chappati and *Phulka* (*Whole-wheat Griddle Breads*)

½ lb. whole-wheat flour	1 teaspoon salt
(preferably hand ground)	7½ fl. oz. water (approx.)

Mix the flour and salt and place on a pastry board. Sprinkle some water in the middle, and gradually work until the flour has absorbed most of the water. Stop as soon as the dough is supple and elastic. The exact quantity of water required will vary according to the flour and the prevailing weather. Knead the dough well – the longer the better. Ten minutes gives a specially light finish, but on average most people find that 5 minutes is adequate. Cover with a wet muslin cloth and leave for 30 minutes. Knead lightly again before shaping the dough. If the dough is left for a longer period of time, it should be kept in a cool place.

Form the dough (or *atta*) into small round balls, and flatten with the palm of the hand. Dust with a little flour on each side, place on a board and roll out as thin as a sheet of parchment paper. Your chappati must fit the griddle or tawa used (they come in all sizes); the smaller griddle is for the phulka and the larger for the chappati. Have the griddle at a medium heat (a little hotter if it is an authentic thick one) and turn the pancake on to it. Wait until the first bubbles rise in the bread. Turn, using a spatula or hand. After a minute or so, press on the edges a little and gently rotate the bread. Now pick up the bread on a fish slice, and if you are using gas, hold over a high flame without turning. The bread will puff up and is then ready to eat.

With a little experience, each chappati or phulka will take ½ minute or so to cook. To serve, heat a deep dish, line with hot napkins and stack the bread. Keep covered, and take to the table.

A few tablespoons of milk can be used in the dough, and the addition of a tablespoon of clarified butter will make the dough more elastic, and the bread more supple. The addition of two tablespoons of bessan to 4 oz. whole-wheat flour makes a nutritive, pleasing change from the usual chappati. For tandoori roti, make cakes 5 inches in diameter, $\frac{1}{4}$ inch thick. Place in kitchen foil in medium-hot oven till cooked. Dot with butter, and serve hot.

Paratha (*Whole-wheat Buttered Griddle Bread*)

7 oz. whole-wheat flour	Butter
$\frac{1}{2}$ pint liquid, part of which should be milk, the rest water	Milk
	12–16 grains lovage seed (roughly bruised)
$\frac{3}{4}$ teaspoon salt	

Prepare the dough as for chappati, mixing in the lovage seeds, and again using only enough liquid to make a slack almost batter-like dough. Cover with damp cloth and leave to rest for at least $1\frac{1}{2}$ hours, but preferably 8 hours or more.

Roll out the small balls of dough into perfect circles and brush the surface with a very little melted butter. Fold to make a semi-circle, then again to make a triangle. Roll out to full size. Brush again with melted butter and repeat. The more times you repeat the process, the crisper your bread will be. Make a pancake 6–8 inches in diameter. Cook on a lightly buttered griddle until pale brown and mottled. Turn, and cook other side. Serve hot.

Stuffed Parathas

These are extremely good. Various stuffings are used: potato purée, minced cauliflower, grated radish, minced meat, cooked lentils, etc. For *Potato Paratha* use 8 oz. mashed potatoes mixed with 1 tablespoon chopped parsley, $\frac{1}{4}$ teaspoon dry ginger powder, juice of $\frac{1}{4}$ lime, $\frac{1}{2}$ teaspoon salt, $\frac{1}{2}$ teaspoon ground fennel or aniseed, $\frac{1}{4}$ teaspoon paprika and 2 tablespoons minced onion fried in a little butter. Roll out the dough and place a little of the purée in the centre. Cover with a second circle of dough, press down the edges and fold to make a triangle. Flour lightly and carefully, roll out again into an enlarged triangular shape. Griddle fry on both sides till brown and mottled with red in places. Serve hot.

For a cauliflower filling, chop 6 oz. cauliflower very fine and sauté in a little butter with 1 tablespoon grated green ginger, 1 tablespoon ground pomegranate seed, 1 teaspoon black cumin, green minced herbs and salt. The addition of ground chillies will make the paratha hot; other aromatics, like amchoor or ground tart mango powder, or garam masala (see p. 249) can be used. Green peas also make a good stuffing. They should be cooked in akni and pressed and flattened lightly before mixing with aromatics.

Makki Ki Roti (Maize Griddle Bread)

8 oz. sifted maize (cornmeal) flour	¼ pint or less water
	1 teaspoon salt

Make a thick dough by working the water into the maize flour and salt. The quantity of water varies according to the milling of the maize. Knead the mixture to give a pliant but very stiff dough for rolling.

To make the roti: make a medium-size ball of dough, coat it on both sides in maize flour; place on the rolling board and smack it down with your palm and fingers with a short, circular, clockwise movement. Repeat this a few times, revolving the dough clockwise and you will have ⅛ inch thick pancake about 4½ to 5 inches in diameter. The dough can be flattened with a rolling pin but the above method is quickest and simplest. Heat a griddle or heavy frypan. Do *not* butter it. Place the maize pancakes on the griddle and cook on medium-high heat. Revolve it clockwise once or twice. Turn once, taking care not to break the roti. Cook till the other side is also deep golden and mottled with specks of brown. Serve hot with a nugget of butter. This bread is traditionally eaten with spinach and is good with dried vegetables; it is not eaten with meat or fish.

Bessani Pura (Legume Pancakes)

2 oz. sifted bessan	¼ pint water (approx.)
1 tablespoon chopped parsley or coriander leaves	Clarified butter for griddle frying
1 tablespoon salt	

Make a thin pouring batter with the bessan and water. Season with salt. Mix in the parsley. Beat lightly and let rest for 10 to 15 minutes.

Heat a griddle or a heavy frying pan. Butter it copiously. Raise the heat high. When the butter is just beginning to smoke, pour in a ladle of batter with a circular motion. At once smooth the top surface and spread the batter a little, using a spatula. Lift the side of the pancake when it has set a little to let the butter run under it. Cook on fairly high heat and turn once. About 20–30 seconds should suffice for each side. Do not over-cook the pancake. It should be a deep gold and mottled with a little brown and red.

A very pungent pancake can be made by adding a little chopped green chilli, replacing the salt by ½ teaspoon each of garlic and onion salt and ¼ teaspoon cayenne.

Missi Roti (*Legume Bread*)

½ lb. whole-wheat flour
½ lb. bessan
4 tablespoons chopped
  coriander or parsley
3 tablespoons chopped
  pimento
1 chopped green chilli
12 ground lovage seeds
1–2 tablespoons chopped
  spinach leaves

1 teaspoon salt
1 teaspoon freshly ground
  black pepper
Butter for frying
2 tablespoons finely chopped
  spring onions or chives
Water

Mix the flours together with salt and pepper, add water and make into a dough. Mix in the other ingredients and knead well. Leave for 2 hours or more covered with a damp cloth. Shape into thick pancakes and cook on a well-buttered griddle. Turn once and serve hot.

Puri (*Deep-fried Whole-wheat Puffed Bread*)

10 oz. whole-wheat flour
¼ pint warm water
¼ teaspoon salt

1½ teaspoons clarified butter
Cooking oil

Sieve the flour and mix in the salt. Make a well in the centre, add water and work to a dough. Add melted butter and knead until dough is elastic, smooth and springy; it should be resistant to the touch and only break when pulled with some force. The entire operation should take about 10 to 15 minutes. Leave to rest for ½ hour.

Butter or oil your hands before shaping the dough into rounds about 2½ to 2¾ inches in diameter. Roll out on a lightly oiled board into circular pancakes 4 inches in diameter. Heat the cooking oil until it just begins to smoke and carefully slide in each pancake. (The professional cook swirls each pancake into the oil with a flick and turn of his wrist.) Press down with a spatula or skimmer. Turn once and press down again. In 10–14 seconds, the puri will puff up, its colour a light, even gold. Drain at once, and serve.

To make Kasta or crisp Puri, knead the flour with a mixture of whipped yoghourt and water in the proportion of 2 to 1, and work a little less than 2 oz. clarified butter into the dough before leaving to rest for ½ hour before deep frying.

Poppadoms

Poppadoms are extremely difficult to make and much the best method is to buy them ready made in packets at an Indian grocer's. Deep frying is the safest way of cooking because it ensures that the whole of the poppadom is fried a rich gold uniform colour. The oil must be smoking hot and the poppadoms immersed for seconds only in order to avoid burning. If they are very large it is advisable to break them into halves or even quarters. Poppadoms can also be roasted over a gas burner on a low flame, turned frequently with prongs.

Kasta Katchori (Lentil-stuffed Fried Bread)

12 oz. flour
7 oz. butter
4 oz. lentils
8 oz. yoghourt

1 teaspoon salt
½ teaspoon paprika
1 teaspoon ground cumin

Clean and wash the lentils, then soak overnight. Add salt to the flour and work in melted butter. Gradually blend in the yog-hourt. Mix well and knead until dough is smooth and springy. Cover with a wet cloth and leave 30 minutes. Make the stuffing as follows: drain lentils and grind or pound finely; mix in the salt, paprika and cumin; set aside. Butter or oil your hands and shape dough into small rounds about $2\frac{1}{2}$ to $2\frac{3}{4}$ inches in diameter; place a little lentil mixture in the centre, fold over, damp the edges to seal, and shape round again. Flatten out into pancakes, each about $\frac{1}{4}$ inch thick and $2\frac{1}{2}$ inches in diameter. Deep-fry, drain and serve hot or cold.

Bhatura (Whole-wheat Leavened Bread)

The *bhatura* is usually made from white flour, and is deep-fried. This recipe is for griddle-baked bread, using whole grain flour, and the result is much lighter than the fried bread. This bhatura should be about $4\frac{1}{2}$–5 inches in diameter and $\frac{1}{4}$–$\frac{1}{2}$ inch thick. Though fully cooked, the inside will be a little soft.

10 oz. whole-wheat flour	5 fl. oz. yoghourt
Good pinch salt	1 teaspoon sugar
$\frac{1}{2}$ teaspoon bicarbonate of soda	

Warm the flour in a very low oven, mix in the soda and salt, then sift. Use mild yoghourt (unless you do not object to the bread tasting sour) slightly warmed, and gradually work it into the flour. Add sugar, sprinkle on a little water and knead to produce a dough much less elastic and springy than that used for puri, paratha or chappati breads. Continue kneading until it is smooth enough to pull clean away from the board. Moisten your hands with butter and knead until the dough is silky. Cover with a damp cloth and leave in a warm place for about $4\frac{1}{2}$ hours. Take out the dough, punch it well and shape into small balls. Flatten and roll out to 5 inches diameter and $\frac{1}{8}$ inch thick. Cook on an unbuttered griddle, pressing down with a napkin to ensure even contact. Turn and repeat. The bread should be light golden brown and risen to a thickness of $\frac{1}{4}$ inch. Serve smoking hot.

Roghni Roti (*Whole-wheat Flat Baked Bread*)

10 oz. whole-wheat flour
  (refined flour can be used)
1¼ oz. clarified butter

¼ teaspoon salt
4 tablespoons milk
Water

Mix the flour and salt, and work in the clarified butter. Knead well, first with milk and then with enough water to make a soft dough for rolling out. Make cakes about 12 inches in diameter and ¼ inch thick. Bake in a hot oven until crisp and light brown.

Roghni Nan (*Leavened Flat Baked Bread*)

10 oz. plain flour
1 teaspoon sugar
5 tablespoons yoghourt
1 oz. clarified butter
¼ teaspoon salt
½ teaspoon bicarbonate of
  soda

2 whole eggs
1 tablespoon dried yeast
5 tablespoons milk
3 tablespoons sesame seed
1 tablespoon kalonji

Whip the yoghourt, heat, and stir in the milk. Remove from fire and combine with the soda, lightly beaten eggs, and melted butter. Sift together salt, sugar and flour. Gradually work in the milk mixture. Add yeast and knead vigorously for 15 minutes, until the dough is springy. Cover and leave in a warm place until it has risen to rather less than double its bulk (about 2 hours). Dust hands with plenty of flour and shape into large balls; then make these into flat, oval pancakes about 10 inches in diameter, pulling the dough gently into shape. The edges may be raised if desired. Brush one side with melted butter and the other with warm milk. Scatter with sesame and kalonji and bake in a hot oven.

This nan bread is cooked in the tandoor. In an ordinary oven, spread lightly buttered kitchen foil over the rack and place the pancakes on this. They are cooked when lightest gold, or oyster in colour and soft to the touch.

A savoury nan can be cooked until it is much drier. The colour should then be medium brown, and the seeds and additional slivers of onion are scattered on half-way through cooking, and pressed down lightly with a cloth. This bread is very tasty for snacks.

Dosha (Rolled Rice Pancakes)

4 oz. rice	1½ teaspoons salt
4 oz. urd or maahn dahl or pink lentils	1 oz. clarified butter

There are two methods of preparing this bread and many ways of achieving different textures. In general, a thin crisp *dosha* has a higher proportion of rice to lentil. And where the directions say 'cover the dosha', a thinner pancake will result if left uncovered.

Steamed Dosha. Wash and clean both lentils and rice, and soak separately for 12 hours. Drain. Grind the lentils extremely fine, and whisk to a light frothy paste. Grind the rice more coarsely and mix the two. Add salt and leave in a warm place for about 12 hours. Stir well and, if necessary, add water to make a thick pouring batter. Fill buttered moulds (those used in India are about 4 inches in diameter, 1¼ inches deep) about two-thirds full. Place on a trivet in a large pan of water and steam for 45 minutes or less, depending on the size of the moulds. Or stand the moulds in a pan of water and bake in the oven. When a skewer comes out clean, the dosha is ready. Serve hot, with a selection of chutneys.

This steamed dosha can also be made with the addition of aromatics like chopped chives, pimento or green chilli, minced onions, and a little asafoetida.

Masala Dosha. Add a good pinch bicarbonate of soda to the batter after it has fermented for 12 hours, and about 2 tablespoons rice flour (or refined flour). Lightly butter a heavy frying pan and pour in some batter. Tilt the pan to spread batter evenly. Now is the time to cover the pan if you want a thick dosha. Cook 2 minutes, turn and cook a further 2 minutes. Remove, place a filling in the centre, fold over and serve hot.

The filling for a dosha is made with minced potatoes cooked with aromatics like cumin, paprika, black pepper, green herbs, chopped onion, mustard seed – all simmered in a little water, then dried off and rolled in a little butter. Turmeric and other spices can be added but they tend to compete with the vegetables and garnishes of the main dish.

Samosa (*Stuffed Pastry Cones*)

10 oz. white flour
¾ tablespoon salt
1 oz. clarified butter

5 tablespoons yoghourt
Stuffing (see below)

Sift the flour and salt and work in melted butter. Then knead in the yoghourt and make a stiff dough. Shape into small balls, press flat, and roll out into very thin circular pancakes. Cut each pancake in half and make into a cone shape. Fill the hollow with stuffing, and seal the flap by damping the edges and pinching together. Deep fry the cones, taking care not to crowd the pan. Remove when crisp and dark gold in colour. Drain. They may be served cold but are better hot.

Make the stuffing with mashed potatoes, chopped green peas, chives and parsley, chopped mint, paprika, salt, and a little lime juice or ground pomegranate seed. Stuffings are also made from cooked minced meat, green herbs and seasonings.

CHAPTER THIRTEEN

Sweets and Desserts

THOUGH there are many sweets and desserts which can be made in the home, this is one area of Indian cookery best left to professionals, if only because of the time and expense involved.

Whole milk, cream and *khoia* (see Appendix p. 252) form the basis of many Indian sweets. Khoia is a milk preparation in which milk is reduced to a thick paste, the texture of a pliable though crumbly dough. The process is very long, and a substitute can be made by mixing one part plain flour to three parts powdered milk with a very little water, so as to make a thick paste. The khoia is mixed with grated, slivered or powdered almonds, pistachio, sesame or poppy seeds, dried melon seeds, coconut, fruits and vegetables, and with granular or whole Indian cheese. Cereals and a type of jelly made from cereals are a feature of the pudding course. Some sweetmeats can be kept for several days; others must be eaten fresh. There are two main kinds of conserve: the whole vegetable, fruit or berry cooked in syrup, or the minced conserve.

A whole range of splendid sherbets and soft drinks is giving way to bottled drinks with synthetic flavours. However, Indian ice cream (there are four main varieties) is still a firm favourite. It was made in ancient India, before the introduction of ice, by filling metal cones with the ice cream mixture, sealing the top with a stiff paste and placing them in a large *chatti* or vessel of unglazed clay together with specially selected pebbles, salt-petre and other natural chemicals. The chatti was rocked continuously until the ice-cold pebbles had set the ice cream. The ice cream mixture was thicker and firmer than that of modern commercial ice cream (a recipe is given on page 229).

Kheer or Sheer (Creamed Rice)

2 pints milk	2 cloves, or ¾ inch cinnamon
3 oz. washed rice	6 tablespoons blanched,
6 oz. sugar	slivered almonds
1 oz. raisins	2 teaspoons kewara or rose
Bruised seeds of 4 cardamoms	water

Boil the milk and add the washed rice. Stir and boil for 1 minute on medium heat, then cook over a low heat, stirring constantly for 15 minutes, continue cooking for about 1½ hours, stirring occasionally. Add sugar, raisins, cardamoms and cloves. Cook again, stirring slowly from time to time until raisins plump out and the mixture thickens: it should be of a very thick pouring consistency. Add the almonds and place in a moderate oven for 25 minutes. Mix in the rose water just before serving. It can be served hot, but is best well chilled and served in individual cups with a light scattering of slivered blanched almonds and pistachios. It is also customary to decorate the chilled kheer with edible silver or gold leaf.

Firni (Rice Compote)

1 lb. rice	1 tablespoon slivered
6 pints milk	pistachios
1 lb. sugar	2–3 tablespoons rose water
1 oz. blanched and slivered	
almonds	

Wash, clean and drain the rice. Soak overnight, then grind. Bring milk to the boil and add rice. Cook on medium heat until stiff and creamy. Draw aside from the heat, and stir in sugar. Put back on the fire and cook, stirring continuously until the sugar is dissolved and well mixed in. Cook and stir on a very high heat for 2 minutes. Remove and cool. Add the rose water when the *firni* is cool, but before it is set. A few extra drops may be added on serving. Serve chilled in small shallow dishes or moulds and scatter with slivered almonds and pistachio.

The smoothness of the firni depends on grinding the soaked rice extremely fine. Use a mincer, pestle and mortar or electric blender.

Amphulia (*Baked Mango and Rice*)

This should be made with mango purée. As a substitute sieve peaches, apricots or any smooth fleshed fruit.

1 lb. rice	4 fl. oz. double cream
2 oz. sugar	¼ teaspoon ground saffron
4 fl. oz. milk	1 grain musk (if available)
1 lb. sweet mango purée	2 teaspoons rose water

Soak rice overnight. Boil the milk and stir over a medium heat until reduced by half. Mix the mango purée, cream and boiled milk in a bowl, then add sugar, musk, saffron and rose water. Boil the rice until very soft. Put a layer in a deep oval dish and top with a layer of creamed mango. Repeat until used up. Dot with a little butter and place in a slow oven until set and lightly browned. Serve hot or chilled.

SWEET PILAUS

These puddings are served with malai, Indian cream, or double cream whipped up with a little egg white. Sweet pilaus are sometimes served before dinner, as it is traditional in India to offer something to sweeten the mouth. In this case, the quantity served would be small. Not unnaturally, if there is a rice pudding, no other rice is served with the meal. Breads of various kinds would be served with the other dishes.

Zarda or *Kesar Pilau* (*Sweet Rice with Saffron*)

1 lb. rice	6 oz. blanched, halved almonds
8 oz. sugar	4 oz. halved cashews
¼ teaspoon ground saffron	4 oz. coarsely chopped chirongi or hazel nuts
8 oz. butter	
10 crushed cardamoms	1½ inches splintered stick cinnamon
Good pinch nutmeg	
5 cloves	¼ teaspoon salt
Juice of ½ lemon	Whipped cream or malai (see p. 252)
5 oz. raisins	
3 oz. sultanas	

Prepare the nuts and spices. Parboil the rice (about 9 minutes) with salt, saffron and as much water as it will absorb. Reserve. Make a syrup of sugar and nutmeg in 2 cups of water: stir until completely dissolved, then boil 1 minute and remove from fire.

Melt butter in a heavy casserole and fry cardamoms and cloves on a low heat. Moisten with all but ¼ cup of syrup. Bring to the boil and add rice. Stir a little and cover. Steam on lowest heat until all moisture has been absorbed. Uncover and add lemon juice, raisins, sultanas, slivered or halved almonds, halved cashews and chirongi or hazel nuts. Add splintered cinnamon. Stir well but once only and replace cover. Give the zarda a dum in a slow oven for 12 minutes. Leave in a cool place for 5 minutes and serve with whipped cream or malai, and some syrup for those who may want it.

This is but one variety of zarda pilau. There is also the *dugna* (double) zarda and the *chughna* (fourfold) zarda, which use the same quantity of rice, but twice and four times the amount of butter. The zardas are rich and meant only for special feast days.

Pilau Darbeheysht (*Sweet Pilau with Musk*)

1 lb. preserving sugar (or ½ lb. candy sugar if possible)	4 oz. raisins
½ lb. rice	Grain of musk (optional)
4 oz. butter	Good pinch ground saffron
6 cardamoms	4 oz. blanched almonds
2 cloves	4 oz. shelled pistachios
1 inch cinnamon stick	2 teaspoons rose water

Pulverize the sugar and mix with 2 pints water to make a medium thick syrup. (Or dissolve 1 lb. preserving sugar in 1½ pints water.) Soak rice overnight; drain. Melt butter in a saucepan, add the rice together with cardamoms, cloves, cinnamon and raisins and fry until the grains become translucent. Grind the musk (or get a drop or so from the chemist), dissolve it in a little water and add to the syrup. Cook rice in syrup until done.

Fry the ground saffron in a little butter and water. Add almonds, pistachio and aromatize with rose water. When almost dry, serve as a garnish with the rice.

Pilau Suffaida (*Sweet Pilau with Fruits*)

1 lb. rice
2 oz. blanched almonds
2 oz. cashew nuts
4 tablespoons each of the
    following dried seeds:
    melon, cucumber, marrow,
    sesame
2 pints milk
10 oz. sugar
½ lb. butter
9 bruised cardamoms
5 ground cloves

Few drops almond oil
Good pinch salt
¼ teaspoon nutmeg
½ lime or lemon
1 orange (peeled, seeded and
    sliced)
6 mango or peach slices
2 oz. peeled and seeded
    white grapes
2 oz. white raisins
2 fl. oz. double cream

Chop almonds, cashews and other seeds, or put through coarse plate of mincer. Stir in the milk, whip well and reserve. Make a syrup with 1 pint water and the sugar. Reserve. Parboil the rice (about 8–9 minutes) and also reserve.

Melt the butter in a heavy casserole and fry the cardamoms and cloves, adding a few drops of pure almond oil (from your chemist) and salt. Moisten with milk, strained from minced nuts, and syrup, aromatize with nutmeg and cook over low heat for about 10 minutes, stirring well. Add rice, mix in the juice of ½ a lime or lemon and stir. Cover and cook very gently until rice is tender, about 8–10 minutes. Aromatize the fresh and dried fruits with rose water, and mix with the minced nuts and double cream very gently into the rice so as not to break it up. Cover and give it a dum for 15 minutes in a slow oven. Leave aside for 7 minutes before serving.

These are only a few of the many sweet rice pilaus. Others use cheese, many kinds of fruit, both dried and fresh, as well as honey and herbs.

Here are some *Karrah* or Halva recipes.

Gajjar Karrah (Halva of Carrots)

1½ lb. carrots
4 pints milk
½ inch stick cinnamon
3 cardamom seeds
¼ teaspoon ground saffron
2 oz. washed raisins

2 oz. butter
2 tablespoons honey
6 oz. sugar
2 oz. blanched almonds
½ teaspoon rose water
(optional)

Grate the carrots and set aside with their juice. Scald the milk, add carrots and cinnamon and boil for 1 minute. Now simmer and stir frequently over low heat. (The more stirring the better for this recipe.) When the milk has reduced to less than a quarter, stir in the cardamoms, the saffron dissolved in 1 tablespoon boiling water and the raisins. Mix and stir until the milk is dry. Enrich with butter and stir over a medium heat until the butter has been absorbed and coats the mixture. Add honey and sugar. Stir and cook for another 8 minutes or so until a rich translucent red. Add the slivered or halved almonds, aromatize with rose water and serve. It may also be served chilled with cream.

Karrah Pehlwani (Halva Titan)

4 lb. carrots
8 oz. sugar
¼ teaspoon nutmeg

½ teaspoon ground saffron
¼ lb. butter
2 lb. blanched almonds

Grate or blend the carrots and put aside. Make a syrup with the sugar and 5 oz. water and cook until the thread stage (217°F.). Take off any scum. Add carrots, nutmeg and saffron and cook until all moisture and syrup has dried up. Add melted butter and almonds freshly ground (no more than 5 minutes before use) or chopped very fine. This is an extremely nourishing dish, said to be eaten by wrestlers and strong men in earlier times. It comes from an old Indian cookery book, and is no less subtle than the next recipe.

Karrah Mahali (Halva Royale)

1 lb. semolina	¼ teaspoon ground mace
¾ lb. butter	4 oz. blanched slivered
2½ fl. oz. rice water	almonds
6 oz. sugar	Rose water

Soak the semolina in just enough water to cover, and leave overnight. Stir in 2 cups water and knead the semolina. Strain well and reserve liquid. Heat butter and add the semolina liquid and the rice water. Stir in the semolina and cook until the mixture becomes clear. Add sugar and mace, and keep stirring for 6 minutes. Now add the almonds slivered fine, and cook until mixture becomes transparent. It is ready when a skewer or knife thrust in comes out clean. Aromatize with ½ teaspoon or more of rose water and serve either hot or chilled.

Halva Petha I (Pumpkin Halva)

1 lb. pumpkin	2 oz. blanched slivered
3–4 oz. brown sugar	almonds
¼ pint milk	8 bruised cardamom seeds
2 oz. butter	½ teaspoon nutmeg

Remove the seeds from the pumpkin, peel, scrape, grate and weigh it. Place in a saucepan with all its juice and simmer to dry off all moisture. Add its own weight in sugar; stir and cook over medium heat until the mixture thickens and becomes stiff. Do not let it burn. Moisten with milk, stirring all the time, and then enrich with butter. Stir slowly and cook until the mixture stands away from the pan. Scatter with almonds, cardamom and nutmeg. Put in a buttered mould and smooth with a spatula. Place in a moderate oven for 10 minutes, then serve.

Halva Petha II (Pumpkin and Coconut Halva)

½ pint milk	½ inch stick cinnamon
1 lb. pumpkin	2½ oz. butter
1 lb. brown sugar	2 oz. cashew nuts
1 oz. raisins	2 oz. blanched almonds
4 oz. grated fresh coconut	¼ teaspoon nutmeg
or 2½ oz. desiccated	

Peel and grate pumpkin, bring milk to the boil and add pumpkin. Boil about 12 minutes, stirring constantly. Mash the softened pumpkin and continue cooking on low heat until all moisture has evaporated. Add brown sugar and stir over a brisk heat for 10 minutes. Add the raisins, coconut, cinnamon and melted butter. Stir and cook for another 6–7 minutes. Pour into a buttered dish and leave for 15 minutes in a medium oven. Sprinkle with chopped cashews, chopped almonds and nutmeg, and serve hot.

Halva Badam (*Almond Halva*)

2 lb. blanched almonds
About ½ lb. flour
About ¼ lb. butter

6 oz. sugar
Rose water or kewara water

Damp the almonds and dredge or coat with flour. Fry in butter until well browned, remove, cool, and rub off all trace of flour. Grind or pound the almonds to a fine flour. Make a syrup of the sugar and a little water and boil to the thread (217°F.). Add almond flour and 1 oz. butter. Cook on medium heat until it thickens. Flavour with a little rose water and serve hot, or chilled.

Halva Kela (*Banana Halva*)

6 large ripe bananas
2 oz. butter
7½ fl. oz. water
2 oz. sugar
Pinch of nutmeg

1 ground cardamom
A little almond essence
2 tablespoons blanched
    slivered almonds

Peel and slice the bananas in 1 inch pieces, and fry in butter in a heavy frying pan for 7 minutes, over a medium heat stirring frequently. Take out and mash. Moisten with 5 tablespoons water, and replace. Simmer on a low heat, stirring continuously for about 3 minutes. Dissolve sugar in the remaining water and add to the banana purée. Boil together for 10–12 minutes, stirring when necessary to prevent burning, and keep the mixture smooth. Cook until thick, then turn into a bowl and whisk until smooth and light. Sprinkle with nutmeg, cardamom seed, and almond essence, and scatter with almonds. Chill before serving. The amount of butter can be varied according to taste. Really, it is necessary only to prevent the banana from sticking or burning. Any surplus can be drained off before cooking in water.

Halva Anda (*Egg and Coconut Halva*)

6 eggs	½ inch stick cinnamon
2 oz. butter	1 oz. raisins
¼ pint milk	2 tablespoons slivered
3 oz. sugar	pistachio
Good pinch nutmeg	1 oz. grated coconut

Beat the eggs until frothy. Heat the butter and pour in the eggs. Cook and stir lightly over a low heat for about 5 minutes. Have prepared a syrup of milk and sugar flavoured with nutmeg and cinnamon, with raisins added. Pour over the eggs and simmer on a gentle heat for 9–10 minutes. Cook until the mixture thickens. Add the pistachio and coconut. Serve hot. (Twice as much coconut may be used if preferred.)

Shahi Tukra (*an Indian Bread Pudding*)

10 medium-thick slices bread	milk powder to a thick paste
3 oz. butter	with water, and fry in a
Good pinch saffron	little butter until light gold)
6 tablespoons milk	2 fl. oz. double cream
5 oz. sugar	16 pistachio nuts, shelled
4 oz. khoia (Indian dried	Few drops rose water
coagulated milk: mix whole	

Trim bread of all crusts and fry in butter until a deep gold. Dissolve the saffron in boiling milk; add sugar and stir until melted. Pour over the bread and leave to steep for 7 minutes. Remove carefully and drain. Combine the milk left over from steeping the bread with the khoia and double cream and stir over a low heat for about 1 minute. Add the fried bread and cook gently, turning once. Now thicken the mixture over a high heat until very little liquid remains. Arrange on a platter, sprinkle with coarsely ground pistachio nuts and sprinkle with rose water. Chill before serving.

Bakarkhani (*a Sweet Raisin Bread*)

1 lb. refined flour	Rose water
2 oz. raisins	1 tablespoon dried yeast
12 oz. sugar	2 oz. blanched almonds
8 oz. clarified butter	

Mix yeast with the flour and work with enough water to make a soft dough. Roll out to a thin platter-shape about 22 inches in diameter. Brush generously with butter and scatter with half the raisins. Fold in the edges. Use more butter and remaining raisins and fold again. The cake should now measure about 6 inches in diameter. Seal the edges well with a little water or milk. Punch the top full of small holes and bake in a hot oven. When half-cooked spike with slivered almonds. Remove from the oven when a medium gold and steep in a syrup of butter and sugar. Sprinkle with rose water when cool. Chill and serve sliced. This type of bread is served as a pudding or a sweet snack. A variation of it – the Shahi Tukra – is often made today with white leavened bread.

Kela Mithai (*Banana Cheese-cake*)

10 ripe bananas	6 oz. sugar
10 oz. cream of wheat or semolina	½ oz. butter (for buttering dish)
¼ teaspoon nutmeg	¼ pint milk
½ inch stick cinnamon	Water

Peel the bananas and mash or purée. Combine with the cream of wheat or semolina and flavour with nutmeg and ground cinnamon. Add milk and sugar, and enough water to produce a medium thick paste. Cook slowly in a double boiler for 3–3½ hours until the mixture thickens and begins to set. Turn into a buttered dish and allow to cool before cutting into squares for serving.

Karrah Paneer (*Indian Cheese-cake*)

1¾ pints milk
Juice of 1 lemon
2 egg yolks
4 oz. sugar

½ oz. butter
4 oz. blanched chopped
   almonds

Bring milk to boiling point and add lemon juice. Mix well and allow the milk to curdle. Drain thoroughly, then knead the resulting curd well with all the other ingredients except almonds. Use a blender. Butter a mould and stud the sides and bottom with coarsely ground or broken almonds, to make a coating at least ⅛ inch thick. Pour in the curd mixture. Dust the top with a little more sugar and bake in a medium oven for about 15 minutes or until set. Serve hot or chilled.

Tiltandula (*Sesame Seed Meringue*)

This is a modern version of a recipe given in a narrative drama written in A.D. 400.

½ lb. butter
1 lb. brown sugar
16 eggs

Juice of 8 limes or lemons
½ lb. roasted sesame seed
½ teaspoon ground saffron

The recipe should include a grain of sandalwood but this may be difficult to get outside India where the wood is specially selected and ground. Use almond, kewara or orange as a substitute, or any essence that will go with the nutty flavour of sesame seed.

Mix thoroughly the roasted sesame seed and saffron. Separate the eggs. Cream the butter and sugar and mix in the beaten egg yolks. Stir in the lime juice. Gradually mix in the sesame seed and saffron. Cover with water and cook until the mixture is quite soft to the touch. Dry off all moisture, add the whipped whites of egg and bake in the oven until the top is well browned. Cool, and cut into wedges for serving.

Shakar Parre (Sugar Puffs)

For the syrup:

6 oz. brown sugar   2 tablespoons honey

For the pastry:

8 oz. white flour   ¼ teaspoon powdered
2½ oz. clarified butter   cinnamon
¼ teaspoon ground mace   4 tablespoons milk

Make a syrup of the sugar in ¾ cup water, and cook until reduced
to the consistency of honey. Mix in the honey and set aside.

Sift the flour. Heat the clarified butter to just below smoking
point, and quickly but vigorously work it into the flour. Add
mace and cinnamon. Knead the mixture well. Now bring milk to
boil and gradually work it in. Knead thoroughly and roll out
into a rectangular shape, about ½ inch thick. Cut into ¾ inch
squares. Deep fry the pastry, taking care not to crowd the
pan. Remove when a light gold in colour. Drain on kitchen
paper, then steep in the warm syrup for 7 minutes. Arrange
neatly on a plate, reduce the syrup by a quarter and pour it
over the pastry cubes. Cool or chill before serving.

Bombai Halva (Semolina Halva)

1 lb. semolina   5 cardamom seeds
2 lb. sugar   2 oz. slivered blanched
8 oz. butter   almonds
2 tablespoons rose water   2 oz. chopped pistachio

Steep the semolina in plenty of water and leave overnight.
Place a large piece of muslin over a basin and strain the semolina
through this, squeezing out all the liquid into the basin. Dip
the muslin bag in the water again and squeeze a second time.
Repeat several times until a lot of the semolina starch has
collected in the water. Discard semolina. Let the water stand
until the sediment has sunk to the bottom. Carefully drain off
the top water.

Boil the sugar in an equal quantity of water until it reaches
the fondant or soft ball stage (240°F.). Mix in the sediment.

Stir and boil until a thick paste. Enrich with melted butter and cook until it becomes almost too thick to stir with a spoon. Flavour with rose water and cardamoms and sprinkle with almonds and pistachio. Cool. When set, cut into cubes with a hot knife. The semolina jelly has a chewy texture and is very filling.

Sevian (*Vermicelli Halva*)

½ pint water	3 oz. butter
3 oz. sugar	Good pinch ground saffron
1½ tablespoons honey	¼ teaspoon grated nutmeg
7 oz. vermicelli	

Make a syrup of the water, sugar and honey, boiling for 7 minutes. Reserve. Break the vermicelli into small pieces, and, using a heavy frying pan, cook in butter until a rich, gold colour, slightly mottled with red and brown. Add saffron dissolved in a little water, then the syrup. Boil for 3 minutes. Cook and stir until the butter separates; then cook until all moisture has dried. Add nutmeg, mix and serve.

A *richer* preparation is made by frying the vermicelli and then simmering it in milk with slivered, blanched almonds. It is then mixed with a very thick sugar syrup incorporating khoia. Rose water is added, plus slivered pistachio and finely chopped raisins. It is then given a dum, and the dissolved saffron is added just before it is served.

A kheer or sheer of *sevian* (vermicelli) is made in the same way as the creamed rice recipe (p. 215). To the vermicelli, add one eighth its own weight of blanched ground almonds, and boil in milk, stirring continuously. When the vermicelli is soft, add sugar and stir briefly to dissolve it. Cook until it begins to stick to the bottom and come away from the sides of the pan. It should be like a thick pouring batter. It can be served hot or chilled.

Nareal Pitta (*Coconut Dumplings*)

½ lb. grated coconut	3 crushed cardamom seeds
¼ lb. brown sugar	Puff pastry

Lightly brown the coconut, sugar and cardamom in a heavy

frying pan. Add chopped raisins if you like. Take a small circle
of puff pastry and fill the centre with the coconut mixture. Fold
in half, pinch the edges and seal with a little water or milk.
Deep fry in oil to a golden brown so that the casing is crisp
with a soft filling. Serve hot or cold. They may be brushed with
a little melted butter and then beaten egg white, and browned
in the oven.

Barfi Pista (Creamed Milk Sweetmeat)

1 lb. powdered whole milk, (a
   substitute for khoia (see
   p. 252))
4 oz. castor sugar

2 oz. ground pistachio
Slivered pistachios
4 cardamom seeds

Sift the powdered milk (or make khoia: see p. 252). Gradually
mix in 1½ cups water, bring to the boil and cook over a moderate
heat, stirring continuously, until reduced to a very thick paste.
Make a thick syrup with the castor sugar and a little water, and
add to the creamed milk. Add ground pistachios and stir
thoroughly. Cook again until it is a thick paste. Turn into square
shallow tins or dishes, spreading about 2 inches thick. Leave to
stand for 8 hours. Press into it roughly broken cardamom seeds
and slivered pistachio. Cut into diamond shaped lozenges to
serve. The *barfi*, like most Indian sweets, are decorated with
silver and gold leaf (see p. 44).

Bole Comadare (Coconut Cake)

½ pint sugar syrup
½ lb. rice flour
¾ lb. grated coconut
3 egg yolks
½ lb. brown sugar
1 teaspoon anise seed

½ pint coconut milk
4 oz. coarsely broken
   cashews
Good pinch ground mace
Good pinch ground cloves

Make a medium-thick syrup and stir in the rice flour, mixing
well. Reserve. In a heavy frying pan, brown the coconut for one
minute, then add the beaten egg yolks, anise seed and brown
sugar, stirring constantly. Moisten with the coconut milk,

and then the syrup. Cook and stir to reduce. Add cashews, mace and cloves. Turn out into a buttered dish and cool. Cut into cubes to serve.

Jalebi (*Sweet Spirals in Syrup*)

1 tablespoon dried yeast	½ teaspoon ground saffron
10 oz. sifted flour	strands
2½ fl. oz. warm water	1 pint light syrup (¼ lb. sugar
2½ fl. oz. hot water	melted in ¾ pint water)

Soften the yeast in the warm water. In a mixing bowl, combine the flour with the yeast and ¾ pint of water. Beat hard with a wooden spoon until mixture is very smooth. Soak the saffron in a very little boiling water and add. Let it stand a few minutes.

Heat cooking fat in a deep pan. Now take a small nozzled funnel, place your finger over the end and fill with batter. With a circular motion release into the smoking hot fat as many spirals about 2 inches in diameter as possible, without crowding the pan. Remove and drain. Have the syrup kept warm in a double boiler and dip in the *jalebi* while still hot. Steep for 15 seconds. Remove and drain. The syrup will glaze when the jalebi are cool. They may be eaten hot or cold, and can be served with cream or with ice cream. The sugar tastes like honey.

Rasgullas (*Cheese Quenelles in Syrup*)

1 pint milk	2 pints water
4 tablespoons lime juice	2 tablespoons rose water
2 tablespoons ground semolina	2 oz. blanched almonds
1 lb. sugar	

Bring milk to the boil stirring continuously. Add lukewarm lime or lemon juice and boil until the milk curdles. Drain overnight through a cloth to make curd cheese. If necessary, place under a weight to remove all trace of moisture. Rub the cheese to make a smooth paste and knead together with the semolina. Shape into perfectly smooth, round walnut-size balls. Press some chopped almonds and a little sugar into the middle of each ball. Make a syrup of the sugar and water, bring to the boil and add the *rasgullas*. Poach for 1½ hours. Remove and cool slightly. Sprinkle with rose water, and serve hot or chilled.

The same preparation can be served in a smooth cream sauce. When perfectly cooked, drain the rasgullas and cover with milk. Leave for 6 hours, or overnight. Remove and set aside. Heat milk, and reduce by three-quarters, stirring all the time. Now add beaten double cream or malai, and stir. Add a very little almond essence and a suspicion of rose water. Pour over the rasgullas and serve chilled.

Sandesh (Cheese Fudge)

3 pints milk	½ lb. castor sugar
6 tablespoons pistachio	Seed of 8 cardamoms
5 tablespoons lime juice	¼ teaspoon nutmeg

Make curd cheese as in the previous recipe. Put cheese together with sugar into a heavy frying pan and cook over a medium heat, crumbling the mixture until it thickens and is smooth. Remove, knead well and put into small moulds or dishes about 2½ inches by 1 inch. Press bruised cardamoms and grated nutmeg into the *sandesh*. Cool, prize from moulds and serve. Larger moulds can be used, but the sandesh is liable to break on turning out.

Gulab Jamun

½ lb. blanched almonds ground very fine	5 fl. oz. yoghourt
½ lb. sifted flour	1 teaspoon baking powder
	¼ lb. butter

Mix almonds and flour and work in the butter. Add baking powder, then work in the yoghourt. Let it rest for 15 minutes. Roll into sausage shapes 2 inches long and carefully deep fry. Do not let them break. Remove when coloured a rich red-brown. Place in prepared syrup for 15 minutes and serve hot, or cool for 8 hours and serve chilled.

Kulfi (Indian Ice Cream)

2 pints full cream milk	2 tablespoons ground almonds
2 tablespoons rice flour or ground sesame seed	4 oz. khoia (see p. 252)
5½ oz. sugar	

A fairly commonplace way of making ice cream in India, where refrigerators are still rather rare, is to put the mixture into metal moulds shaped like cones, which are then pushed into earthenware pots filled with chopped ice, salt and saltpetre. The pot is then rotated until the ice cream sets. This method is similar to the principle of the hand-turned freezer of Europe. The cones are about 5–6 inches long, fitted with a tight screw cap and sealed with a ribbon of dough to prevent leakage. They can be placed in the bucket-type freezer or even a large enamel pail and rocked by hand. The important point is that the rotation or movement must be continuous or the resulting ice cream will be hard and icy rather than creamy. The *kulfi* or ice cream is removed by rolling the cones in the palms for a few seconds, then smartly tapping them out on to a plate. Moulds made of silver, stainless steel or other lined metals may be used in place of cones.

Scald the cones. Simmer and stir the milk until reduced to little over half the original quantity. Add the ground sesame or rice flour and cook until reduced to a thick paste. Add sugar, and cook until dissolved and perfectly amalgamated. Cool, then add first the almonds, and then the khoia. Mix well and pour the thick mixture into the cones. Freeze as described above. The consistency will be thicker and harder than ordinary ice creams; it melts quickly and must be eaten within a few minutes.

Màll-Pura (*Sweet Pancakes*)

This is a type of Indian pancake. They are usually made with flour – whole-wheat, wholemeal, or refined white flour – milk and sugar. Of the two main varieties of *màll-pura*, one uses white granulated sugar, and the other a brown sugar, either demerara or brown Barbados. The best pancakes are made with malai (p. 252). You can also try adding a small quantity of khoia (p. 252). I have found that milk just going sour makes superb puras. Leave a pint bottle in the warmth of the kitchen, and in about 24 hours it should be right – a taste-test will tell when. The milk must not be left over-long, or it curdles to a junket-like consistency.

This recipe will yield 4 to 6 puras, depending on the thickness.

3 oz. sifted whole-wheat flour, or semolina	1¼ teaspoons fennel seed
24 whole peppercorns	1 pint fresh milk
2 oz. granulated sugar	Pinch of salt
	Clarified butter for cooking

Melt the sugar in the milk stirring well. Pour milk into bowl containing the flour, and gradually mix it in, making sure there are no lumps. Lightly whisk if necessary. Add the peppercorns, fennel seeds and salt.

Heat a thick, heavy griddle, failing that the thickest frying pan you have. Melt about 1–2 tablespoons butter on the griddle. Raise the heat high, till the butter is smoking faintly. With a ladle pour on a pancake, making circular motions to complete the pancake. It should be about 4–5 inches in diameter. Smooth it on the top, with a spatula or knife. Keep the heat fairly high (the heavy griddle can bear a very high heat), and with the knife lift the edges of the pancake to let the butter run under it. As soon as it is set, lift gently and turn over. Give the second side another minute or so. It is now ready. Lift it, allowing as much fat as possible to drip back on to the griddle. Add a little more butter for the next pancake if necessary. The peppercorns and fennel seed give the pura a piquant flavour. The sugar can be slightly increased for those with a sweet tooth. The finished pura is mottled red and brown, crisped at the edges and fairly pliant inside, especially if cooked on a true Indian griddle which is slightly concave in the centre. It should be between ⅛ and ¼ inch thick. The màll-pura is not like other Indian or European thin pancakes, but is substantial and rich, and eaten much on cold days and during the rainy season, especially for breakfast or at teatime. Serve pura hot but, if liked, cook the day before as they will re-heat well. In a refrigerator, or in cold weather they keep two or three days. Those who like things sweet can dip the màll-pura in warm syrup for 10 minutes.

CHAPTER FOURTEEN

Chutneys and Pickles

THE preparations in this section may be divided into three main groups. There is the *chatni* or chutney made with vinegar, sugar and spices; there are fresh chutneys which will keep several days in a cool place; and there are *achars*, pickled fruits, vegetables, meat, game or fish given a long marination in oil. Only the chutneys are known outside India.

Pickles and chutneys of all kinds can be mild, hot, or very hot; they can be bland or highly aromatic, sharp or sweet-sour. Many Indian homes used to keep a veritable treasure trove of pickles and chutneys, but today much of the pickle-making has passed into commercial hands. These pickles are good, but they lack finesse and most are far too highly seasoned, over-cooked and over-marinated.

Pickles should never be allowed to overwhelm the foods they accompany. The flavour of a delicate fish preparation, for instance, cannot compete with strong-tasting pickles and chutneys. On the other hand, a rich korma or pilau needs no pickles. It is the plainer foods that give scope for the use of pickles: breads, cheese, rice, simple pilaus, or dishes where vegetables and other accompaniments are only mildly spiced or flavoured. An interesting way to enjoy pickles is to serve a dozen or more kinds accompanied by steaming hot boiled rice and a large bowl of yoghourt punch (*raita*, see Appendix, p. 250) or even plain yoghourt. The pickles may cover the full range from sweet to sour, mild to hot, and the yoghourt will refresh the palate and damp the fires of the hotter seasoning. Followed by plenty of fresh fruit, this makes a nourishing and tasty supper, and provides an adventurous change in food tasting.

TECHNIQUE OF MARINATION

Pickles are marinated, rarely cooked. Chutneys are cooked. Both pickles and chutneys may require a mellowing or maturation period, varying from a fortnight to six months.

Pickles being marinated require exposure to gentle heat for a few days. In India (except during the monsoon) the pickle jar is kept in the sun, the mouth covered with cheese cloth or muslin. The jar is shaken once or twice daily and once or twice stirred gently with a wooden pickling spoon. Usually salt is added daily in small quantities to let ingredients absorb it gradually. In the evening the pickle is removed to the kitchen, put on a cool dry shelf and covered with its lid. This process is repeated for a few days according to the instructions for each recipe. Overlong exposure to sunshine tends to cook the pickle and make it musty.

In lieu of sunshine an initial half hour in a just perceptibly warm oven, then several days in a dry warm place (near the boiler, hot water pipes, or kitchen stove), will do as well. Rotate jar towards heat source, keep it dry, do not use lid during the day, and at night cap properly. Leave in a cool, *dry* place. The lemon pickle for instance needs about three days marinating in a warm place. (The maturation period for this pickle after it is completed and sealed, for example, will be a week to a fortnight.)

Here is a recipe for an unusual pickle.

Lassan Achar (Garlic Pickle)

½ lb. garlic
1¾ tablespoons salt
4 tablespoons fennel or aniseed
1 teaspoon lovage seed
1 tablespoon cayenne pepper
1 tablespoon whole peppercorns
1 tablespoon Kashmir garam masala or ordinary garam masala (see p. 249)

½–¾ teaspoon turmeric
1½ tablespoons kalonji (nigella indica)
6 bay leaves
¼ teaspoon powdered asafoetida
3 *pippal* (long black pepper)
1½–2 pints oil

Peel the garlic and see that it is free from all moisture. This means that hands and spoons must also be dry. Place the whole garlic cloves and all the aromatics in a pickling jar and cover to $\frac{1}{2}$ inch depth with good oil (olive or mustard). Stir well and cover with a stretched muslin cloth. Put in a warm place (in the sun, or next to the boiler or stove) and stir 3 or 4 times daily. At night, cover the pickle with a lid. Repeat for 3 or 4 days, then allow to stand for a week in a dry atmosphere before using. During this time the garlic loses much of its pungency yet retains its flavour. In time, it becomes translucent, and still milder, losing its crispness. One keeps it, therefore, according to 'taste'. After some months, you may also sieve or pound it to a chutney.

Nimboo Achar (*Lime or Lemon Pickle in Lime Juice*)

24 whole limes or lemons	4 oz. green chillies
Juice of 6–8 limes	5–6 tablespoons salt
8 oz. green ginger	4 bay leaves

Peel and slice the ginger in julienne strips. Slit the chillies and remove the seeds (unless you want the pickle very hot). Wash the whole limes and dry carefully. Roll on the table with the palm of the hand to soften them a little. Cut into quarters using a silver or stainless steel knife and remove the pips.

Arrange a layer of quartered limes or lemons, with any juices that may have run from them in a pickling jar, dust with salt and broken bay leaf and add a few chillies and strips of ginger. Repeat until the jar is full, then pour in the lime juice. Shake thoroughly. Cover the jar with a muslin cloth and leave in the sun, or in a warm place for 4 days. Add a little of the salt each day. Before it is ready, the pickle will be crusted with salt and the taste excessive. This salt is soon absorbed and the taste balance rectified. The pickle is ready to eat in 4–7 days but is best after two weeks, by which time the skins will be tender (lime softens more quickly then lemon) and the juices thick and aromatic.

If green ginger is not in season, it can be omitted. The addition of 3 tablespoons of cayenne pepper produces a more 'lively', but less subtle pickle, and would suit few Western palates.

Garam Nimboo Achar (*Spiced Lime Pickle in Oil*)

16 limes or lemons
4 tablespoons salt
2 tablespoons crushed dried chillies (seed for milder pickle)
1 tablespoon black pepper
2 tablespoons minced garlic
1 teaspoon ginger powder

2 tablespoons roasted yellow mustard seed
1 teaspoon roasted and finely ground fenugreek
About 1½ pints good oil
1 tablespoon coarsely broken cumin

Prepare the aromatics. Wash limes and dry thoroughly. Cut into halves or quarters or, if you prefer, into narrow wedges. Spread on a large platter and dust with salt, garlic, ginger, mustard and fenugreek. Heat oil until it begins to 'smoke', then keep warm on a very low heat for 10 minutes. Allow it to cool. Put the limes with seasonings into a large pickle jar, add cumin and cover with oil. Leave for 6 days or so in a warm dry place. Stir once or twice every day. Cover with a muslin cloth during the day; put on the lid at night. Can be used within the week, but will be better after a fortnight or more.

Phul-Gobi Achar (*Cauliflower Pickle*)

1 medium-size cauliflower
3 tablespoons crushed yellow mustard seed

1 tablespoon salt
½ teaspoon cayenne pepper

Cut the flowerets from the cauliflower and cook in boiling salted water for 30 seconds if you want a crisp pickle; 1 minute for a softer pickle. Drain well and pack into a large jar. Aromatize with mustard seed, cayenne and salt. Shake the jar and keep in a warm place for 2 to 3 days, stirring or shaking often. Cover with muslin during the day, and the lid at night. The texture should be crisp. The salt will extract some moisture from the cauliflower, otherwise this pickle has no sauce. The pickle will keep for a fortnight or more in a cool dry place.

To make this same pickle with oil, prepare the cauliflower as above and add half its weight in quartered turnips. Mix with the same aromatics plus 2 teaspoons turmeric, 2 tablepoons garam masala (see p. 249), 1 teaspoon crushed red chillies, 2 teaspoons freshly ground black pepper, 1 teaspoon paprika, ¼ teaspoon roasted asafoetida, 1 teaspoon garlic salt, 1 teaspoon onion salt. Heat the oil to boiling point and leave 12 minutes on a very low heat. Cool and strain over the vegetables. Keep in a warm place for 1 week with a muslin covering by day and a lid by night. For those who prefer a softer pickle, marinate for 3 weeks before use.

Mirchi Achar (Pickle of Green Chillies)

This pickle can also be made with small green pimentos which will produce a much blander taste.

1½–2 lb. green chillies or pimentos
2 pints or more of good quality oil
1 tablespoon paprika
2 tablespoons dry mustard
¼ lb. bruised fennel or aniseed
¼ lb. bruised yellow mustard seed
6 tablespoons salt
6 dried finely ground bay leaves
½ teaspoon cayenne

Heat the oil and leave on the lowest possible heat for 15 minutes. Remove, let stand for one minute and add paprika and mustard powder. Slit and seed the peppers without severing them. Mix coarsely bruised fennel or aniseed and mustard seed, with salt and ground bay leaves and use to stuff the peppers.

Arrange the peppers in a large jar and cover with the cooled flavoured oil. Keep in a warm place for 1 week stirring once or twice every day and shaking occasionally. Add more salt – about 2 tablespoons – on the fourth day. Keep well covered and in a dry place for another week or 10 days before using.

Achar Tandal (Marinated Cauliflower Stalks)

1 lb. cauliflower stalks
2¼ tablespoons salt
1¾ tablespoons pounded yellow mustard seeds
½ teaspoon cayenne
Water to cover

Remove the flowerets from two or three large cauliflowers

so that a length of the thickest part of the stalk remains. Wash well, dry. Cut into equal 3-inch sticks about finger thickness. Boil enough water to cover and immerse the sticks for 30 to 60 seconds. Drain. (The longer time will give a tender pickle and the shorter time a crisper one.) Pack into a large pickle jar and dust with salt and cayenne. Aromatize with fairly well pounded mustard seeds. Boil then cool about 3 pints water, and pour over the cauliflower sticks to cover completely. This forms a brine. Place the jar in the sun, or a warm place, covered with muslin. Stir once a day. Remove at night to a dry warm place and cover with the lid. Repeat for two days, then leave covered in cool dry place for a week or ten days before using. This is an economical tasty pickle.

Anda Achar (Pickled Eggs)

24 hard boiled eggs
¼ teaspoon asafoetida
¾ lb. ground or minced onions
24 minced cloves garlic
1¼ teaspoons turmeric
5 inches minced green ginger
6 tablespoons coarsely ground coriander
8 bay leaves
2 tablespoons salt
1 tablespoon sugar

1 teaspoon paprika
3 tablespoons bruised kalonji (nigella indica)
1 lb. skinned, seeded tomatoes
¾ tablespoon dried basil
2 pints vinegar
Seed of 14 cardamoms
6 cloves
2 inches cinnamon
1 pint mustard or olive oil
Oil for frying

Prepare the tomatoes and aromatics as listed. Shell the eggs and see that they are quite dry. Deep fry for 1 minute in very hot oil. Add the asafoetida in the last 10 seconds. Remove and drain. Now fry the onions grated fine, remove when light brown, and drain. Prick the eggs all over with a skewer or larding needle, making sure it penetrates to the centre. Heat some oil in a frying pan and add the minced garlic and turmeric. Cook over the lowest possible heat (use an asbestos mat) until the aromatics are a rich red colour. Stir until the oil separates. Mix in onions and green ginger, coriander seed, bay leaves, sugar, salt, paprika, kalonji, tomatoes and the basil. Add the vinegar, stir well and boil for 7 minutes. Put in the eggs. Add cardamoms, cloves, cinnamon and 1 pint oil. Keep on a low heat without simmering for 15 minutes. Cool and place in a jar. Cover, and keep in a dry warm place for a week before using. It is best after four to six weeks at least. Stir lightly once a week.

I have also found this recipe excellent for button mushrooms. Clean the mushrooms and peel. Dry thoroughly with a cloth and proceed as for the eggs. Use grated beetroot to colour the cooked marinade. This will make a fine pickle and also an unusual hors d'oeuvre. Serve a little marinade with the mushrooms.

Khumbi Achar (Marinated Whole Mushrooms)

1½ lb. small button mushrooms
½ pint best olive oil
15 minced cloves garlic
Juice of two limes
2 tablespoons paprika*
¼ teaspoon cayenne*
3 tablespoons ground coriander*
1 tablespoon onion salt
1 teaspoon ground fennel seed
*roasted together

1 teaspoon dried, crushed basil
1½ teaspoons fresh black pepper
2 minced or ground bay leaves
2 tablespoons salt
2 grated medium beetroots
Pulp of 4 sieved tomatoes
2 tablespoons tomato purée
4 minced tinned pimentos

Prepare the various aromatics as above. Wash, clean and dry the mushrooms, so all moisture is dried off. Make a marinade by mixing well into the olive oil garlic, lime juice, paprika, cayenne, coriander, onion salt, fennel seed, basil, black pepper, bay leaves and salt. Put in muslin bag the beetroot, tomatoes, tomato purée and pimentos. Heat the marinade in 2 pints boiled water, and simmer gently till it is reduced to half its quantity. Now put in the mushrooms, and simmer or preferably poach. About 12 minutes should be enough. Allow to cool, remove beetroot and reject; serve cold or chilled. The marinated mushrooms should keep for a fortnight or more, and longer in cold weather. I have often made a marinade combining French and Indian techniques, by omitting the water, and substituting three-quarters of a bottle of medium sweet white wine, fortified with 4 fl. oz. good cognac. In this case the olive oil is reduced to a quarter pint. This will keep a long time. Either recipe makes a delectable hors d'oeuvre or snack.

Machchi Achar (Fish Pickle)

8 lb. fish	2 teaspoons ginger powder
Vinegar for cleaning	2 tablespoons freshly ground
1 lb. 2 oz. salt	black pepper
4 pints vinegar	4 oz. pounded raisins
1 lb. 2 oz. sugar	8 bay leaves
2 tablespoons onion salt	1 teaspoon strand saffron,
1 teaspoon ground mace	ground finely

Choose fine, firm-fleshed fish. Clean and wash with a little vinegar. Cut into slices $\frac{1}{2}$ to $\frac{3}{4}$ inches thick and about 3 inches by 2 inches. Sprinkle on both sides with salt and leave for 6 hours. Meanwhile prepare other ingredients. Wipe fish with a cloth steeped in vinegar, then with a dry cloth. Mix the 4 pints vinegar with sugar, onion salt, mace, ginger powder and black pepper and raisins washed in a little vinegar. Place fish in a jar with the bay leaves and saffron, and cover with the strained liquor. Seal tightly and leave for 1 month before using.

Achar Ban-Sooer (Pickled Meat)

Wild boar, venison, pork, beef or mutton can be used for this recipe.

3 lb. boned meat	10 bay leaves
4 oz. salt	2 tablespoons dried parsley
2 tablespoons black cumin	or coriander
1 tablespoon turmeric	2 tablespoons dried basil
12 red chillies	1 tablespoon kalonji (nigella
3 oz. yellow mustard seed	indica)
4 inches green ginger	1 oz. garam masala (see p. 249)
4 oz. garlic	(optional)
3 oz. peppercorns	About 2 pints good oil
3 tablespoons onion salt	Vinegar
1 teaspoon powdered	
asafoetida	

Cut the meat into $1\frac{1}{4}$ inch cubes. Rub thoroughly with salt and place under a heavy weight for 24 hours. Meanwhile prepare aromatics as below, and bring oil to the boil, leave on low heat for 20 minutes, cool and strain. Remove meat and wipe with a vinegared cloth. Grind or pound three quarters of the aromatics with enough vinegar to make a paste. Rub over the meat, using a wooden spoon or ladle. Pack into a large jar, scattering in the remaining aromatics roughly chopped. With a little vinegar, scrape up any remains of the aromatic paste and add. Pour on enough oil to cover the pickle by 1½ inches. Cover with muslin and keep in a warm place for 1 week, stirring contents with a long wooden ladle. Seal, and leave in a cool dry place for at least 1 month. This pickle makes a good snack and can also be grilled after draining. It should keep for a year or more.

Mhaans Achar (Pickled Meat)

4 lb. pork, boar, venison or beef, mutton or chicken	6 oz. roughly crushed yellow mustard seed
4 tablespoons minced garlic	½ tablespoon cayenne
4 tablespoons minced green ginger	2 tablespoons paprika
	6 ground bay leaves
2½ tablespoons salt	4 tablespoons garam masala
About 3 pints oil (enough to cover the meat)	(see p. 249)

Take the meat and cut into medium-sized pieces. Wash well but quickly so as not to let juices run out. Let the meat drain in a colander.

Prepare the meat as follows: in a heavy casserole put in the meat with garlic and ginger; stir and add the salt; stir and cover well and, over medium heat, let steam in its own juices (the excess moisture should be extracted); cook till every drop of moisture has been dried and meat tends to stick to the pan.

Meanwhile heat the oil, using best olive oil for preference, or a good salad oil; mustard oil is good for pickling and gives a distinctive aroma and flavour. In a heavy casserole or pan, heat the oil till it begins to smoke. Lower heat slightly, leave for 12–13 minutes.

Into the hot oil, put the mustard seed. Remove the oil from the heat at once. Stir well, add all the other aromatics, and put

in the meat. Stir and simmer gently. If the meat is already
tender, the simmering should not last more than 10 minutes.
Venison and other game meats, unless they have been hung for
a while, may require another half hour. Test to see if tender with
a knife point or a needle. Let the pickle cool in the marinade and
pack into a stone or glass jar, with all the marinade. Cover well
and use when required. It will last a long time. If kept in a dry,
cool place, this pickle should be good for a year or more. The
two points to watch are that the meat, garlic and ginger in the
casserole are perfectly dried off, which also tenderizes the meat;
secondly, to let the oil smoke well on medium heat for 12–13
minutes without burning it; this rids the oil of all its moisture.
As the smoke may cause your eyes to smart, the oil is best
heated near an open window, or in the open if you are in the
country.

The following chutneys are suitable for storing.

Revand Chutney (Rhubarb Chutney)

1½ lb. rhubarb
8 oz. sugar
2¾ pints vinegar
1 teaspoon cayenne
2 teaspoons ginger powder
2 tablespoons ground, roasted
  yellow mustard seed

1 tablespoon minced garlic
¼ teaspoon nutmeg
2 oz. blanched, finely chopped
  almonds

Clean rhubarb, wipe with a vinegared cloth and chop into inch
pieces. Dissolve sugar in vinegar, add rhubarb, and cook until
reduced to a purée. Meanwhile prepare and add aromatics and
almonds. Simmer, adding more vinegar if necessary. Cool and
turn into pickle jars. Leave in a warm place for 2 weeks with a
muslin covering by day, and a lid at night. Keep for 3 weeks
to a month before using.

Gajjar Chutney (Cooked Carrot Chutney)

2 lb. carrots
4 oz. salt
4 minced cloves garlic

2 tablespoons ground yellow
  mustard seed
2 teaspoons cumin

2 teaspoons powdered ginger
1 tablespoon bruised black
  peppercorns

2 chopped green pimentos
Approx. 1 pint vinegar

Scrape and trim the carrots and cut into small dice. Dust liberally with salt, and spread on trays leaving in the sun for 3 days (or keep in a warm place for 5 days). Prepare the aromatics. Mix carrots with garlic, mustard seed, cumin, pimentos, ginger and black pepper. Use enough vinegar to cover. Stir well and leave to stand for 5 days, stirring once or twice daily. Use when the texture is to your liking.

Brabarr Tamattar Chutney
(Half-and-half Tomato Chutney)

2 lb. each ripe and green
  tomatoes
4 pints vinegar
½ lb. tamarind (or capers
  ground with 4 tablespoons
  Worcestershire Sauce)
6 tablespoons brown sugar
2 lb. raisins
¼ lb. garlic
¼ lb. onions

3 tablespoons roasted ground
  coriander
1 tablespoon cayenne
2 teaspoons ground mace
10 cardamoms
1 teaspoon basil
2 teaspoons roasted ground
  fenugreek seed
4 oz. salt

Mince the tomatoes and boil in 2 pints of vinegar until reduced to a paste. Bring remaining vinegar to the boil and pour over the tamarind. Add 3 tablespoons brown sugar and stir well with a wooden spoon. Leave for ½ hour, then strain through muslin; reserve the flavoured vinegar.

Mix the raisins, garlic, onions, coriander, cayenne – all pounded – into the flavoured vinegar. Heat this mixture over medium heat; do not boil. Aromatize with mace, cardamoms, basil, fenugreek seeds, and add 3 tablespoons of brown sugar and the salt. Cook this together, without boiling, for 15 minutes. Cool, then pour into airtight jars for 5 to 6 months before using. It is a slow maturing chutney.

Tiparee Chutney (Gooseberry Chutney)

½ lb. yellow mustard seed
¼ lb. salt
8 oz. brown sugar
1 tablespoon freshly ground
 black pepper

1¼ pints vinegar
2½ lb. tart gooseberries
¾ tablespoon cayenne
½ lb. minced garlic
½ lb. seedless raisins

Lightly roast the mustard seed and then grind. Make a syrup with the salt, sugar, black pepper and half the vinegar. Cook the gooseberries in the remaining vinegar together with mustard seed, cayenne, garlic and raisins. Add syrup, and cook until a thick purée texture. Bottle and seal well. Keep 6 months before using.

Chutney Ananas (Pineapple Chutney)

1½ lb. pineapple, peeled
 and cored
1 oz. salt
8 cloves garlic
3 oz. green ginger

½ lb. raisins
7 oz. sugar
¼ teaspoon ground nutmeg
1 pint vinegar

Chop the pineapple, sprinkle liberally with salt and leave it for 1½ hours. Mince the garlic and ginger and chop the raisins. Now drain the pineapple and rinse it lightly with a little spare vinegar. Mix aromatics with pineapple. Simmer vinegar with sugar and nutmeg for 10 minutes, then add pineapple. Cook until reduced to a medium thick paste. Cool and bottle. Use after 2 weeks.

Chutney Nashpati (Pear Chutney)

3 lb. pears, peeled, cored
 and chopped
1½ lb. minced seedless
 raisins
10 oz. sugar
Juice and rind of 2 oranges
¼ teaspoon nutmeg
Seeds of 12 cardamoms

10 green chillies
1 teaspoon paprika
2 oz. roasted poppy seed
3 inch stick cinnamon
10 cloves
8 fl. oz. vinegar
½ lb. chopped cashews

Combine chopped pears with the raisins and all other ingredients except vinegar and cashews. Add 5½ fl. oz. of the vinegar and bring to boil. Simmer for about 2½ hours. Mix in the chopped cashews and moisten with 5 tablespoons vinegar. Simmer and reduce again. Bottle for use after 1 month.

Chutney Khasa (*Exotic Chutney*)

3 lb. *ampappar* (mango paste) or use Spanish *membrillo* (quince paste)
1 quart vinegar
1¾ lb. sugar
1 tablespoon paprika
1¾ lb. salt
1 lb. roasted ground yellow mustard seed
½ lb. sesame seed
½ lb. ground poppy seed
¼ lb. minced green chillies
8 tablespoons broken red chillies

1 teaspoon ground mace
12 bay leaves
4 tablespoons kalonji
1 teaspoon ground saffron
1 teaspoon lovage seed
1¼ lb. blanched and ground almonds
8 oz. garlic
12 cardamoms ground with husks
6 oz. green ginger
1¾ lb. raisins

Rinse the mango or quince paste in a little extra vinegar. Make a syrup of 1 pint vinegar and sugar and add the paprika, salt, mustard seed, sesame seed, poppy seed, green and red chillies, mace, whole bay leaves, kalonji and lovage seed. Boil for 2 minutes then chop, and add ampappar. Simmer until reduced to a thick paste. Mix in the saffron with the ground almonds, garlic, cardamoms, green ginger and raisins. Add more vinegar to cover and simmer for 2½ hours. Cool and fill jars. Use after 2 months.

Fresh chutneys or *sambals* take only a few minutes to make. Some of these are uncooked. They will not keep more than a few days in a refrigerator.

Chutney Pudeena (*Mint Chutney*)

¼ lb. fresh mint
1 medium onion
Juice 1½ limes

4 tablespoons minced parsley or coriander

½ teaspoon cayenne (pinch for
   mild chutney)

1½ teaspoons salt
3 teaspoons sugar

Wash, and shake the mint dry. Use only the leaves, except for about half a dozen stalks. Mince the onion or pulverize in blender, adding a moistening of lime juice, then the mint, parsley, and the remaining lime juice. Add cayenne, salt and sugar. Blend or grind well, and serve, preferably chilled.

Chutney Gajjar (Fresh Carrot Chutney)

½ lb. carrots
½ onion
2 tablespoons finely chopped
   coriander leaves or parsley

1 tablespoon minced green
   ginger
1 teaspoon salt
Juice of ¾ lime

Grate or mince the carrots and onion finely and mix with green herb, ginger, salt, and moisten with lime juice. Mix, and leave to marinate for ½ hour before serving. Like all fresh chutneys it is better if slightly chilled.

Chutney Tamattar Bhurta (Tomato Chutney)

1 lb. tomatoes
Rind of ½ lime, thinly
   pared
1 teaspoon freshly ground
   black pepper

¼ teaspoon basil
¼ teaspoon paprika
1 grated medium onion
2 inches minced green ginger
Good pinch turmeric

Grill tomatoes until skin is scorched. Remove skin and chop tomatoes. Pound (or use blender) with the lime rind, add other ingredients. Chill and serve.

Chutney Nareal (Coconut Chutney)

4 oz. grated coconut
1 oz. sesame seed
1 teaspoon chopped kari
   phulia leaves
½ teaspoon cayenne

2 tablespoons grated orange
   rind
Juice of 2–3 limes
Pinch of ground saffron

Pound the coconut and sesame seed. Add other ingredients, with saffron last. Heat the chutney without cooking it. Cool, and chill before serving. Also use mixed in yoghourt or cream.

Chutney Kheera (Cucumber Chutney)

1 lb. peeled cucumbers
1½ teaspoons salt
2 cloves garlic
2 green chillies or 1 green
   pimento
Pinch of cayenne
Pinch of sugar
1 chopped red pimento (fresh
   or tinned)

2 teaspoons chopped
   fenugreek leaves, or ½
   teaspoon fenugreek seeds
   (ground)
Juice of 2 limes
1 tablespoon coriander leaves
   or parsley

Cut up the cucumber and salt well. Leave to stand for 1 hour then rinse off salt and drain. Prepare rest of ingredients. Pound or blend cucumber with them, using as much lime or lemon juice as is required to make a thick purée. Chill well and mix with chopped coriander leaves or chives before serving.

Chutney Kela (Banana Chutney)

6 large green bananas
10 dates
¼ cup lime juice or vinegar
Coconut milk (see p. 252)
3 oz. grated coconut

Good pinch ground mustard
2 medium onions
½ tablespoon mint leaves
½ teaspoon paprika
¼ teaspoon cayenne

Stone dates and boil in lime juice until soft. Peel bananas and remove strings. Grind or blend with the coconut milk and other ingredients to make a thick chutney. Chill before serving.

This chutney can also be made with beetroots instead of bananas, with the addition of good pinch nutmeg and ¼ teaspoon black pepper.

Chutney Petha (Pumpkin Chutney)

1 lb. pumpkin or marrow
4 onions
1 large pimento
4 red chillies
1 pint thick coconut milk
2 tablespoons lime juice

1 tablespoon sesame seed
1 tablespoon roasted and
   ground kalonji
1 ground, dried bay leaf
1 teaspoon ground aniseed

Peel, seed and cut up the pumpkin or marrow into small chunks.
Pound and blend with the other ingredients. Reduce to a thick
paste and chill before serving. Like all these chutneys, more
green pepper or red pepper can be added to taste.

Chutney Tilli (Sesame Seed Chutney)

4 oz. sesame seed
1 teaspoon black cumin
2 ground cloves
4 tablespoons chopped chives
1 inch green ginger
1 green pimento

1 teaspoon salt
Juice of 2 limes
$\frac{1}{2}$ teaspoon ground black
    pepper
1 cardamom

Roast the sesame seed and cumin without browning. Mince or
pound with all other ingredients. Chill and serve. Blend in a
little oil if preferred to make the chutney into a thick creamy
paste.

Chutney Kashmiri

2 lb. brown sugar
2 quarts vinegar
2 lb. green ginger
1$\frac{1}{2}$ lb. garlic

$\frac{1}{4}$ lb. red peppers
$\frac{1}{2}$ lb. mustard seed
$\frac{1}{4}$ teaspoon ground saffron
1$\frac{1}{4}$ tablespoons cayenne

Mix sugar with sufficient vinegar to dissolve it (1$\frac{1}{2}$–2 pints).
Pound or mince all the ingredients separately. Mix together
and moisten with about 2 pints of vinegar. Add the sugar and
vinegar syrup and blend to a paste. Put aside for 3 to 4 weeks
before using. Quantities of vinegar may vary slightly, but use
enough to produce the usual chutney consistency.

Chutney Lakhnavi (Lucknow Chutney)

3 lb. green mangoes (or
    tart quinces)
2 quarts vinegar
$\frac{1}{2}$ lb. brown sugar
6–8 oz. salt
$\frac{1}{2}$ lb. mustard seed

$\frac{1}{2}$ lb. garlic
1 lb. green ginger
$\frac{1}{2}$ oz. cayenne
$\frac{1}{2}$ tablespoon paprika
1 lb. raisins
1$\frac{1}{2}$ tablespoons turmeric

Peel the mangoes or quinces and chop. Cook in vinegar, to

come no more than half way up fruit, until reduced to a pulp. Boil 2 pints of vinegar with the sugar and salt and add to mango pulp. Grind or blend the remaining ingredients. Mix all together and cover with vinegar then cook about 2½ hours, until well reduced. Turn into pickling jars and keep in the sun or a warm place for 7 to 10 days. Cover tightly and store in a cool dry place for 1 month before using.

This recipe was a secret concoction, and learning its ingredients was like the slow painful extraction of a tooth. The taste however is excellent and unusual and the recipe is not complicated. It is not a chutney for everyday use though, as the ingredients are not cheap.

Farmer's Garlic Chutney

2 oz. peeled garlic
1 large bunch coriander or parsley leaves
2 green chillies
1 large red chilli (or ¾ teaspoon cayenne)

3–4 tablespoons dried mango powder
1 teaspoon salt
4–6 tablespoons mustard oil (olive oil as a substitute)

Grind, pound and blend all the ingredients except the oil with a little sprinkling of water. Mix, add oil, chill and serve. Pungent with garlic, but a delicious chutney.

Basic Recipes

Garam Masala (*Hot Aromatics*)

6 tablespoons freshly ground
black pepper
5 tablespoons black cumin
1¾ tablespoons ground
cinnamon
1½ tablespoons ground cloves
1 tablespoon ground mace

2½ tablespoons ground
cardamom seeds
6 tablespoons ground
coriander seed (optional)
2 tablespoons ground bay leaf
(optional)

Pick over the spices, discarding any husks, and grind very fine or medium fine if preferred. Keep in an airtight jar.

This fragrant powder has many uses: for sautées, grills and skewered foods; for curries and braised foods, when it is added during the last 5 minutes of cooking; for yoghourt and yoghourt punch. It may be sprinkled on food just before serving, or mixed in before the cooking is complete. It is not a curry powder, and can be used on its own, though it will blend well with all the other aromatics.

Spiced Salt

2 lbs. table or rock salt
(crushed)
2 oz. red pepper
1 oz. asafoetida
2 oz. cumin

2 oz. coriander seed
2 oz. grey or black salt
2½ teaspoons mace
1 oz. black pepper

Pound the ingredients until very fine and mix with the salt. Bottle.

This salt will be more aromatic if the seasonings are first heated gently in a heavy frying pan which is quite free of grease. Place over a low heat and stir gently. Do not allow the spices to brown or darken. The heating enhances the flavour and aroma of the essential oils and will give the aromatics better keeping qualities.

Spiced salt can be used when poaching; it can be rubbed into a roast during the last few minutes of cooking; used on steamed vegetables, salads and in preparations made with yoghourt.

Dhai (*Yoghourt*)

Yoghourt is used in cooking and marinades. Mixed with salt, pepper and green herbs it is a cooling summer accompaniment to salads. Certain Indian breads like griddle-fried paratha are eaten with yoghourt as the only side dish.

For a simple method of making yoghourt, take 1 to 2 pints of milk, bring to the boil and allow to cool. When lukewarm add 1 to 2 tablespoons commercial yoghourt. Stir well and leave to stand for 10–12 hours in a warm place. Always keep back two tablespoons or so of the yoghourt to mix with the next batch of milk. By the third or fourth batch the yoghourt should be of the consistency used in India: thick blancmange.

If the resulting yoghourt is too liquid, the milk must have been too hot when the 'starter' yoghourt was added; if too milky and sweet, the milk must have been too cool or the place where it was left to stand, insufficiently warm. Many people believe in keeping the pan covered and wrapping it in an old flannel cloth. Only porcelain, earthenware or glass dishes should be used, and ladles should be made of wood or stainless steel.

Moisture-free yoghourt. The yoghourt used in many dishes should be squeezed in a close, finely woven cloth or napkin to expel surplus moisture. The yoghourt left is creamy and fluffy and is the best for eating plain as well as for cooking with.

Raita (*Whipped Yoghourt Punch*)

Take 4 oz. sliced cucumber roundels (salted and drained), 2 oz. chopped onions or spring onions and 4 oz. boiled grated marrow and mix with $\frac{1}{2}$–$\frac{3}{4}$ pint yoghourt whipped with $\frac{3}{4}$ teaspoon salt, $\frac{1}{4}$ crushed clove garlic, $\frac{1}{4}$–$\frac{1}{2}$ teaspoon freshly ground black pepper. Leave in the refrigerator for several hours. Decorate with a circle of finely chopped parsley, a circle of paprika, another of ground black cumin and sprinkle with a little black pepper. Serve with other dishes or on its own.

Paneer (*Indian Cheese*)

For the simplest way of making this cheese, boil 2 to 3 pints of milk, remove from heat and stir in 1 teaspoon powdered alum (available from any chemist). Return to fire and stir until the milk curdles and the liquid has separated completely. Drain in a fine colander. Place cheese in a muslin bag and squeeze out all moisture. You now have crumbly cheese, called paneer *chennah*. It can be sautéed in a little butter with an aromatic or two, or used in a more elaborate way as in a dish of dry green peas (see p. 178).

Paneer Tikki (*Wedge Cheese*)

Take some cheese made as in the previous recipe, and place in a double muslin cloth or thin napkin. Fold the cloth securely and shape with hands into a rectangle about $\frac{1}{2}$–$\frac{3}{4}$ inch thick. Place a heavy board on the cheese and on top of this a heavy weight (a large casserole full of water is a good weight). Leave for a few hours, or overnight until set. Now cut into shapes. The cheese is firm but not hard. If sautéed plain it will colour a beautiful red and brown, or it may have a touch of saffron or turmeric added. If it is to be added to a curry the paneer should first be sautéed and added to the other ingredients five minutes before serving, otherwise the paneer will harden.

To grill, cut the cheese into 2-inch squares. Rub with a little onion salt and garlic salt, then with saffron or turmeric dissolved in hot milk. Cook under a hot grill for a minute or two. As it dries, baste with butter. Turn once, continuing to baste. Sprinkle with salt and freshly milled black pepper before serving.

This cheese is also used to make many Indian sweetmeats and confections.

Khoia

This is a milk coagulate with a cheese-like texture. It is made by heating milk over the lowest possible heat, stirring slowly all the time. Six pints of milk should reduce to produce ½ pint of cream. The process is laborious and best left to professional cooks. Personally, I like to add dried full cream milk to ordinary milk to produce a richer mixture.

Malai (Indian Cream)

Use best full-cream milk. Bring to the boil, cool a little, then place in refrigerator. When chilled carefully remove the cream which has risen to the top and put aside. This is easier to do if you use a shallow vessel. Alternatively, the milk may be cooked over a gentle heat and the skin of cream spooned to one side. These clottings are removed and used as required. Unlike fresh cream, malai will not pour; it is more like a layered paste. The second method is that traditionally used on farms to make Cornish cream. To make a reasonable amount about 2 quarts good milk are needed at least.

Coconut Milk

Grate flesh of one fresh coconut. Steep in just enough milk to cover. Mix or blend, and leave overnight. Collect the coconut cream on top. Reserve. Strain the milk in muslin, and reserve. N.B. When coconut milk is added to a dish do *not* cook covered – it is likely to curdle.

Ghee or Ghrt (Clarified Butter)

Take 2 lb. of best butter and melt it in a *heavy* pan with an asbestos mat underneath. Heat it to just below simmering point and maintain this heat for about 40 minutes (increase the time for a larger quantity of butter). Much of the moisture in the butter will have evaporated and impurities will sink to the bottom of the pan. Carefully pour off the clear butter, straining through several thicknesses of muslin. If kept in a cool place, this ghee will last for a year or more without turning rancid. It is the best of all cooking fats (and the most expensive) and can be heated to a higher temperature than even the best olive or mustard oil. For this reason it is ideal for frying and will give the crispest results – the high temperature preventing seepage of fat inside the food. It is excellent for searing meat prior to braising.

Akni (Indian Court Bouillon)

1 small onion
2 teaspoons crushed coriander
  seed
3 cloves crushed garlic
1 tablespoon minced green
  ginger

$1\frac{1}{2}$ teaspoons fennel seed
2 pints water
1 chopped capsicum

Chop and fry the onion and bruise the aromatics. Tie everything together in a small muslin bag, place in cold water and bring to the boil. Put the lid on the saucepan and simmer for 20–30 minutes. Strain and cool. Akni can be kept for several days and is used to steam, poach and flavour foods. Quantities of aromatics may be doubled to make a stronger akni. Alternative versions use the following ingredients:

1. 1 teaspoon black or white cumin; 1 teaspoon mustard seed; 1 teaspoon thyme or fenugreek leaves; 6 bay leaves; 1 teaspoon onion powder; 1 teaspoon ginger.

2. 1 tablespoon ground coriander; 10 cloves garlic; 5 cardamoms (with skin); 1 inch stick cinnamon; bunch lemon leaves (or a few bay leaves); small bunch coriander leaves or parsley; 1 tablespoon minced mint leaves; 10 lovage seeds.

The method is the same in each case. Bottle, or keep in a covered basin.

Yakhni

Yakhni, or stock, is similar to stock made in Europe. Meat, game and poultry are used, although I prefer lamb or chicken for light stock, and beef for heavier yakhni. For a brown stock meat and bones may be lightly roasted before cooking. Wine or thickening is never used; fresh herbs and light spicing are customary. Here is a typical recipe.

1 lb. meat (all fat removed)	2 turnips
½ lb. cracked bones	2 carrots
1 teaspoon salt	4–6 lemon leaves or thinly
2 large onions	pared rind of ½ lemon
2 cloves garlic	1 small green chilli
Large bunch parsley	1 bay leaf
1½ inches green root ginger	2–3 capsicums

Chop meat into cubes. Season with salt, cover by 3½ inches water. Leave 1 hour if possible. Bring slowly to the boil, raise heat, clear scum, add rest of ingredients, coarsely chopped or broken, and boil fast for 5 minutes. Lower heat, and barely simmer as follows:

for light yakhni, 2–3 hours
for medium yakhni, 5–8 hours
for thicker yakhni, 8–12 hours, in two simmerings
for jellied yakhni, up to 24 hours, in two or three simmerings, rejecting the vegetables after 3–4 hours.

Note that for the heavier stocks the pan lid must be sealed (foil between lid and saucepan will do), and the heat should be minimal. A low oven or the side of a coal range is best.

Heavy yakhni may be clarified and reduced to a *glace de viande* for the glazing of grills.

I have a delicious method for boiled chicken. Boil the bird in heavy yakhni, and when almost done add 2 oz. butter and about 16 fl. oz. of double cream or yoghourt. The sauce thus produced is of course served with the bird.

Tamarind Infusion

The fruit has stones, pulp, rind and stringy roots. Take 2 oz., wash lightly and cover with water. Steep for 1 hour, and when soft rub with the fingers, mixing thoroughly with enough water to give the consistency of a light sauce. Strain through a fine muslin cloth and use the acidulated water (imli) for vegetable, fish, pork or lentil preparations as called for.

Dried pomegranate seeds can be treated in the same way or used finely ground to add a piquant flavour.

Batter Flours

The best batters are made from chick-pea (bessan), split-pea or lentil flour. This can be made at home in an electric blender or even a mincer. The legumes should be pulverized and then sifted, producing a fine flour. The lentils are improved if lightly heated in a frying pan before grinding.

Plain Batter

Take 6 oz. white flour, mix in the yolk of 1 egg, then beat in sufficient milk to make a thin pouring batter. Allow to stand 15 minutes then stir lightly. Use to make thin, crisp pancakes which are then stuffed with vegetables, the edges folded in and the flap sealed with a little water or milk. Dip the rolls in beaten egg yolk and either deep fry or use a frying pan with about an inch of very hot cooking fat. Drain well. They should be a light golden colour. One of the best stuffings is made with sprouting lentils (see p. 194) a few chopped green herbs, salt, a pinch of pepper or paprika.

Kastha Bessan (Special Batter)

8 oz. bessan (chick-pea) flour for preference	3 fl. oz. yoghourt
Seeds of 3 cardamoms	¼ teaspoon chilli powder
Good pinch strand saffron	¼ teaspoon black pepper
1 tablespoon coriander	2 teaspoons minced chives
2 cloves	1 teaspoon salt

Grind the aromatics, mix well with chives and make a paste with the flour and yoghourt and aromatize with seasonings. Beat well and allow to stand for ½ hour. Beat again lightly before using to coat vegetables, fish, chicken etc. which are then deep fried until a rich brown in colour.

Savoury Dumplings

½ lb. patna rice   Salt to taste
2 oz. split chick peas

Wash rice and drain. Dry it on a cloth in the sun or in a very
low oven, turning now and again. When crisp, dry, break up
fairly fine in a grinder, and then remove any fine flour through
a sieve. Wash and boil the split chick peas until soft. Add salt
when the peas are cooked and the broken rice, stirring constantly to avoid any lumps. Remove the mixture, let it cool,
and then make it into round balls slightly larger than a lemon.
Place these balls on a fine muslin cloth and tie up. Steam or
cook in boiling water for 20–25 minutes and the dumplings are
ready. They are normally eaten with ghee or butter.

෯෯෯෯෯෯෯෯෯෯෯෯෯෯෯෯෯෯෯෯෯෯෯෯෯෯෯෯

APPENDIX TWO

Weights and Measures

STANDARD English measures are used throughout this book.

A standard English measuring cup holds ten fluid ounces, that is half a pint (Imperial measure). An American measuring cup, however, holds only eight fluid ounces, an American half pint.

When dry ingredients are measured in a cup their weight will obviously vary with their density. All spoon measurements should be level. One American tablespoon = one English dessertspoon. The following table gives equivalent measures for common ingredients:

American	*English*
1 cup flour	4 oz.
3 tablespoons flour	1 oz.
1 cup sugar	$\frac{1}{2}$ lb.
1 cup fat	$\frac{1}{2}$ lb.
1 cup uncooked rice	$\frac{1}{2}$ lb.

Metric	*English*
$\frac{1}{2}$ litre	approx. 1 pint
28 grammes	approx. 1 oz.
450 grammes	approx. 1 lb.

Oven Temperatures

	Degrees Fahrenheit	Regulo (for gas cookers)	Degrees Centigrade
Very slow	240–80	$\frac{1}{4}$–$\frac{1}{2}$	115–35
Slow	280–320	1	135–60
Warm	320–40	3	160–70
Moderate	340–70	4	170–85
Fairly hot	370–400	5–6	185–205
Hot	400–40	7	205–25
Very hot	440–80	8–9	225–50

English Index

Almond
-coconut mutton curry, 50
cream chicken, 104
fish with cream and, 134
halva, 221
lamb with, 87
-milk pork chops, 59
Aromatics, notes on, 13–18
hot (*garam masala*), 249
Aubergines
pilau with spinach and, 164
purée of, 188
spiced, 188
on the spit, 189

Baking, notes on, 32
Banana
chutney, 246
halva, 221
Batter, 255
Beans, *see* Green beans *and*
French beans
Beef, aromatic sautéed steak, 78
Bhoona, notes on, 28–9
Birianis
notes on, 167–8
with fish and cheese, 169
(*see also* Pilaus)
Black-eyed peas, 198
Boiling, notes on, 34
Brains
braised, 69
fried, 79
Braising, notes on, 24–7
Bread pudding, Indian, 222
Breads, Indian
notes on, 204–5
leavened flat baked, 211
legume, 208

lentil-stuffed fried, 209
maize griddle, 207
pancakes, legume, 207
pancakes, rolled rice, 212
pastry cones, stuffed, 213
poppadoms, 209
sweet raisin bread, 223
whole-wheat buttered griddle,
206
whole-wheat flat baked, 211
whole-wheat griddle, 205
whole-wheat leavened, 210
whole-wheat puffed, deep
fried, 208
Brill, in simple fish curry, 130
Butter, clarified, 252

Cabbage
curry, 190
rolls with mushrooms, 190
Carrot
chutney, cooked, 241
chutney, fresh, 245
halva of, 219
Cauliflower
braised, 183
braised lamb with, 65
pickle, 235
purée, 184
stalks, marinated, 236
Chamak, notes on, 33
Cheese
biriani with fish and, 169
fudge, 229
Indian, 251
Indian, with green peas, 178
meat-cheese sandwich *en
brochette*, 88
quenelles in syrup, 228

259

INDEX

Indian Index

MORE ABOUT PENGUINS

Penguinews, which appears every month, contains details of all the new books issued by Penguins as they are published. From time to time it is supplemented by *Penguins in Print*, which is a complete list of all books published by Penguins which are in print. (There are well over three thousand of these.)

A specimen copy of *Penguinews* will be sent to you free on request, and you can become a subscriber for the price of the postage. For a year's issues (including the complete lists) please send 4s. if you live in the United Kingdom, or 8s. if you live elsewhere. Just write to Dept, EP, Penguin Books Ltd, Harmondsworth, Middlesex, enclosing a cheque or postal order, and your name will be added to the mailing list.

Another Penguin Handbook is described on the following page.

Note: *Penguinews* and *Penguins in Print* are not available in the U.S.A. or Canada

Another Penguin Handbook

SOUTH EAST ASIAN FOOD

ROSEMARY BRISSENDEN

Indian and Chinese styles of cooking have since the war become gastronomically common-place in Britain. This unusual book introduces the British or American cook to a much rarer tradition of cookery – the subtle styles of South East Asia.

Mrs Brissenden takes great care to make her subject clear. As well as recipes she gives detailed information about local herbs and spices, about utensils, and about conventions of work which won't be immediately obvious to the outsider. So you needn't be baffled by the mysterious customs of Indonesia, Malaysia or Thailand. Especially as the surprising message of South East Asia seems to be – relax!